BACKPACKER
The Magazine Of Wilderness Travel

Trekking
Washington

BACKPACKER

The Magazine Of Wilderness Travel

Trekking
Washington

Mike Woodmansee

THE MOUNTAINEERS BOOKS

Published by
The Mountaineers Books
1001 SW Klickitat Way, Suite 201
Seattle, WA 98134

BACKPACKER The Magazine Of Wilderness Travel
33 East Minor Street
Emmaus, PA 18098

Published simultaneously in Great Britain by Cordee, 3a DeMontfort Street, Leicester, England, LE1 7HD

Manufactured in China

Acquisitions Editor: Cassandra Conyers
Project Editors: Laura Slavik and Julie Van Pelt
Copy Editor: Paula Thurman
Cover and Book Design: Ani Rucki
Layout: Jennifer LaRock Shontz
Mapmaker: Brian Metz, Green Rino Graphics
Photographer: Mike Woodmansee unless otherwise noted

Cover photograph:
Frontispiece: *Cirque Mountain near High Pass*

Library of Congress Cataloging-in-Publication Data

Woodmansee, Mike.
  Trekking Washington / by Mike Woodmansee.—1st ed.
    p.   cm.
  ISBN 0-89886-904-8 (pbk.)
  1. Hiking—Washington (State)—Guidebooks. 2. Hiking—Cascade Range—Guidebooks. 3. Hiking—Washington (State)—Olympic Mountains—Guidebooks. 4. Washington (State)—Guidebooks. 5. Cascade Range—Guidebooks. 6. Olympic Mountains (Wash.)—Guidebooks. I. Title.

GV199.42.W2W66 2003
796.52'09797—dc21
                                                              2003006033

Contents

Fisher Creek Valley from Easy Pass

Legend

———————	paved road	] [	bridge
··············	dirt road	⌣	pass
■■■■■■■■■	trail		river or stream
•••••••••••	off-trail		lake
———▶	secondary trail		
——▶	trek direction	▲	campground
(I-90)	interstate highway	❶	camp 10 miles per day
(97)	U.S. highway	❶	camp 10–15 miles per day
(153)	state route	❶	camp 15–20 miles per day
3060	Forest Service road		
/643/	trail number		

Trekking near the Stehekin River (Trek 7)

Introduction

I write this Introduction having returned last evening from a trek of 66 miles over three days. My sore feet are a vivid reminder of the terrain traveled. The absolute peace within me is another memory of having experienced the very best of nature on its terms. My brain is still processing the landscapes—scenes that will be etched in my mind's picture book forever—and the experiences: picking our way down a seldom-visited valley from an idyllic alpine lake to trail below; snowflakes that spewed from the July sky and the chill wind that arose so quickly while setting up camp that my gloved hands did not warm for two hours; blue sky the following morning that enabled me to see with vivid clarity from Liberty Bell and Silver Star Peaks in one direction to Cathedral Peak in the opposite, a view I didn't even know was possible given the remote location; six deer grazing in meadows and lolling about on a snowfield beneath Whistler Pass; shrill calls of picas and marmots; glacier lilies blooming from ground still covered with snow only a week before; and the rolling white water of one wilderness river after another. Trekking is really living!

The beauty, challenge, and inspiration of mountains caught hold of me in my teens. For thirty years I have been enthralled, humbled, enriched, and renewed by experiences in mountain ranges and wilderness areas across the globe. Closer to home, the trails and wild lands of Washington have filled my mind with memories of overpowering beauty, daunting challenges, elegant paths across rugged terrain, the deep solitude of primeval forests, and the eternal inspiration of alpine meadows ablaze in summer colors. I've shared my pictures, stories, and adventures with anyone willing to watch, listen, or, better yet, come along.

Beginning as a hiker, I transitioned to mountaineering and mountain climbing, and then evolved to trekking. My first partners were family, then friends. I have trekked alone or with partners ranging in age from seven to seventy-eight—evidence that a person can trek for a lifetime.

The What, Where, and Why of Trekking

A dear friend once said the exulting feeling of being in the mountains was akin to receiving a million bucks in small change. Whoopee! Run your hands through it.

Lake Augusta shoreline (Trek 13)

Throw it in the air. Share it with friends. But really, why trek? Why this affinity for toil? Why this desire to load home on your back, exhaust muscles to reach a meadow ridge, shiver in predawn alpine air, sweat in the afternoon sun, exult over a mountain vista only to be caught by a summer storm brewing over the Pacific Ocean? And to do this to family and friends whom you actually have to get along with day to day. What is the attraction?

Why we trek. Trekking is an antidote to the burdensome aspects of modern living. Think of day-to-day living as buttered popcorn, grabbed by the handful and tasty for a while. Like buttered popcorn, daily living can be severely lacking in essential nutrients and upsetting to the stomach. Without renewal, daily living, like buttered popcorn, accumulates within us until we are stuffed and stifled, out of touch with our real and complete selves. Trekking is the ultimate antidote for daily living, an antioxidant for the soul, but so much more than that! Trekking is imagination, anticipation, and an investment in your life that pays a dividend every single day. Trekking is *physical*—challenging your preparation skills and testing your levels of personal risk and commitment, resulting in the opportunity to live your dreams. You will walk away from a trek a different person, better for having created a synergy with nature, your partners, and yourself.

What is a trek? A trek is defined by distance: 30 miles or more. An outdoor trip that entails hiking 8 miles to a lake and camping out for two days is just that, a hike. It lacks the distance, continuity, and ever-changing adventure that define trekking.

Trekking distances are such that you will have to will yourself to keep moving, at times with sore feet, tired back, and screaming quads, in order to reach that camp with a view, that stream to slake your thirst, or that trail junction leading you home. Every step of the journey is meaningful, and everywhere nature is at its surreal best. When the challenges seem too daunting, the scenery reminds you of the value. In sum, a trek is an outdoor hiking experience of sufficient length, beauty, solitude, and challenge to touch your inner being.

Where to trek. Washington State offers a wealth of trekking opportunities rivaling any on earth. The treks I've experienced in the state span at least three national parks, two national recreation areas, seven wilderness areas, and one national monument. They reach from Horseshoe Basin in the Pasayten Wilderness to the Loowit Trail in Mount St. Helens National Monument and across Puget Sound to the deep valleys and ridge-top vistas of Olympic National Park. Four treks are dedicated to traversing the premier segments of the Pacific Crest Trail (PCT) through Washington, arguably the finest 300 miles of this entire daunting 2,638-mile route from Mexico to Canada.

In creating *Trekking Washington,* I challenged myself to identify, complete, and document the best experiences possible. Each trek is a classic, substantially different from the others, and several offer truly unique experiences. Each trek provides an intensely rewarding array of natural beauty in the form of old-growth forests, pristine rivers and streams, lush alpine meadows, and breathtaking vistas. Beyond natural beauty, each trek also offers solitude, a discernable path that rarely encounters civilization, and enough distance so that the concerns of daily living disappear in favor of the trekking realities. Satisfying the search for more adventure, deeper meaning, and more powerful experiences is the purpose of documenting and describing these classic treks. Hikers, scramblers, trekkers, endurance athletes, solo travelers, friends, or families will all find enrichment.

Trekking Fundamentals

There are several fundamental aspects of trekking that require your consideration, from who to trek with and what to carry, through preparation and the sorts of challenges that can end your trek. While everyone is different and your attributes and experiences are unique, you will do well to carefully consider the following guidance.

Solo vs. group trekking. Begin by trekking with companions. Solo travel and group trekking are extremely rewarding, but there are trade-offs to both. However, if you travel by yourself and get in a "pickle" or injure yourself, you have no choice but to get yourself out of trouble. Only after you have experienced the challenges of the wilderness and feel quite confident in your ability to deal with outdoor calamities of every type and combination should you consider solo trekking.

Responsibility. Always leave a descriptive itinerary of your trek with a responsible person, including beginning and exit trailheads and description and license numbers of vehicles left at trailheads. Describe your daily trekking plans, including likely camping spots, the color of your tent(s), the color of your raingear, and the color of your jackets. Be sure to mention the date/time to activate a search response if you haven't been heard from. Finally, leave the telephone numbers of the agencies with jurisdiction over the land on which you are trekking. All this information will be essential to anyone trying to find you in the wilderness. Always carry your wallet, a check or two, and a credit card, because you never know when you might be forced to exit the wilderness far from where you planned.

Pack weight and physical conditioning. You must be in good enough physical condition to at a *minimum* carry your essential gear uphill and down at least 10 miles per day for up to three or four days. This level of fitness will get you through the physically easiest treks, which are still very challenging, beautiful, and rewarding. The amount of gear you carry is your choice. The goal is to carry as little as possible but everything you need. For a solo trekker, a pack weight of 30+ pounds is about the least you can expect to carry for a 3- to 4-day trek, but you can likely keep your pack weight under 40 pounds. If you have trekking partners, you can shave a few pounds off these numbers by each carrying a portion of the common gear (tent, stove, fuel, etc.). When I want company and I'm in recruitment mode, I volunteer to carry the group gear and more of the food in order to keep my partners' pack weights lower.

The amount of weight you can carry comfortably varies greatly based upon your own size, physical strength, overall fitness level, and your trekking itinerary. Here are my rules of thumb for pack weights and fitness. The lighter your pack, the more freely you move and the greater distances you can travel in a day. For trekking, I try to keep my pack weight at about 25 percent of my body weight, but I will go up to 33 percent. The best preparatory fitness regimen is to get out and hike. If you do not have access to hiking as a normal part of your fitness regimen, apply the following test: if you can run 5 miles without stopping or walk briskly (3 mph +) uphill on a treadmill for 60 minutes and walk through a park or around town with a 30-pound backpack on, then you can likely complete a 30- to 40-mile trek following a 10-miles-per-day itinerary.

If you want to attempt the longer treks or accept the more challenging itineraries, then I suggest the following regimen. A minimum of four times per week complete at least one consecutive hour of high-intensity aerobic activity (running, hill climbing, or cycling) with one of these workouts lasting two hours in duration. A minimum of twice per week, complete a strength-training regimen that includes pushups, sit-ups, pull-ups, dips, and curls, plus any other routines you enjoy. In addition, hike on a trail, ride a bike, or take a long walk/run one day per week and experience three to five hours of largely continuous exertion, choosing trails or routes that are hilly. The ideal would be to supplement the foregoing with backpacking, snowshoeing, or cross-country skiing as the season allows.

Trekking Essentials

Knowing you can carry 25 to 33 percent of your body weight is relevant, but not very useful by itself. What should you carry for a trekking adventure? Specific gear and equipment suggestions are listed in Appendix A. Use the appendix as a handy checklist and modify it as you gain experience trekking.

Food. Many books have been written about outdoor cooking and meal preparation. My first suggestion is to buy one! Organizations such as National Outdoor Leadership School and Outward Bound have developed weight-conscious backcountry nutrition and meal preparation to an art form. Access these sorts of resources as well. For general planning purposes, anticipate carrying and consuming 24 to 32 ounces of food per day, divided into three meals, plus morning and afternoon snacks. Your goal is to come up with a diet equal to about 2,500 to 3,000 calories per day. Appendix A has a sample menu for a day's worth of trekking meals.

Bring items such as salt and pepper, a small amount of olive oil, and powdered milk to enhance tastiness. Be creative! As long as you can carry it and it won't spoil on the trail, try it. I avoid freeze-dried meals because I don't like their taste or texture.

Water. Carry at least 1 quart of water at all times. The only time I would carry just 1 quart is if I were walking in a valley where I knew every few miles I would either cross a stream coming down the side hill or have access to the main valley stream. When ascending to or traversing the high country, always carry at least 2

Aaron Woodmansee trying dad's pack (Trek 16)

Mature buck grazing in alpine meadows (Trek 10)

quarts of water, perhaps 3 quarts, and from using your map always have a good idea where the next water opportunities are. I've never had to carry more than 3 quarts of water for my trekking in Washington *except* for short distances when I filled my water bag and carried it to a dry camp.

Drinking untreated or nonboiled water exposes you to organisms that will wreak havoc with your digestive system. It is very easy in the mountains to differentiate between water that looks appealing to drink and water that doesn't. It is *impossible,* however, to tell safe drinking water from unsafe water. The smart choice is to carry a water filter and filter your drinking and cooking water.

Compress all gear and food into a single backpack at a load weight of 30 to 50 pounds (including 2 quarts of water) and you are equipped to trek.

Wildlife Encounters

The mountains of Washington are full of wild creatures large and small. Most (deer, elk, marmots, pica, fox, bobcat, etc.) are a thrill to see and only the most unfortunate among us could get in harm's way encountering these animals. There is another category of beasts that can stir fear in the heart of any trekker. These beasts are the bear, the cougar, and the mouse. Yes, I did say mouse, likely the scariest of all Washington's wild creatures. Honestly, which would you really rather deal with in your tent, a smelly clumsy bear rummaging for your stashed candy bar or a mouse that might run up your pant leg?

Fortunately, the prescription for avoiding both bear and mouse intrusions is similar. Simply be certain that all of your foodstuffs and fragrant items are stored off the ground and away from your sleeping area. Properly stored food must be at least 10 feet high and 4 feet from a tree trunk or branch capable of holding a bear. All land management agencies are only too happy to provide a wealth of detailed information on avoiding both bear and mouse encounters. The good news is that in thirty years I've only been lucky enough to see thirty or so bears. In every instance I either stopped or kept walking as seemed appropriate and the bear either kept doing what it was doing or ran away at a startling speed. I've never had a bear in my tent, and only one mouse. We all survived the mouse encounter unscathed, although there was some screaming and a lot of scrambling!

The only way you will see a cougar is through dumb luck or because it is thinking about eating you and doesn't mind you knowing it. I've only seen one cougar in the wild and that experience was of the dumb luck variety. If you are traveling in a group, you have nothing to fear from a cougar, unless you leave the group. Solo trekkers need to be aware as they trek that a cougar could be stalking them and that the appropriate response to an interaction is unbridled aggression. Scream, throw things, expand your chest, flap your arms, make yourself appear bigger, do anything to make the cougar decide it can get an easier meal elsewhere. Two things to never do: don't turn your back and don't run.

Smooth Trekking

The following strategies will help you deal with the situations or conditions that are most likely to ruin your trek.

Trek at your ability level. This is number one, the most likely premature ending to that trek you planned but didn't prepare for. If you can run 5 miles *and* walk around town or through a park for three straight hours with a pack weighing 30 pounds on your back, then you can likely handle the easiest trek with the easiest itinerary, a 30- to 40-mile trek in three to four days. This also presumes that you kept your pack weight in the 35-pound range. Now, if you reason that seven years ago you ran 5 miles and as a scout you carried a 50-pound pack, and you've been working out at the gym "regularly" a couple of times per month, therefore, you are ready to trek, you are so wrong. I urge you to adopt a fitness regimen as outlined earlier *and* if at all possible, make an overnight hiking trip with gear similar to that which you'll carry when trekking. This sort of shake-down trip will give you real-life feedback on what you need to carry and don't need to carry, and how rigorous a trek your *current* fitness level can handle.

Wear a shoe that fits. You're in great shape and your pack weight is right, but you didn't think through footgear. The little bit of rubbing on your heel that you ignored turned into a hot spot that you ignored, which now rages as a blister the size of a quarter that will *not* be ignored. If you can't treat it, trek's over. Footgear is the single most essential piece of equipment you will carry, or correctly said, that carries you. Innovation in trekking footgear has eliminated much foot suffering. I recommend one of the many similar brands of low-top or above-the-ankle hiking shoes. Any shoe you consider should have a lug sole for traction in dirt, mud, and snow; a firm internal arch; a protected toe box; and enough heel-to-toe plus side-to-side rigidity to support your foot while traversing on a snow slope or on a trail-less slope. The rigidity tests require a comparison. Compare the hiking shoe you are considering to a climbing boot and a running shoe. A climbing boot is way too stiff; it bends very little from heel to toe or side to side. A running shoe is way too soft and offers little resistance. Much like the childhood tale of the Three Bears, you want the trail shoe that is just right, neither too rigid nor too flimsy. I would likely choose a Gore-Tex or equivalent model, simply for the water-resistant benefit. Beyond this, you want a shoe that is comfortable on your foot. I'd suggest a fitting that provides up to a half-size of room when you are wearing two pairs of socks—one liner sock, and one slightly thicker synthetic outdoor sock. Regarding liner socks, I usually choose polypropylene liners over nylon or silk because my experience with the more slippery-feeling socks is that they don't stay up and instead always find a way to lump up inside my shoe. For trekking, never wear a pair of those heavy old leather hiking boots.

Make your feet happy. If you trek much at all, your feet will incur abrasions, hot spots, and blisters. An abrasion is a place on your foot where repetitive rubbing, if not corrected, eventually makes an open wound. A hot spot is a blister in

Angie Woodmansee wading in alpine tarn (Trek 16)

Glacier Peak reflected in Image Lake (Trek 11)

the making, wherein repetitive rubbing creates friction within the skin itself, turning it red and tender to the touch. A blister is repetitive friction within the skin to such an extent that the surfaces are damaged and fluid gathers between skin layers. Your body declares the outer layer of skin "finished" and forms a fluid sack to protect the underlying skin. The process works, amplifying sensitivity within the trillion or more ever-present nerve endings so that even the slightest pressure sends a screaming signal to your brain.

Treatment options are simple: mole foam and callous cushions. For abrasions, cut out a piece of cushy mole foam three to four times larger than the abrasion and then apply, covering the abrasion. This should send you along the trail in a much improved state. If the abrasion is already through the skin, which is raw and oozing, use a callous cushion to protect the tender area within its inner circle after applying a Band-Aid. Put the mole foam over the top if more cushioning is required. Do not put the mole foam directly upon an open wound. For hot spots, the goal is to remove pressure from the spot being rubbed. Put a callous cushion or even two (one atop the other) over the hot spot so that the protective inner circle of the cushion is over the hot spot. This should relieve pressure by transferring the rubbing and related friction to the cushion, which has no nerve endings. For blisters the treatment is the same as for hot spots, except that since a fluid sack has developed, you can consider cutting the skin to allow the fluid to escape and reduce the overall sensitivity of the region. I simply snip the skin over the blister with the scissors on my multifunction knife and release the fluid. Gross! If you don't like my barbaric method, most first-aid books have a whole chapter dedicated to blister repair. One final bit of advice, I recommend callous cushions because they are usually just the right size to properly fit over a blister. Therefore, they are simple to use; just peel them off their packaging material and place them on your feet. If the callous cushion isn't big enough, fashion a doughnut-like protective pad out of your mole foam simply by folding it over and cutting a semicircle from the folded edge.

Be weather savvy. To trek in Washington is to deal with the prospects and realities of poor weather. Treks have been compromised and ruined by bad weather. In Washington State the maritime weather influence guarantees that stable, sunny weather will be the exception. The Cascade and Olympic Mountain Ranges, rising in the path of moisture-laden clouds, become the location where clouds drop most of their moisture in the form of rain or snow. Of course, since most trekking occurs in the mountains, you have poor foglike visibility to deal with in addition to that damp, cold feeling that comes from water running off your backpack and seeping through the seams of your rain jacket or pants.

The easiest way to cope with bad weather is to leave a day or so later, or whenever the weather forecast begins to promise that elusive 3- to 5-day good-weather window. If dates can't be changed and your planned trek is in the Olympic Mountains or in the Cascade Mountains west of the crest, have an east-side trekking option planned as a backup. The weather in the Pasayten or Lake Chelan–Sawtooth Wilderness Areas is invariably better than west of the crest. Also consider going to southern Washington, Mount Adams, Mount St. Helens, or the Goat Rocks if the forecast for weather out of the Portland area is better than the Seattle forecast.

If your primary approach is going to be simply walking into the bad weather, or if you get caught in bad weather while trekking, think again. Even with the world's best raingear you will get soaking wet trekking on a rainy day. It is hard to stay warm in the mountains when you are soaking wet unless you are walking steadily. The rain and clouds take away the view, which is one of the main reasons for trekking, and it is sometimes an essential element of routefinding. Finally, bad weather, especially above 5,000 feet elevation, usually means rain and wind, perhaps snow. This combination introduces hypothermia into the equation. Here are six strategies for beating the weather.

1. Build one extra day into your trekking itinerary as a rest day, a day of exploring, or a bad weather day. This would enable you to delay your start by one day if you are facing a downpour, or to sit tight one day on the trail while staying dry and comfortable.

2. If you must trek in poor weather, protect as much of your clothing as possible, and your sleeping bag, from moisture. Carrying a couple of small plastic garbage bags can be the difference between comfort and misery.

3. Realize you will become soaked. Wear relatively little clothing under your raingear and rely more on exertion from walking to keep you warm than your clothing.

4. When trekking in poor weather walk as quickly as possible and take fewer breaks because you will chill very rapidly while stopped. Varying fitness and trekking speeds will cause problems within your group, as one person's "just

staying warm" pace might be too fast for others to keep up with. To even the pace, faster trekkers may have to carry some of the slower trekkers' gear. Try to take breaks in constructed shelters, under a rock outcropping, or beneath a large tree where you can be protected from rain. In these cases stop longer, breaking out some of your dry clothes for warmth as you eat, drink, and gather yourself for more fast walking.

5. If you are ascending into higher elevations toward ridges or through passes, realize you are walking into trouble and will have little margin for error. Wind will be a significant added detriment not experienced in the valleys, and the effective temperature could drop 30 degrees or more. Keep your group together and moving. Know where you intend to camp, how long it should take to get there, where the camp water source is, and if there will be any indicators that camp is near (a trail junction, noteworthy stream, etc). If people are tiring or lagging, cut your losses and set up tents on the spot. Warmth and dryness are the two big issues, not comfort. Upon reaching camp, take charge. People will be cold and tired, not up to doing the quick thinking and moving it takes to get tents set up, gear stowed, water gathered, stoves fired up, and recovery underway. Whoever got the group this far needs to get them through camp setup. Put all gear except backpacks, shoes, and possibly stoves inside the tent. Packs and shoes go under the fly, cook inside or outside depending on what you prefer and how crowded the tent is. If you are traveling solo, this is one of those opportunities for personal growth!

6. Now that you know what a crummy day in the mountains is all about, are you ready for another one? You know the drill but for one twist, a camp breakdown tip. When getting ready to break camp while it is raining, have everything packed while you are still inside your tent. Step out, slap your shoes on, take down the tent, and put it on the outside of your pack, for the tent is soaked already.

Plan well. Lack of preparedness is a severe mental lapse that might have taken place weeks or months before the trek, caused by not accurately visualizing what the trek would entail. Perhaps an off-trail segment carefully described sounded so easy that you skipped over the part about carrying an ice ax and now you face a scary snow slope. Or maybe all the adventure sounded so cool while sitting in the living room, but now only one day into the trek your stove doesn't work, you can't figure out how to set up your tent, and the mosquitoes have you on radar lock. How you deal with lack of preparedness says a lot about the real you. My recommendation is to take a deep breath and a good look around. Do not proceed if it will put you in danger. Usually workable possibilities are available. Maybe now is the time to learn more about yourself.

Manage your itinerary. If your itinerary is too challenging, slow down or lighten your load! Maybe you thought you could average 20 miles per day and it turns out 15 is better. If you've been saving a day for bad weather or side trips, commit the day to your schedule and adjust your itinerary. On one occasion, I placed my tent and other gear carefully behind a log at a trail junction 3 miles from a road end, but 30 miles from trek's end. I went and retrieved my gear when I finished.

Change your route. Suppose you just don't have it in you to gain 5,000 feet elevation climbing over two more ridges. In this case, check out the map. What are your alternatives? Rather than quit the trek, choose a different line for a day. Often there are valley trails that can connect ridge routes. While not as scenic in a panoramic sense, valley trails are beautiful and usually are less strenuous because of comparatively less elevation change. Or maybe steep snow blocks the path and you lack an ice ax. Look for an alternate route, even if you have to climb or descend 500 feet to avoid the obstacle.

Use your routefinding tools. Armed with the recommended map and trek narrative, routefinding will seldom be a problem as only a handful of treks have trail segments crossing permanent snowfields, unmaintained trail sections, or modest cross-country navigation. Even so, if you aren't sure which trail to take at a junction, look for other evidence. Is one trail heading up and one down? Or is one heading north and one south? Use your deductive reasoning to narrow your choices. Once you have chosen a trail, keep your map handy to determine if, within a few minutes, the trail behaves as indicated on the map. If you are dealing with an unmaintained

Kristy Woodmansee snow camping in the Cascades

trail or an off-trail route description and can't quite figure out the detail, use your map, your view, and your mind. Can you determine visually and from your map where the route description is directing you? If you can, simply choose your own path to the next known landmark or trail intersection. Odds are that's what I did.

Enjoy the company of others. If anything, the mystique of trekking alone is overrated. While civilization may give us more togetherness than our human frailties can handle, neither are we wired to spend a great deal of time alone. I say this having trekked alone often. The wilderness areas and national parks traversed and encircled by the treks will provide a great deal of solitude and loneliness. And being alone does amplify the feeling of wilderness and exposure to the dangers, risks, and rewards that come with trekking. Even so, it is common for a solo trekker to get a day or two into a trek and then bail out because of loneliness. There are two things you can do to counter loneliness: don't camp in isolation and be sure to visit with the people you do encounter on the trail. Everyone has their story and by listening first, maybe you will get to share your story of trekking alone and remind yourself why it was such a good idea.

Don't let your companions bring you down. It's really easier than you think to keep a negative partner from bringing you down. Have you ever more appreciated your health than when walking down a hospital corridor to visit family or friend? When I listen to people complain in the mountains, rather than focusing on their plight I focus on how fine I feel. At the same time, there are two types of challenging partners: those who are struggling mentally and physically and those who have a difficult personality. Proper wilderness decorum dictates that you do what it takes to help a struggling partner. You are a team, so volunteer to carry the heavy load or make whatever sacrifices are necessary to get yourself and your partner(s) through or out. For a partner with a negative attitude or difficult personality, wilderness decorum again dictates that you support your partner. Simply ignore the negatives while being as positive as a sunny day in the high country. It can get very funny after a while, for as difficult as it is to be positive around a negative person, it is three times as hard to be grouchy around someone cheerful.

Prepare for insects. For a couple of weeks during the summer, often the prime flowering season of late July and early August, mountains are alive with bugs. Insects are the worst in the forests and by lakes. Learn to trek fast through the valleys and savor your time above 6,000 feet where breezes and cool mornings keep the insects at a tolerable level. Also, carry insect repellant and be prepared to occasionally set up your tent at noon just to have a bug-free lunch.

Bring a variety of simple foods. When dining out, the flavor of food is always 50 percent ambience. Macaroni and cheese for the fifth night in a row? Well, if you are sitting at High Pass, or Lake Beauty, or a hundred other special locations, it will be perfect. Seek variety in the oatmeal you eat and the hot chocolate flavors you drink. Remember a calorie eaten is a calorie to expend.

Stay posititve. Staying motivated while trekking is a distant relative to lack of preparedness. The treks are all magnificent journeys and rival any trekking experiences on earth. But none of them are easy; even the easier treks take a lot of work. My treks have not all gone exactly as planned and on a few occasions I've had to alter or abort my plans.

When traveling in a group, you can either benefit from or be hindered by group attitude or "group think." Do not let the group talk you out of finishing something you can finish. Turn the situation around and help *them* find a way to finish, through encouragement, sharing loads, slowing down, taking a rest day, or even making it a shorter trek. There are lots of ways to finish. While quitting sounds easy, it can create horrendous logistical problems. Sometimes quitting still entails two days of trekking and if you have only four days left to finish the trek, what's the point? Also, all your support is usually organized around where you intended to complete the trek. Choosing an alternate exit point can easily leave a day's worth of logistical challenges.

Now is the time to remind yourself why you thought the trek was important in the first place. What did you really want to see and experience? Can you re-excite yourself about the scenic highlights yet to come? How far have you come versus the distance yet to travel? What's really causing the negative thoughts? If your pack is too heavy or the itinerary is too aggressive, can you slow down or drop some gear that you can somehow pick up later? If you are traveling solo and getting lonely, change camp locations if it means being able to camp by and visit with other people. If you have sore feet, patch them up better. My final advice is always to sleep on it. Last night's negativism borne of fatigue or the day's struggles usually vanishes in the face of a new day filled with opportunities and adventure.

Other Trekking Tips

Trekking in Washington will often involve snow or stream crossings, travel in poor weather, and periodic sections of unmaintained trail or cross-country travel. Here are more tips to make trekking safe and more enjoyable.

Snow travel. Snow travel adds three challenges to the trek: how to stop a slipped step or slide; where to find the trail on the other side of the snow slope; and how to walk on this variable surface, which can be icy hard or mushy soft.

I strongly recommend that trekkers acquire an ice ax and learn how to perform self-arrest with the tool by either taking a class or learning from a friend, as an unstopped slide guarantees injury. Mountaineering textbooks and training courses offer instructions in proper snow travel and ice ax arrest techniques. Avail yourself of these resources.

Where to find the trail? If the snow slope is narrow, look on the other side; the continuing trail likely appears out of the snow at or near the same elevation where you are standing. If the snow slope is wide and the snow is deep, you could face walking 0.5 mile or more across snow. In these cases, your primary goal is to determine key locations in the terrain that are used by the trail (such as a mountain pass, ridge crossing, bridge across a stream, etc.) and where you want or need to intersect the trail again. Assume a cross-country travel mindset when crossing large expanses of snow, which means that you take a path-of-least-resistance course toward your desired objective, without worrying about where the trail is for any particular step. For example, if I encounter snow near Fire Creek Pass and my map indicates my desired trail goes through Fire Creek Pass, then I visually identify where the pass is and head there by the easiest or most convenient route available to me, knowing I will either find bare trail at the pass or pick a new destination point for continued snow travel.

Soft snow is easier and safer to walk across than hard snow for three reasons. First, it is easier to make flat, secure platform steps for your feet in soft snow. Second, if you happen to slip, you tend to slide more slowly on soft snow. Third, while you are sliding it is easier to stop by planting your ice ax, or your knees, toes, elbows, and fingers, if the snow is soft.

When eyeing a snow crossing, if you are frightened and uncomfortable, don't do it! Find a route above or below the snow, or turn around. If the crossing would be okay except the snow is frozen too hard, again either find a route above or below the snow passage or wait until the warmth of day softens the snow surface (usually by 11 A.M.). When you are out on the snow, stand with your weight straight over your feet (don't lean in). Kick as complete a platform as you can for each successive footstep. When climbing or traversing a snow slope, everyone uses the same kicked steps, therefore the steps tend to get progressively better as each person kicks into them. When descending a snow slope, the preferred method is to face out on the slope, making your own path by sinking your heels deeply into the snow with a straight-legged gait known as the "plunge step." Again, you want to keep your weight out over your feet, leaning forward much like a skier would when descending a slope.

Most of the snow crossings encountered by trekkers will be affected by melting from underneath, meaning the snow you are walking on could be very thin and concealing a cavernous hole beneath it. This is guaranteed to be true whenever a stream runs beneath a snow slope. Be extremely aware of the thickness of the snow surface and what might be happening beneath the surface. If in doubt, get on your hands and knees and poke the snow surface with your ice ax, a rock, or other tool until you are satisfied the surface is safe.

Stream crossings. Most large and mid-size streams have either bridges or logs in place that provide predictable alternatives to fording the stream. However, there are still occasions when fording a stream is necessary. Following are helpful rules of thumb. For all but the most benign stream crossings, keep your footgear on your feet instead of crossing barefoot. Streams are icy cold and the underlying cobbles

Crossing of raging Doubtful Creek (Trek 6)

very slippery, adding considerable pain and instability to the crossing, especially barefoot. Water less than knee deep, whether fast or slow moving, will not cause dangerous difficulties. Water more than knee deep that is fast moving will boil up your legs to mid-thigh, making balance more difficult. Using a stout stick as a tripodlike support or locking arms with a trekking partner often provides substantial additional stability for crossing a knee- or thigh-deep stream. Water thigh deep or greater that is fast moving can create a life-threatening situation, as you will very likely be swept downstream by the current's substantial power coupled with the poor footing of slippery rocks in the streambed. If faced with a dangerous crossing, don't do it! Find a log or wait until early morning when most mountain streams are at least a foot lower in depth than during high runoff hours—anything but thrusting yourself forward into the mercy of the rolling white water.

Routefinding with map, altimeter, compass, and GPS device. Books and outdoor training courses are available that discuss issues relative to navigation. It is vitally important to learn how to interpret data on a map and to learn at least how an altimeter and compass work, if not a GPS device, too. Then you can decide what tools you need in order to successfully complete the treks you undertake. The limitations of navigation by compass are so significant from a trekking perspective that over the years I've relegated this tool to very basic "north-south" utilization. So far I've found no personal need for a GPS device within the realm of mountain activities I undertake. I do, however, use maps and an altimeter, and I find them extraordinarily useful and essential tools.

Most trekking situations involve walking on a trail, leaving little need for extensive navigational equipment. With a contour map (one showing contour lines and elevations) and an altimeter, you can readily figure out where you are. The altimeter is also very useful for helping to determine how much elevation you've gained, how much farther in elevation it is to a ridge top, etc. For cross-country navigation, determine an approximate route to your desired objective following the path of least resistance by examining both the contour intervals on your map (which indicate relative steepness, ridges, gulleys, etc.) and by looking at the terrain in front of you (brush, cliffs, bogs, fallen timber, etc.). Choose a route based not on a compass heading but on the elevation where you are versus the elevation of your objective, taking into account the physical obstacles in between. The altitudes presented by the altimeter change over the course of a day because they are based on barometric pressure, so making adjustments at known elevation points is important. Still, plus or minus 100 feet in accuracy is plenty good enough for trekking purposes, as most trekking maps have a contour interval of 80 to 100 feet. You can get an altimeter that's built into a wristwatch, so it will always be available at a glance.

Hygiene. Hygiene suffers in the mountains. People who typically primp for hours do good just to brush their teeth once per day. Still, being clean removes not only dirt and odor but also has a very positive effect mentally, helping you to maintain your perspective after days of toil. Here are some hygiene don'ts and do's. Don't wash with soap in a lake or stream. It is okay to swim in a lake or wade in a stream, but don't wash there. The only soap I ever carry is a liquid biodegradable soap that can be applied to hair, body, pots/pans, or clothes with equal ease. Fill your water bag or bottles and walk well away from the water source before soaping up. Given how cold mountain water usually is, you'll be surprised how little water it takes to rinse your body off. If you have lots of time and fuel, it is possible to warm water over the stove for a little extra bathing comfort, shaving, etc. Usually I just wash my hair. I use moist towelettes to clean the rest of my body. Also, if you carry an extra shirt or pair of pants, try for the first two or three days to wear them in camp only. That way you'll have clean clothes to put on after a physical day on the trail. If your trekking itinerary allows a few active hours in camp each day, it is helpful and a good idea to wash out your soiled clothes so that they will be ready for reuse the next morning or later in the trek.

Injuries and first aid. Take a class on wilderness first aid. The Mountaineers offer a Mountaineering-Oriented First Aid (MOFA) class that is very useful. Pocket first-aid books are available that can fit in your backpack with your first-aid kit.

The good news is that trekking on the whole is an arduous but fairly safe activity. Most injuries involve the feet (see the section on "Smooth Trekking"). Beyond that, it's bug bites, burns (stoves and sun), cuts (usually from your own knife), pokes, and abrasions. The next injuries you might see are ankle and knee sprains. In a slip on snow or with a severe misstep, you could experience a broken ankle or leg. Unplanned slides on snow and the resulting crash at the bottom could cause serious back, neck, and head injuries. For injuries minor or serious, you will have to rely on yourself and the people you are trekking with for treatment of your injuries and possible evacuation. So everyone in your party needs to know the

ABCs of first aid (airway maintenance, breathing, and circulatory system function). For cuts, burns, and abrasions, stop any bleeding, keep wounds as sterile as possible, and bandage the injuries as appropriate to protect from dirt or further bleeding or injury. For an injured joint or broken limb, splinting above and below the injury provides stability for comfort, if not movement. And with all of the padding and strapping materials typically carried by trekkers, you'll be surprised how good a splint you can improvise. Help may be one to five days away, so for all but the most serious injuries the best strategy is to get yourselves out.

Evacuations. Evacuation by professional, military, or volunteer rescuers is costly, risky, and often untimely. Forget the quick cell phone call out. The chances of getting reception, connecting, and conveniently effecting your own cavalry response are less than 1 percent. If you don't end up responsible for paying the rescue bill, you will be held morally responsible for any harm caused to your rescuers. No, if there is any way to limp, hop, or crawl out, either on your own or with the help of friends, do it!

If evacuation by outside parties is the only option, that likely means one of your partners must hike out to get you help. In order to be evacuated by helicopter, the weather must be good and the crew must know exactly where you are.

How to Use this Book

Each trek write-up includes introductory information, the trek description, and tables summarizing directions, mileage, elevations, and camping options.

The information block includes the specifics for each trek. Determining a trek's level of difficulty is subjective, so here are the levels I established and the criteria I used to gauge them:

Easier. Can likely be completed by a trekker for whom 10 miles per day with moderate elevation gain is a hard effort.

Strenuous. The distance of the trek lengthens and the number or length of long climbs rises to an extent that better all-around fitness and some trekking experience is necessary to complete and enjoy the trek.

Very strenuous. Another ratcheting up of trek length and/or physical exertion. Likely some tread is difficult to follow, perhaps even some modest off-trail rambling is required. May include other challenges, such as snow or water crossings that add complexity. Three or more climbs of 3,000+ feet in elevation are probably encountered on the trek.

Most strenuous. Treks at a length of near 100 miles or more. Requires the ability to travel 15+ miles per day for a week's time and with a moderately heavy backpack. Definitely includes five or more climbs of 3,000+ feet in elevation gain or persistently rolling high country that results in daily elevation gains of 4,000 or more feet.

Toughest. Self-explanatory.

The information block also includes specifics on elevation gain, best season, recommended itinerary, water availability, logistics, jurisdictions, maps, and trail location. In Treks 3 and 13, elevation loss is also given in order to show that these treks would be more demanding if done in reverse.

The trek descriptions outline the treks and give an inkling of the adventures awaiting you. Where a particular trek presents specific challenges, snow crossings, water crossings, off-trail navigation, etc., the trek description discusses the issues in detail. Obligatory and recommended side trips are also included.

To review trek directions at a glance, use the "Trail Summary and Mileage Estimates" table included with each trek. Note that each trek's elevation profile will give you a general sense of a trip's ups and downs, but does not reflect every bump and dip along the way.

Distances. Although the trek description offers a recommended itinerary, you can alter the miles-per-day (mpd) distances you travel based on your abilities and schedule. Use the "Suggested Camps Based on Different Trekking Itineraries" table included with each trek to identify travel and campsite options.

Trekking Washington is intended to provide you with a lifetime of challenging trekking enjoyment. As you traverse these magnificent routes through protected lands, be mindful of the value of trekking and the value of the scarce lands. Our protected wild lands are constantly under threat and should be expanded to provide for the needs of an ever more frenetic civilization searching more than ever for peace, natural beauty, reflection, and renewal. Go trek! Tell others! Share your natural world!

A Note About Safety

Safety is an important concern in all outdoor activities. No guidebook can alert you to every hazard or anticipate the limitations of every reader. Therefore, the descriptions of roads, trails, routes, and natural features in this book are not representations that a particular place or excursion will be safe for your party. When you follow any of the routes described in this book, you assume responsibility for your own safety. Under normal conditions, such excursions require the usual attention to traffic, road and trail conditions, weather, terrain, the capabilities of your party, and other factors. Keeping informed on current conditions and exercising common sense are the keys to a safe, enjoyable outing.

The Mountaineers Books

TREK 1

The Complete Boundary Trail

Freezeout Ridge and Freezeout Mountain

Difficulty:	Most strenuous
Distance:	141 miles
Elevation gain:	27,000 feet
Best season:	Mid-July through September; late July is best for flowers.
Recommended itinerary:	8 days (15–20+ miles per day)
Water availability:	Good except between Peeve Pass and the Pasayten River, and along Copper Ridge. Do not leave the Peeve Pass area or the Chilliwack River without 2 quarts of liquid.
Logistics:	A boat ride is required across Ross Lake at mid-trek. Contact the concessionaire at Ross Lake Resort, 206-386-4437, for boat taxi service. This must be arranged prior to trek departure. Scheduling the boat

shuttle for early morning is recommended. It is possible to travel via bus from Seattle or Vancouver, B.C., to Omak. Contact Greyhound, 206-628-5508, or *www.greyhound.com.* From Omak or even Seattle, you can arrange for a ride to the trailhead from Mountian Transporter, 509-996-8294, or *www.mountain transporter.com.* On the return home, if transportation cannot be arranged personally, it is 50+ miles to Bellingham, where you can connect with commercial bus service again. Travel to the trailhead vicinity the day before starting the trek, as the drive from western Washington is 7 hours. Several campgrounds are along the route, including at the trailhead, or lodging is available in Omak or Okanogan.

Jurisdictions: Pasayten Wilderness, 509-996-4000; North Cascades National Park, 360-856-5700. Permits are required by both agencies and camping reservations are required in the national park complex.

Maps: Green Trails: Horseshoe Basin, Coleman Peak, Billy Goat Mountain, Pasayten Peak, Jack Mountain, Ross Lake, Mt. Challenger, and Mt. Shuksan

Trail location: Linking up with U.S. Highway 97 at Wenatchee (US 2) or Okanogan (State Route 20), drive east beyond milepost 309 to Highway 7 South. Turn left and follow this road past Tonasket. Turn left on the Loomis-Oroville Road. Continue through Loomis on the Loomis-Oroville Road. About 2 miles beyond Loomis, reach Forest Service Road 39 (there may be signs indicating Toats Coulee). Turn left, following Road 39 approximately 14 miles before turning right on Road 500 and traveling approximately 7 miles to the trailhead at Iron Gate Campground, elevation 6,100 feet. For pickup at trek's end, drive Interstate 5 north to Bellingham, taking exit 255. Turn right (east) and follow SR 542 to beyond milepost 46. Turn left on Road 32 (Hannegan Road; could be labeled Road 402) and drive approximately 6 miles to the road end and trailhead, elevation 3,100 feet.

Paralleling the international border from the eastern reaches of the Pasayten Wilderness at Horseshoe Basin to lowland old-growth forests north of Mount Baker

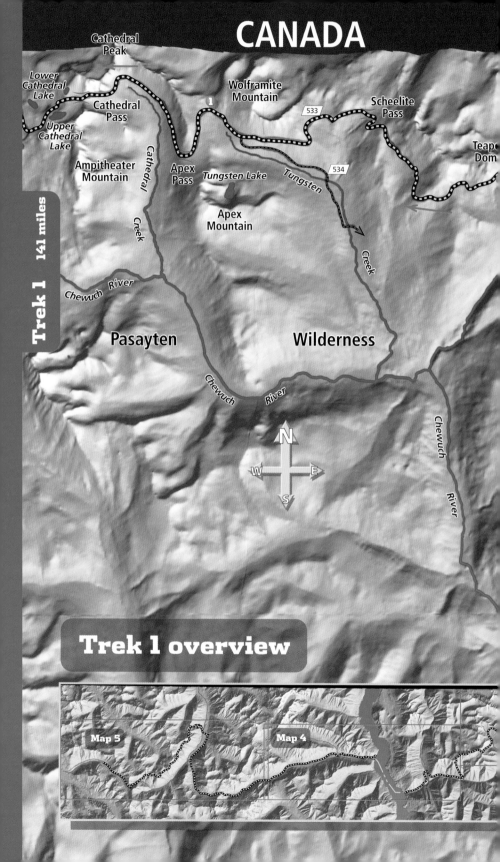

CANADA

Cathedral Peak

Lower Cathedral Lake

Wolframite Mountain

Scheelite Pass

Cathedral Pass

Upper Cathedral Lake

Teap Dom

Ampitheater Mountain

Apex Pass

Tungsten Lake

Cathedral

Apex Mountain

Tungsten

Creek

Creek

Chewuch River

Pasayten

Wilderness

Chewuch River

Chewuch River

N

W E

S

Trek 1 overview

Map 5

Map 4

533

Louden Lake

Horseshoe Pass

340

Rock Mountain

361

Creek

Horseshoe

Sunny Pass

342

375

Pick Peak

533

Iron Gate Campground

Road 500

Map 1

Map 3

Map 2

Map 1

Bunker
Hill

533

456

N
W   E
S

Quartz Mountain

Sheep
Mountain

Peeve Pass

533

Quartz
Lake

3

2

52

502

Sand Ridge

East Fork Pasayten River

Pasayten

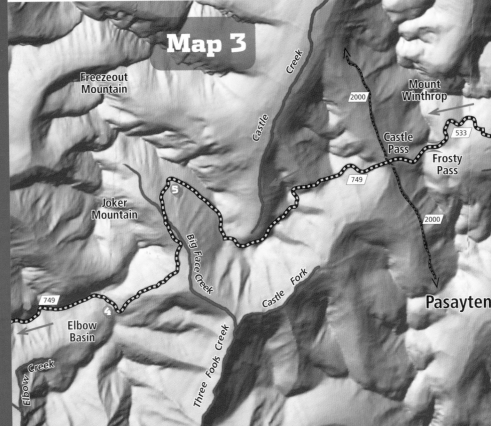

Map 3

Freezeout
Mountain

Castle Creek

Mount
Winthrop

2000

Castle
Pass

533

Frosty
Pass

749

5

Joker
Mountain

Big Face Creek

Castle Fork

2000

749

4

Elbow
Basin

Three Fools Creek

Elbow Creek

Pasayten

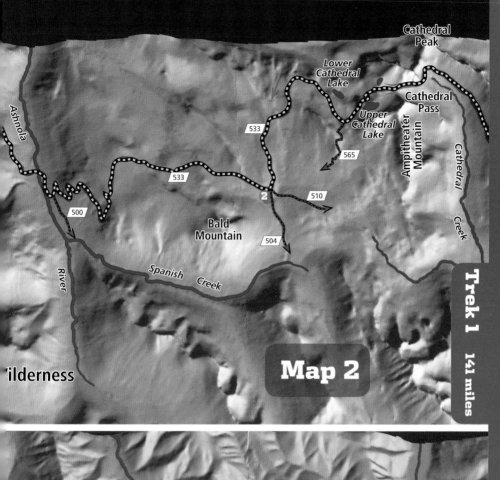

Cathedral
Peak

Lower
Cathedral
Lake

Cathedral
Pass

Upper
Cathedral
Lake

Ampitheater
Mountain

533

565

510

2

504

Ashnola

533

500

River

Bald
Mountain

Spanish Creek

Cathedral Creek

ilderness

Map 2

461

533

95

454

477

482

Creek

Frosty Creek

3

River

Pasayten

huchuwanteen

533

Dead Lake

533

Vilderness

Creek

Soda

4

478

N
W E
S

Perry

Creek

Ross Lak

Recreation

Trail

Beaver

Beaver

Creek

Little

Little

N

W   E

S

Big
Beaver
Trail

Beaver
Pass

Map 5

North Cascades

Cop
Mou

National Park

Copper

Road 32

Hannegan
Trailhead

Loo

Ruth

Creek

T

674

Hannegan
Peak

Ridge   Trail

Copper

9

Sil
Ca

Chilliwack
Trail

Hannegan
Pass

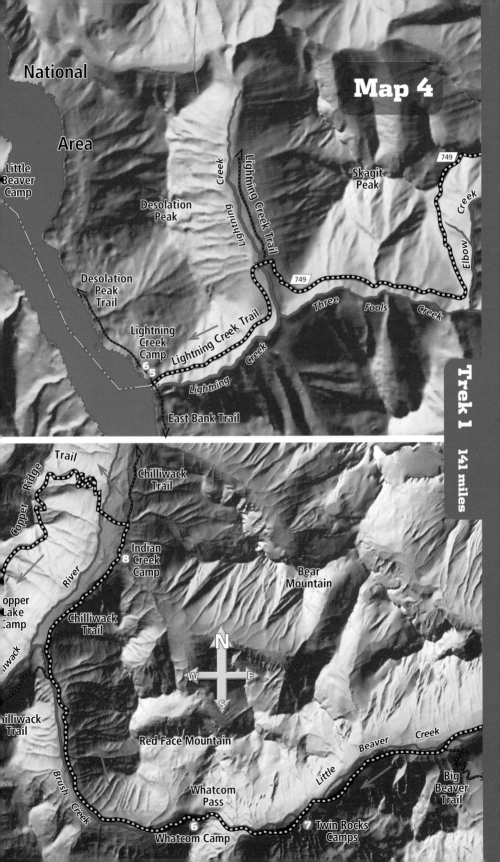

Map 4

National

Area

Little
Beaver
Camp

Desolation
Peak

Creek

Lightning Creek Trail

Lightning

Skagit
Peak

749

Elbow

Creek

749

Desolation
Peak
Trail

Lightning
Creek
Camp

Lightning Creek Trail

Lightning Creek Trail

Lightning

Creek

Three   Fools   Creek

6

East Bank Trail

Trail

Copper Ridge

Chilliwack
Trail

Indian
Creek
Camp

8

River

Chilliwack
Trail

Bear
Mountain

opper
Lake
Camp

hilliwack
Trail

hilliwack

Red Face Mountain

Brush Creek

N

W   E

S

Little   Beaver   Creek

Big
Beaver
Trail

Whatcom
Pass

6

Whatcom Camp

7   Twin Rocks
Camps

and displaying all the diversity, ruggedness, and scenic splendors that mountains can offer, the Complete Boundary Trail is Washington's marquee wilderness trek.

The Complete Boundary Trail should be completed only after accepting and meeting the challenges of many other treks. Seasoned trekkers who are capable of traveling 20 miles a day even in poor weather, comfortable with encountering few fellow hikers, and confident of ascertaining the appropriate path at lonesome junctions or across distances of sparse tread will have an unforgettable experience—the time of their lives! The unprepared will have an unforgettable experience as well.

DAY ONE   21+ miles   3,000 feet gain

The first day of trekking places you deep into the core of the vast Pasayten Wilderness. The distance is slightly more than 20 miles simply because water availability dictates camping locations. The elevation gain is a steady 1,200 feet initially, with the remaining gain earned in increments of a few hundred feet as the trail undulates through the high country meadows and escarpments.

Leave Iron Gate Campground and take your first steps on the Boundary Trail, elevation 6,100 feet. Staying straight ahead at the junctions with Clutch Creek and Deer Park Trails, transition into the lush meadows of Horseshoe Basin adjacent to Pick Peak. Sparkling sunshine will only enhance the vivid green meadows and flowers stretching to Arnold Peak and Rock Mountain. Traverse the broad basin, passing straight through the junction with Windy Creek/Albert Camp Trails, while staying left at the junction with Long Draw Trail #340, elevation 7,000 feet. Now established in the Pasayten high country, you'll notice the feeling is more of Colorado than the Cascades. No jungle-like slopes teaming with vines and brushy

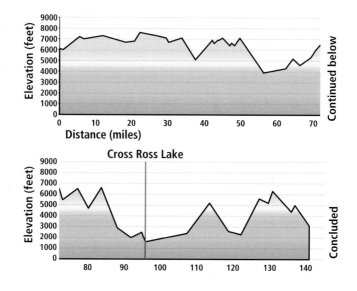

Horseshoe Basin from the Boundary Trail

greenery. Instead, gently sloping pine forests transition to timberline meadows fully 1,000 feet higher than timberline west of the Cascade Crest. The peaks of the Pasayten country are gentle or uplifted, craggy north-facing facades giving way to gentle southern and western slopes. Glaciers are nonexistent, though the graceful valley curves provide evidence of ice from lifetimes before. Endless views around all points of the compass amplify the wilderness aura.

Pass tiny but picturesque Louden Lake and hike behind Rock Mountain, a short mile from Canadian soil. Winding ever higher, flirt with elevations as high as 7,300 feet as you round Teapot Dome and traverse among the silver snags adorning Bauerman Ridge, remnants of a fire long ago. Rounding the ridge into the Tungsten Creek Valley, descend briefly, passing through Scheelite Pass before hiking beneath Wolframite Mountain and reaching the junction with Tungsten Creek Trail #534, elevation 6,800 feet, 20.8 miles from Iron Gate. Obvious mining structures and equipment lie in ruin across the slope, a vivid memento of the frenetic search for wealth that scarred the terrain less than 100 years ago. Tungsten was mined on and off for decades, for among other purposes the manufacture of military armaments, but mining dwindled to nothing during the 1950s.

Staying right on the Boundary Trail past the mining ruins, traverse into the lovely alp headwaters of Tungsten Creek, directly below the gentle slopes leading to the summit of Wolframite Mountain. Find a camp in the attractive basin. You can also camp just prior to reaching the aforementioned trail junction, near a small year-round stream. Or, there are habitable mining "cabins"—maintained by the "Friends of Tungsten"—just a couple of hundred feet above the trail and visible through the trees as you pass through the mining ruins.

DAY TWO   21 miles   4,000 feet gain

Day two of the trek encompasses traversing through spectacular meadows and viewing the most sought-after mountain vistas in the Pasayten. As with day one, much of the elevation gain is measured in increments of hundreds of feet at a time except for the finale, an 1,800-foot climb to Peeve Pass from the Ashnola River.

From camp, stretch your legs and immediately tackle a gentle ascent of 500 feet to the climactic saddle of Apex Pass and stunning views of Cathedral Peak, the complex granitic spire rising starkly to the west. Move ahead, traversing the steep garden terraces far above Cathedral Creek. The beautiful and challenging peak looks like a cathedral, with striking towers and columns of granite sculpted by the artist Nature. Passing directly beneath the peak, climb ever higher before scrambling the granite boulders to Cathedral Pass, elevation 7,600 feet. A short mile below lies Upper Cathedral Lake, tucked beneath the cliffs of Amphitheater Mountain in a larch-speckled, granitic cirque, 5 miles from camp in Tungsten Creek basin.

Depart Upper Cathedral Lake, turning right at the junction with the Lower Cathedral Lake Trail. This represents a revision in the Boundary Trail route, as the trail used to traverse the pond-pocked tundra slopes angling toward Remmel Lake and Mountain. Instead, follow the path 300 feet downhill to beautiful Lower Cathedral Lake and beyond through meadows to a junction with the Border Ridge Trail. Stay left and in 1 mile arrive at the Forest Service cabin and trail junctions with Andrews Creek and the Chewuch River that comprise Spanish Camp, elevation 6,700 feet. Stay right and in alternating open forest and lovely meadows, traverse on the Boundary Trail around the north side of gentle Bald Mountain. Climb over a broad open ridge above 7,000 feet elevation before descending very gradually into thick forest along the Ashnola River, elevation 5,100 feet, 12+ miles from Upper Cathedral Lake. When personally completing this trek, we encountered weather deteriorating from sunshine to thick clouds and rain. Thus we were pleased to enjoy a break in the lean-to shelter adjacent to the splashing river. Upon crossing the river, angle gently uphill through forest, stay left at the Sheep Lake Trail #529 junction, and ascend into lush meadows to arrive amongst the broad meadows, gentle ridges, and small streams near Peeve Pass and the junction with Larch Creek

Trail #502, elevation 6,900 feet. Find a camp 0.25 mile before Peeve Pass near streams flowing from the gentle basin above the trail.

DAY THREE   23+ miles   2,500 feet gain

By now you have reason to wonder why the itinerary is so aggressive, for again you face trekking more than 20 miles. The alternative is to make the distances shorter and add a day of trekking. Although a fine line is reached, on balance this day will not be too difficult as there are no long ascents and much of the mileage quickly passes on gentle valley trails along the Pasayten River and tributaries.

Upon leaving camp, immediately pass the Larch Creek Trail #502 junction and a succession of other junctions, each time remaining on the Boundary Trail #533. Contour on rarely walked tread around Quartz Mountain at 7,100 feet elevation, descending in ups and downs to near 6,400 feet elevation on the complex ridge crest before climbing back to 7,100 feet. Virtually ascend over the top of Bunker Hill to the junction with Dean Creek Trail #456. Stay right and begin the steady descent, losing 3,000 feet of elevation along the gentle ridge before reaching the pine forests of the lovely Pasayten River Valley. Throughout this high traverse the trail is less than 2 miles from the international border. Gaze over endless peaks and valleys in all directions, uninterrupted wilderness but for the slender denuded thread declaring the demarcation between the United States and Canada. By now you are deep into the wilderness core on lonesome terrain viewing scenes witnessed by few. You are more apt to see a bear than a person, and your most frequent trail mate will be white-tailed deer.

Stay right at the junction with the East Fork Pasayten River Trail #477. Cross both the east fork and primary channel of the Pasayten River on bridges, staying left on the Boundary Trail at the junction with the Border Trail #461, elevation 3,900 feet. Make good time as you trek 6+ miles on the gentle tread near the beautiful and wild river. Follow the Boundary Trail upstream past the Harrison Creek Trail #454 junction until reaching a trail junction just past Soda Creek, elevation 4,300 feet and 0.5 mile short of the airstrip. If you happen to reach the airstrip, a meadow carved from the forest for the purpose of landing small airplanes 50+ years ago (since discontinued), you missed the turn. After crossing Soda Creek and reaching the aforementioned junction, turn right and continue along the Boundary Trail as it begins a gentle climb toward the crest of the Cascades.

From the Pasayten River, climb to 5,200 feet and pass through a broad saddle near apt-named Dead Lake before descending back to 4,600 feet elevation as you cross Chuchuwanteen Creek on a foot log and immediately intersect the Frosty Creek Trail #482. Camp here in open forest near the roaring confluence of "ChuChu" and Frosty Creeks.

DAY FOUR   16 miles   5,000 feet gain

Day four is another glorious trekking day that features three significant climbs: the milestone trek to Frosty Pass; the ascent to the lovely shoulder of Freezeout Mountain; and the stern ascent to Elbow Basin. Jack Mountain is among the first of the Cascades that come into view, but Hozomeen is the most spectacular.

Within 1 mile of leaving the comfortable streamside camp and continuing on the Boundary Trail you will need to ford Frosty Creek, as the trail crosses to the north side of the narrow valley. The cold ford will certainly wake you up! After surviving the chilling indignation of wading through Frosty Creek, enjoy the gentle ascent through the valley, transitioning to meadows as you pass by marshy Frosty Lake and an intersection with the Parks Trail #495, elevation 5,300 feet.

Staying left, switchback high above the lake and then contour alp slopes beneath Mount Winthrop toward Frosty Pass. The meadows and nearby scenes are captivating, with views growing at every step. Arrive at Frosty Pass, elevation 6,500 feet, astride the true Cascade Crest, the trek half complete! After enjoying the pass and lovely, lush green meadows, descend easily through steep flower-strewn hillsides amidst cascading streams to a brief union with the Pacific Crest Trail. Be sure to fill up with water at one of the stream crossings, for beyond Castle Pass there is no water until reaching the Big Face Creek Cirque, approximately 6 miles distant.

Upon reaching the PCT #2000 (the official end of the Boundary Trail #533), turn right. In a couple of hundred yards reach Castle Pass, elevation 5,500 feet, and a junction with the Castle Pass Trail #749, 7 miles from camp at Chuchuwanteen Creek. Nearby Three Fools Creek was named in honor of three "foolish" prospectors who mistook pyrite for gold.

Turn west on Castle Pass Trail and begin the journey toward Ross Lake. Climb in ups and downs high on the ridge that extends from Freezeout Mountain and forms the divide between Three Fools and Castle Creeks. After climbing to 6,500 feet once, then twice, traverse into the great cirque of Big Face Creek. Absorb the surrounding wilderness splendor, as this trail is virtually unvisited. The terrain is rugged and beautiful with Joker Mountain just ahead, Three Fools Peak rising sharply above the Cascade Crest to the east, and Jack Mountain rising high above Devils Ridge. Complete the descending traverse of the cirque, the roar of waterfalls resonating throughout the valley.

The crossing of Big Face Creek is only complicated by the amount of effort put toward keeping your feet dry. Once across the stream, the tread becomes overgrown and a bit difficult to follow. As indicated on the map, the trail traverses brushy terrain down valley toward the steep forested slopes ahead. Stick with the tread, sometimes no more than a parting of the grasses, as the trail becomes much more defined upon reaching the big timber. After switchbacking up through the woods for several hundred feet, the tread traverses right onto more open slopes. Still climbing steadily, choose a course that follows the path of least resistance whenever the tread becomes too sparse to follow, as you will always be able to reconnect with tread a bit farther up the hill. Having finished the 1,800-foot climb from Big Face Creek, cross the divide into magnificent Elbow Basin with spine-tingling views in all directions. Camp where you will in this grand park. Water is available lower in the basin, or fill your water containers at the last stream crossing on the ascent to the basin. My first traverse through Elbow Basin was in the evening, as yours likely will be. Jack Mountain and the immense black spires of Hozomeen Mountain are close by and dominating; cliffs plummet thousands of feet from mountain summits into forests below. The evening light on brilliant green Elbow Basin will be soft and cast a golden hue upon the scene. Likely very tired, sit in triumph and relish the splendor that surrounds you.

DAY FIVE   14 miles   2,000 feet gain

While the challenges are by no means completely behind you, the first four trekking days are the most demanding. Your spirits will soar at the prospects for day five, the shortest trekking day with the least elevation gain. Plan your day to arrive at camp along the shore of Ross Lake by midafternoon, allowing for a swim in the chilly water with time to sun yourself dry. You may experience your first encounter with civilization in several days, as there are both human- and motor-powered boats on Ross Lake that share lakeside camp spots. Enjoy the company. In exchange for telling the story of your adventure, your fellow campers will likely share food and beverages you have only been dreaming of.

Leaving camp, traverse through short grasses and flowers along the very top of Elbow Basin. The tread is thin but the route obvious. Tread is always visible ahead, just not under your feet. Once across the basin, look directly down onto frozen and well-named Freezeout Lake. Continue traversing the flower-laden meadows toward Skagit Peak before descending long curving switchbacks across the steep slopes of the valley wall. Ever tightening into a twisting, zigzag path, the trail drops into Three Fools Creek Valley with rare efficiency. The route to Ross Lake remains rugged, with unexpected uphill stretches in the valleys and along the traverse above Lightning Creek to Ross Lake. As you traverse along Three Fools Creek toward Lightning Creek, you will leave the Pasayten Wilderness and enter the Ross Lake National Recreation Area. For the remainder of the trek, camping is regulated and reservations are required.

Upon reaching the junction with Lightning Creek Trail, turn left and immediately cross the roaring stream on an ancient but sturdy bridge. Passing dank Deer Lick Cabin, the same vintage as the bridge, climb 500 feet in forest before curving above the deep, narrow canyon where Lightning Creek roars toward Ross Lake. In ups and downs traverse the cliffs, waiting to glimpse the lake. At long last the lake appears 700 feet below.

Ross Lake is a 22-mile-long reservoir filling the former Skagit River Valley, reaching deep into Washington's wilderness core from SR 20 all the way to the U.S.–Canadian border. The lack of accessibility coupled with the aura of surrounding wild lands maintains the wilderness ambience despite the lake's unnatural creation.

In short switchbacks, descend toward the shoreline, crossing over the East Bank/Desolation Peak Trails and heading straight down to the water's edge at Lightning Creek, with camp and boat landing, elevation 1,600 feet, 14 miles from Elbow Basin. Kick back, relax, dip in the chilly waters of Ross Lake, and befriend the boat campers. Rest up, because the most rugged and beautiful country lies ahead.

All of this relaxation and leisure presumes that you made reservations with the Ross Lake Resort concessionaire to be picked up from Lightning Creek Landing on the morning of day six (or whatever your itinerary is). If you didn't, your option is to bum a ride across the lake from one of the boaters. Or you can hike 17 miles along the East Bank Trail to SR 20 (okay so far), then walk 7 miles or more along SR 20 (ruins the trek), and eventually link up with the Little Beaver Trail near Stillwell Camp after hiking the Ross Lake West Shore and Big Beaver Trails. I recommend an early morning boat reservation because you will have had all the previous day and evening to reach the lake. If you make a 4 P.M. boat reservation and you are trekking behind schedule, you will be out of luck.

DAY SIX   18+ miles   4,100 feet gain

Day six has the potential to be one of the finest and most memorable days of your life, as you trek through the magnificent Little Beaver Valley to the climactic views from Whatcom Pass.

Enjoy your brief boat ride across Ross Lake to the Little Beaver Landing and trailhead. Begin by climbing sharply above Ross Lake, ascending 600 feet with glorious views down the lake to Jack Mountain and beyond, the water darkened by dawn shadows while the spectacular glacier-clad peak is bathed by the pink light of early morning. Now fully awake from the exertion of climbing, you can find your stride as the tread levels. For miles enjoy the walk through morning shadows amongst the old-growth giants. At 4 miles pass the Perry Creek shelter, splash across Perry Creek, and continue onward. Reach the junction with Big Beaver Trail, elevation 2,400 feet, 11+ miles from Ross Lake. Enjoy a break by the powerful, deep green water flowing beside the trail. Staying right at the trail junction, continue up the Little Beaver Valley toward Whatcom Pass. The upper valley is wildly rugged, with waterfalls screaming airborne from cliffs on Wiley Ridge high above. The melting snow and ice from the Challenger Glacier provides the water that froths over polished rock slabs and pours toward the valley floor. The views of Mount Challenger and Whatcom Peak add to the aura that surrounds you.

From 3,000 to 4,800 feet elevation, climb very sharply on narrow switchbacks out of the box canyon and onto more gentle slopes leading to Whatcom Pass.

Ross Lake and Jack Mountain from Little Beaver Trail

Looking back over your shoulder, see all the way down to Ross Lake and across the lake to the twin towers of Hozomeen, rising as two fangs of rock from the forests below. Continue your trek through heather, lupine, and lilies the color of summer, and upon reaching the 5,200-foot pass, drop your pack and savor the surrounding panorama. Walk a short distance farther through meadows and creeklets to Whatcom Camp, 18+ miles from Ross Lake.

Recommended side trip 1. From Whatcom Pass, ascend boot-built trails south on the ridge extending toward Whatcom Peak to reach Challenger Arm. Wander freely on this open ridge, stopping where the views are prettiest, the vistas most astounding, or when the terrain transitions to mountain climbing. Figure on a round trip of 0.5 to 2 hours.

Recommended side trip 2. From Whatcom Pass, ascend boot-built trails north on the ridge extending upward toward Red Face Mountain. Reach a meadow plateau full of brilliant wildflowers and even better views. Descend slightly to delightful Tapto Lakes, one of the ultimate destinations in the North Cascades National Park. Figure on a round trip of 2 to 6 hours.

DAY SEVEN   16–19 miles   3,200–4,700 feet gain

As exceptional as day six was, the aura of Copper Ridge will exceed it. Day seven provides a flexible itinerary, either trekking to the magnificent camp at Copper Lake or ascending over the top of Copper Ridge past the lookout and along the ridge to magnificent Silesia Camp. Choosing Silesia means you get more time to stare at the incredible panorama of peaks, green-mantled meadow ridges, and deep old-growth valleys.

After leaving Whatcom Camp, descend on well-maintained tread angling toward the valley floor. Again the valley rings with waterfalls, this time from high above on Whatcom Peak and Easy Ridge. Passing Graybeal Camp, continue the rapid descent and reach the Chilliwack River Trail, elevation 2,600 feet. Turn right on this grand path through the old-growth forest leading to Chilliwack Lake in Canada. For 3.5 miles follow the valley floor, hiking beyond the suspension bridge over Indian Creek near Indian Creek Camp to a rudimentary junction with the Copper Ridge Trail. Throughout this walk notice the old-growth giants felled by gargantuan avalanches that came crushing down the mountainous slopes during

Mount Shuksan from Copper Ridge

the winter of 1996–97. The trail is now clear, but the evidence of the violence remains.

Because the valley is flat, flood-prone, and subject to avalanches, the trail to and across the Chilliwack River moves a bit from year to year. Be prepared to study your map and keep an open eye for ribbons marking the route. Also be very aware that your chances of fording the Chilliwack River safely are slim and none. The normal crossing is via a giant fallen cedar or fir, usually one of several spanning the deep and fast-moving water. After perhaps a bit more orienteering, rejoin undisturbed trail a couple hundred feet above the valley floor. Steadily ascend steep, adequately maintained trail, striving for Copper Ridge. Briefly gain the ridge crest just below 5,000 feet, then contour and climb beneath Copper Mountain, traversing meadow basins all the way to Copper Lake, which is tucked in a deep cirque directly beneath the ridge crest. The lake is magnificent and offers lounging, exploring, or fishing.

Depending on the time of day, the weather, and your mood, camp here at 16 miles from Whatcom Camp or continue on for 3+ miles through the ultimate climactic views in this land of eye-popping scenery to Copper Ridge Lookout, and beyond to Silesia Camp. Along Copper Ridge one fabulous view follows another as you gaze down the Chilliwack Valley to Chilliwack Lake and across to Mount Redoubt, Bear Mountain, Twin Spires, Whatcom Peak, and more. Climb higher, reaching Copper Ridge Lookout. From the lookout, the views improve from splendid to sublime. Mount Shuksan and the chaotic crevasses of the Price Glacier are framed between Ruth Mountain and Icy Peak. Mount Baker looms above and to the right, brilliant white ice against blue sky. Mounts Slesse and Rexford rise sharply across the Canadian border to the north.

DAY EIGHT   8-11+ miles   1,700-3,200 feet gain

You've done it! The purpose of day eight is to savor and remember all that came before. This is your victory lap for completing what I hope has been one of the finest experiences in your life. Today's distance is only 8 to 12 miles in length, but every step is varied and beautiful.

If you reached Silesia Camp on day seven, you may well find yourself trooping back up to the lookout to marvel at the sunrise panorama. If you stopped at Copper Lake Camp, you may want a crack-of-dawn start just to witness the splendor of early morning light on the most spectacular peaks in the land. Either way, past Silesia Camp contour Copper Ridge for a final mile before dipping into forest, crossing upper Hells Gorge on good tread, and rejoining the Chilliwack River Trail, elevation 4,400 feet. Turn right at the trail junction, climbing in 1 mile to Hannegan Pass. For the first time in your journey, people may become a common sight. Crossing through Hannegan Pass, look back and try to comprehend all you have seen as the peaks surrounding Whatcom Pass remind you of vivid experiences already tucked safely in your memories. Then descend first in switchbacks before contouring down the gentle valley of Ruth Creek. Views up the valley frame gentle snow-covered Ruth Mountain amongst the vegetation of fireweed and slide alder, with Mount Sefrit rising directly above the trail. Reach the Hannegan Pass Trailhead, 141 hiking miles from Iron Gate.

Trail Summary and Mileage Estimates

0.0	Boundary Trail #533 at Iron Gate Campground, elevation 6,100 feet
1.0	Clutch Creek /Deer Park Trails, elevation 6,000 feet, continue on Trail #533
5.5	Windy Creek/Albert Camp Trails, elevation 7,200 feet, continue on Trail #533
6.7	Long Draw Trail #340, elevation 7,000 feet, stay left on Trail #533
20.8	Tungsten Creek Trail #534, elevation 6,800 feet, stay right on Trail #533
27.0	Lower Cathedral Lake Trail, elevation 7,300 feet, stay right on Trail #533
29.5	Border Ridge Trail #545, elevation 7,100 feet, stay left on Trail #533
30.2	Spanish Camp, elevation 6,700 feet, stay right on Trail #533
37.5	Ashnola River Trail #500, elevation 5,100 feet, stay right on Trail #533
42.1	Larch Creek Trail #502, elevation 6,900 feet, stay right on Trail #533
42.6	Park Pass Trail #506, elevation 6,600 feet, stay left on Trail #533
43.6	Sand Ridge Trail, elevation 6,900 feet, stay right on Trail #533
43.9	Quartz Lake Trail, elevation 6,900 feet, stay left on Trail #533
49.7	Dean Creek Trail #456, elevation 7,100 feet, stay right on Trail #533
56.1	East Fork Pasayten River Trail #477, elevation 4,000 feet, stay right on Trail #533
56.2	Border Trail #461, elevation 3,900 feet, stay left on Trail #533
57.8	Harrison Creek Trail #454, elevation 4,000 feet, stay left on Trail #533
62.4	Robinson Creek Trail #478, elevation 4,300 feet, stay right on Trail #533
66.3	Frosty Creek Trail #482, elevation 4,600 feet, stay left on Trail #533
69.3	Parks Trail #495, elevation 5,300 feet, stay left on Trail #533
72.9	PCT #2000, elevation 5,500 feet, turn right on PCT
73.1	Castle Pass Trail #749, elevation 5,500 feet, turn left on Trail #749
92.0	Lightning Creek Trail, elevation 2,000 feet, turn left on Lightning Creek Trail
96.0	Lightning Creek Landing at Ross Lake, elevation 1,600 feet
96.0	Little Beaver Trail, elevation 1,600 feet (resume hike after crossing of Ross Lake)
107.4	Big Beaver Trail, elevation 2,400 feet, stay right on Little Beaver Trail
118.7	Chilliwack River Trail, elevation 2,600 feet, turn right on Chilliwack River Trail
122.2	Copper Ridge Trail, elevation 2,300 feet, turn left on Copper Ridge Trail
136.1	Chilliwack River Trail, elevation 4,400 feet, turn right on Chilliwack River Trail
137.1	Hannegan Peak Trail, elevation 5,000 feet, straight ahead on Hannegan Pass Trail
141.1	Hannegan Pass Trailhead, elevation 3,100 feet

Mounts Whatcom, Shuksan, and Baker above the Little Beaver Valley

Suggested Camps Based on Different Trekking Itineraries

Night	15–20 mpd	10–15 mpd	10 mpd—not feasible
One:	21+ miles - Tungsten Creek	14 miles - near Teapot Dome	
Two:	42+ miles - near Peeve Pass	30 miles - Spanish Camp	
Three:	66+ miles - Chuchuwanteen Creek	44+ miles - Quartz Lake	
Four:	81+ miles - Elbow Basin	62+ miles - near Soda Creek (airstrip)	
Five:	96 miles - Lightning Creek Landing	78 miles - Big Face Creek Cirque	
Six:	114+ miles - Whatcom Camp	96 miles - Lightning Creek Landing	
Seven:	130+ miles - Copper Lake Camp or		
	133+ miles - Silesia Camp	110 miles - Twin Rocks Camp	
Eight:		121 miles - Indian Creek Camp	
Nine:		133+ miles - Silesia Camp	

TREK 2

The Pacific Crest Trail:
Manning Park to Rainy Pass

Meadows above Canyon Creek Valley

Difficulty:	Strenuous
Distance:	70 miles
Elevation gain:	13,100 feet
Best season:	Mid-July through mid-October, late July is best for flowers and late September for fall colors. If periodic snow crossings are not bothersome, the trek can be completed beginning in early July.
Recommended itinerary:	4 days (15–20 miles per day)
Water availability:	Because the trail traverses on or near ridge tops for most of its distance, water is scarce. Do not leave an on-trail water source without 2 quarts of liquid. Camping locations are dictated by available water.
Logistics:	You must report to customs after entering the United States. The North Cascades National Park Ranger

Station at Marblemount, among others, has the capacity to officially sanction your entry into the United States, which likely occurred a few days prior. Contact North Cascades National Park, 360-856-5700, for information. It is possible to travel via bus from Vancouver, B.C., to Manning Park, B.C. Contact Greyhound Canada, 604-482-8747, or *www.greyhound.ca.* On the return home, if transportation cannot be arranged personally, it is 100 miles to the town of Mount Vernon and a reconnection with commercial bus service. Mountain Transporter, 509-996-8294, can pick you up at Rainy Pass and deliver you to a variety of destinations. Because of the likely international border crossing and long drive from metropolitan areas, arrive at the trailhead the day before your planned start, staying at Manning Park Lodge or in nearby campgrounds.

Jurisdictions: Pasayten Wilderness, 509-996-4000. A permit is required for overnight travel in the Pasayten Wilderness. Typically permits are self-issued at the trailhead, but in this case the trailhead is in Canada.

Maps: Green Trails: Jack Mountain, Pasayten Peak, and Washington Pass. Also requires a Manning Park, B.C., map.

Trail location: Drive Interstate 5 north of Bellingham to exit 256A. Turn right (east) and follow signs to Sumas and the international border crossing in that small town. Once across the border, in just a few kilometers intersect the Trans-Canada Highway (Highway 1). Follow Highway 1 east until intersecting Provincial Route 3 near Hope. Follow Provincial Route 3 east to the trailhead for the PCT approximately 1.5 kilometers east of the Manning Park Lodge. For pickup at trek's end, drive I-5 to Burlington, take exit 230, turn right on State Route 20, and drive east, reaching Rainy Pass beyond milepost 157. Turn left into the parking lot and the access point for the PCT coming from the north into Rainy Pass.

Starting in Canada, savor this challenging highland path that takes you through mountain passes, across expansive alpine meadows, and along seldom-visited,

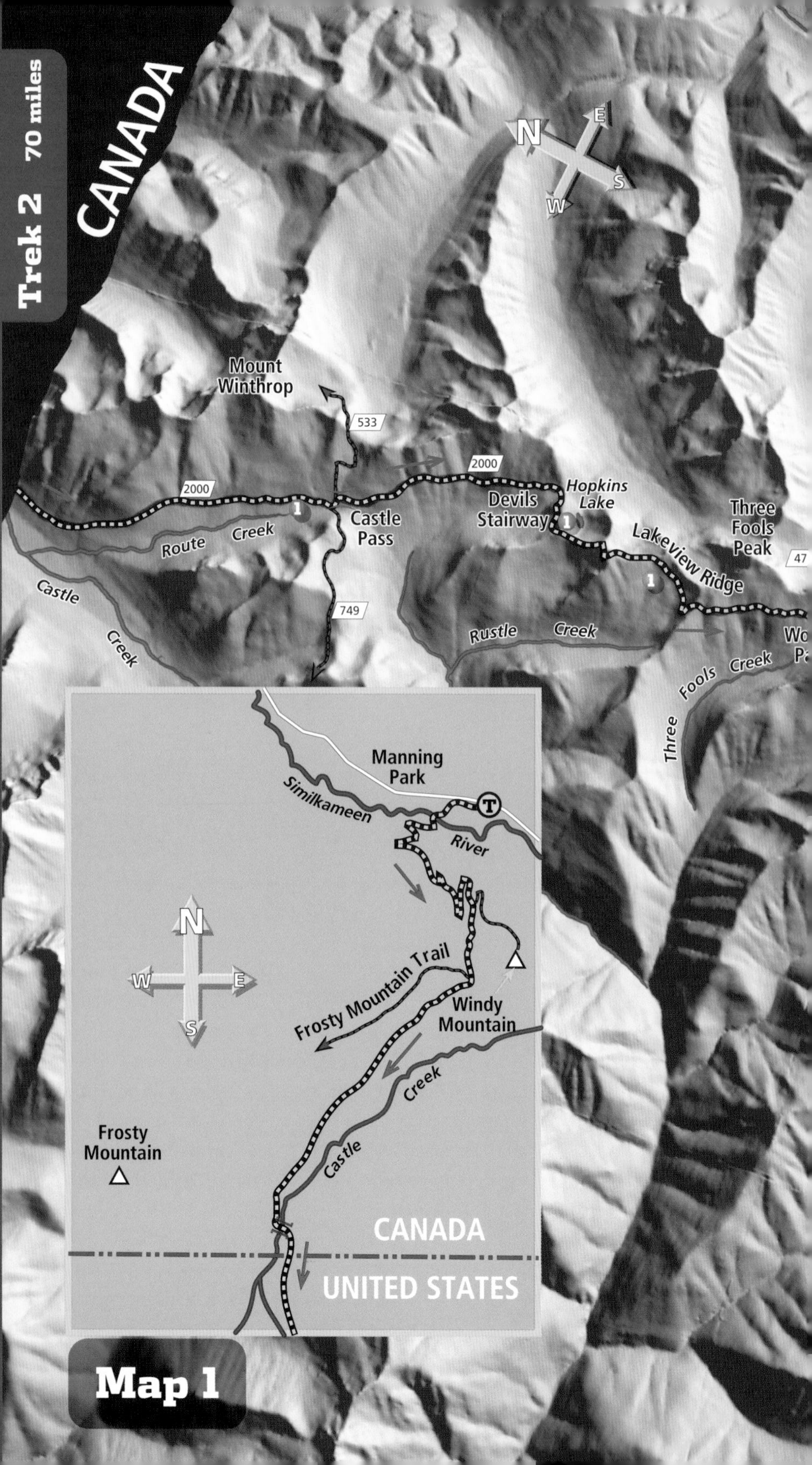

CANADA

Mount
Winthrop

533

2000

Route   Creek

2000

Castle
Pass

Devils
Stairway

Hopkins
Lake

Lakeview Ridge

Three
Fools
Peak

47

Castle

Creek

749

Rustle   Creek

Three   Fools   Creek

Wo
Pa

Similkameen

Manning
Park

T

River

Frosty Mountain Trail

Windy
Mountain

Castle   Creek

Frosty
Mountain

CANADA

UNITED STATES

Map 1

Pasayten

Wilderness

West

Fork

Pasayten

River

Holman
Peak

ck
ss

2000

Holman
Pass

472A

2000

Devils

Backbone

Windy
Pass

wder
untain

752

3 2

2

Road 700

Jim
Peak

Jim
Pass

Tamarack
Peak

Canyon

Creek

Map 1

Map 2

Trek 2 overview

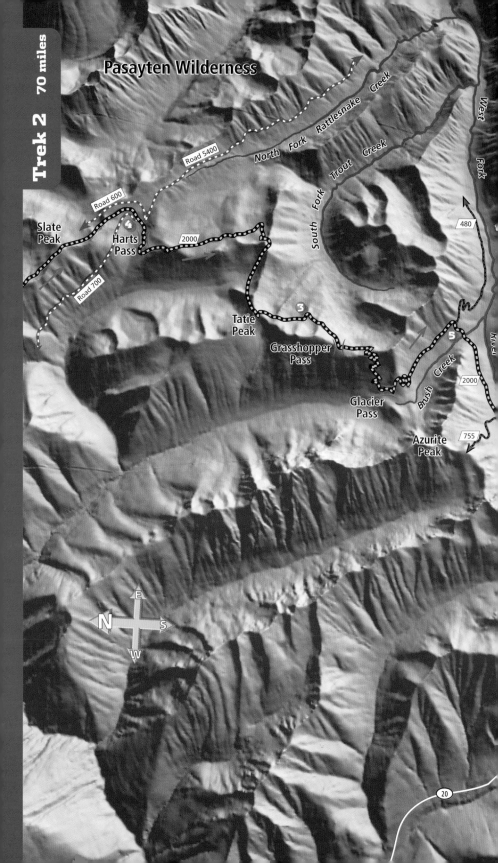

Pasayten Wilderness

Road 5400

North Fork Rattlesnake Creek

South Fork Trout Creek

West Fork

Road 600

480

Slate Peak

4
Harts Pass

2000

Road 700

Tatie Peak

3

Grasshopper Pass

5

Brush Creek

2000

Glacier Pass

River

755

Azurite Peak

N E S W

20

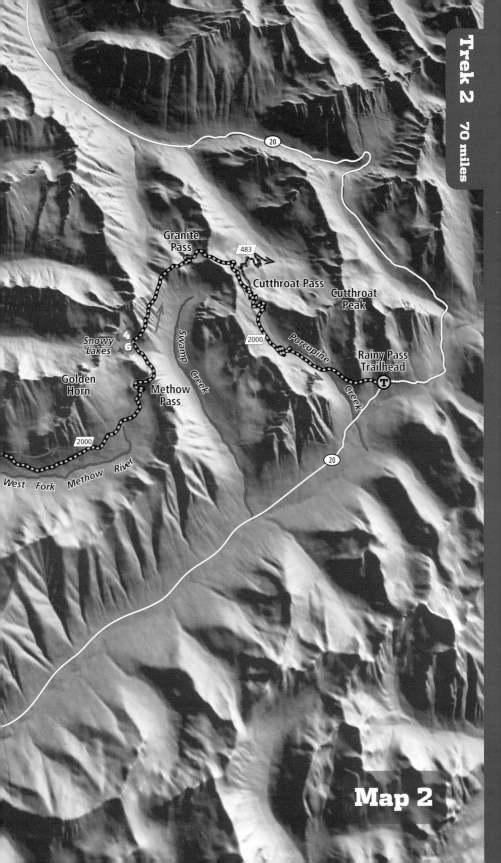

20

Granite
Pass

483

Cutthroat Pass

Cutthroat
Peak

4
6

Snowy
Lakes

2000

Porcupine

Rainy Pass
Trailhead

T

Golden
Horn

Methow
Pass

Swamp Creek

Creek

2000

West Fork Methow River

20

Map 2

remote ridge tops on the true western spine of the continent. Mile for mile, this trek is my favorite segment of the Pacific Crest Trail in Washington.

DAY ONE   18 miles   4,300 feet gain

Begin walking through the flat forests of Manning Park on the Pacific Crest Trail, elevation 3,800 feet. The trail is well marked as it meanders around the developed area near Manning Park Lodge. Soon the wide tread (an old road) turns upward. Stay right at the trail junction with Windy Joe Lookout Trail, then head left as the trail flattens and intersects the Frosty Mountain Trail a short distance later, elevation 5,100 feet. The PCT continues to contour then descends to the bridge crossing of Castle Creek. Once across the stream, the PCT climbs gently upstream, reaching the United States–Canada border approximately 7 miles from the trailhead.

Reaching the border is a special moment, so stop to survey the scene. Monument 78 is a scaled-down version of the Washington Monument. Other monuments are dedicated to the magnificent route and attendant challenges of the PCT. It is humbling to remember this path reaches in a continuous thread all the way to far-off Mexico, more than 2,600 trail miles away. With efforts to establish the trail dating back to 1928, the route of the PCT was defined and first traversed end to end in the early 1970s, but was not completely constructed and dedicated until 1993. The path, one of the grandest walking routes on earth, enjoys the delights of at least seven national parks, thirty-three wilderness areas, and numerous state or provincial parks.

International boundary on the Pacific Crest Trail

Through subalpine forest, adorned with brilliant flowers, climb steadily toward Castle Pass, elevation 5,500 feet. Continue south on the PCT past junctions with Castle Pass Trail and the Boundary Trail, snaking through gorgeous meadows toward Hopkins Pass and Lake, nearly 15 miles from the trailhead.

From mile 7 onward, the wildflowers along the trail are nothing short of spectacular. For hundreds of yards at a

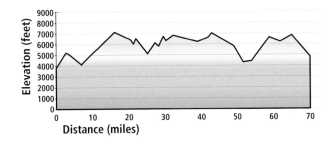

time the trail is lined with lupine, paintbrush, lilies, arnica, and valerian, among other flowers. When I walked this segment of trail, a small deer interrupted my steady march. The trail was too narrow for us to pass. The inquisitive doe did not seem very motivated to leave the trail, nor was I. Finally, when the doe was close enough to touch, she stepped down a few feet below the trail and let me pass.

Once you are past the temptation of Hopkins Lake (0.25 mile off the main trail), begin the steady climb of the Devils Stairway and beyond, winding toward the high terrain of 7,000-foot Lakeview Ridge. Staying on or near the crest, the flowers and expansive scenery from Lakeview Ridge across the Picket Range toward Mount Baker are among the finest views witnessed from the entire PCT. As you descend from the highpoint of Lakeview Ridge, see camp below the trail a hundred feet or so, in a beautiful meadow basin with a small stream, 18 miles from the trailhead. Stream flow may slow to a trickle in late summer, forcing you to descend a few hundred feet for water.

DAY TWO 16 miles 3,200 feet gain

Regain the trail and savor the highland walk along the shoulder of Three Fools Peak to Woody Pass, with views and flowers in abundance. You aren't in heaven, it's the North Cascades! The trail descends 600 feet from Woody Pass before traversing and then climbing to Rock Pass. Staying right at the junction with Rock Creek Trail #473, keep your eyes peeled for signs of water. The stream beneath Woody Pass often disappears into gravel, leaving you thirsty. Confounded, watch as water running from snow patches high above on Powder Mountain disappears into the ground far above the trail. Examine the slopes below the trail as you traverse toward Rock Pass and, with relief, see springs emerge with abundant water about 100 feet below the path.

Switchbacking steadily, the trail climbs through Rock Pass and drops into meadows. Moderately steep at first, the meadows become gentle and grassy, with panoramic views to Mount Ballard and Azurite Peak. As you transition to the respite of forest, cross the first stream of any size since Castle Creek. Continue your gentle meadow descent into the subalpine forests near Holman Pass, elevation 5,100 feet, 7 miles from the camp beneath Lakeview Ridge. Passing junctions with

Devils Ridge Trail on the right and Holman Creek Trail on the left, continue south on the PCT. Climb in light forest to 6,100 feet, then descend before climbing to 6,200 feet elevation as the tread crosses Devils Backbone. From the backbone, gentle forested valleys and the high peaks of the Pasayten Wilderness are visible for miles in the distance.

Soon traverse into the gentle meadows of Jim Pass and head around a knoll into Foggy Pass. Beyond Foggy Pass enter a basin with a creeklet, perhaps the first water since before Holman Pass. Refreshed, gain 700 feet of elevation to cross the high east ridge of Tamarack Peak. Below and beyond is a meadow basin with plenty of camping opportunities. This meadow camp, in sight of Windy Pass and with a small trickle of water running through it, is 34 miles from the trailhead and 16 miles from Lakeview Ridge.

DAY THREE   21 miles   2,400 feet gain

After breaking camp and filling water bottles, in minutes pass through lovely Windy Pass and begin the long gentle descending traverse across rock slopes and high mountain meadows toward Harts Pass, 5 miles distant. Nearing Harts Pass, see the towering lookout atop Slate Peak, which also has the dubious distinction of having the highest roadway in Washington carved into its shoulders. Tactfully, the PCT stays below this winding scar, enabling you to focus on the meadows near and the mountains in the distance, serrated ridges that meld into the horizon. At Harts Pass, walk directly across the dirt road, regaining the PCT on the opposite side. This dirt road and the obvious network of old roads and mining scars are a legacy of the mining frenzy that possessed the Methow region in alternating "rushes" from the 1890s into the 1930s. Towns such as Chancellor and Barron blossomed and then wilted as the harsh climate, mining logistics, and remoteness continually proved the undoing of miners. Harts Pass itself was named for Colonel Thomas Hart, an early mining proponent who proposed the preposterous path we now know as the Harts Pass Road.

The tread climbs gently, traversing through slopes above Rattlesnake Creek. The trail continues its gentle rising contour for miles, reaching an elevation of 7,000 feet near the summit of Tatie Peak. Enjoy this walk high above the valley, with views to the golden granitic forms of Tower Mountain and Golden Horn. From Grasshopper Pass, directly on the Cascade Crest, walk along the ridge before descending into Glacier Pass, the low point in the crest between Brush and Slate Creeks. You must endure the ridiculously gentle switchbacks as the route descends to the pass. Choose to focus on the impressive views of Mount Ballard and Azurite Peak instead of the tedium of the path.

Reach Glacier Pass and a large stand of old growth, elevation 5,800 feet, 15 miles from camp near Windy Pass. The 3 miles of hiking down Brush Creek are mostly in tall and thick subalpine brush, making for a scratchy bit of hiking. Even so, Brush Creek is the first on-trail water source since camp near Windy Pass. Take advantage of this chilling form of renewal. Continue past beaver ponds and finally reach timber just above the Methow Valley. Upon reaching the Methow River Trail #480, elevation 4,300 feet, turn right. The trail is wide and brush-free, a welcome change from Brush Creek.

Enjoy the trail as it winds through old-growth pine trees with their reddish bark. Small streams feed the Methow River and for the first time water is readily available. The river itself is beautiful, transformed to a golden hue caused by the reflection of the granitic pebbles and boulders beneath the crystal surface. Staying left at intersections with trails leading to Azurite and Mebee Passes, cross the river on a sturdy bridge and arrive at a lovely camp in the forest, 21 miles from Windy Pass.

DAY FOUR 16 miles 3,200 feet gain
Climbing gently from alongside the soothing Methow River, leave forest and transition into open meadows. The promise of expansive views is frustrated by more gentle switchbacks. The trail seems inclined to never reach the pass, but eventually

Snowy Lakes Basin

it does. Methow Pass is flat, flowery, and beautiful. See out to Black Peak and other giants of the Cascade Range. Looking back from where you came admire the impressive form of Azurite Peak. Moving along, in a short mile reach a very nice camping spot, with running water, near the way trail to Snowy Lakes.

Recommended side trip. Snowy Lakes are a true delight, and only a 1-hour side trip from the PCT. At the stream crossing and way trail beyond Methow Pass, ascend 600 feet in 1 mile over open terrain toward the obvious basin beneath Golden Horn. Spend an hour or half a day in this paradise. Two of the itineraries call for camping at "Snowy Lakes" Creek, an unofficial name for the stream coming from the basin encompassing Snowy Lakes. This camp can easily be moved up to Snowy Lakes—your choice.

Continuing the trek, traverse on trail blasted into the steep hillside of Swamp Creek, and then climb above Granite Pass to high ridges with glorious views of the Needle, Silver Star, Liberty Bell, and a host of other peaks. Nearing Cutthroat Pass, scan the terrain for mountain goats, nearly always present on the granite outcroppings surrounding the trail. Rock outcroppings and isolated meadows are the normal haunt of "goats," members of the antelope family really, as their rock-climbing proclivities offer a form of protection against predators. Only when forced to by the storms and snows of winter do mountain goats leave their lofty perches and descend into the forests for protection from the elements and to forage.

Staying right at the intersection with the Cutthroat Creek Trail leading up from Cutthroat Lake, keep walking on the PCT, with only 5 miles to go. Savor the winding walk from Cutthroat Pass, along Porcupine Creek, and out to Rainy Pass.

Trail Summary and Mileage Estimates

0.0	Pacific Crest Trailhead at Manning Park, elevation 3,800 feet
2.7	Windy Joe access, elevation 5,200 feet, turn right on PCT #2000
3.4	Frosty Mountain Trail, elevation 5,100 feet, stay left on PCT
7.0	Castle Creek/Monument 78 Trail, elevation 4,100 feet, stay right on PCT
7.2	International boundary at Monument 78, elevation 4,200 feet
11.2	Castle Pass Trail #749, at Castle Pass, elevation 5,500 feet, stay left on PCT
11.3	Boundary Trail #533, elevation 5,500 feet, stay right on PCT
20.5	Rock Creek Trail #473, elevation 6,400 feet, stay right on PCT
25.2	Devils Ridge/Holman Creek Trails at Holman Pass, elevation 5,100 feet, south on PCT
39.0	Harts Pass, elevation 6,200 feet, cross road and regain PCT on opposite side
51.7	Methow River Trail #480, elevation 4,300 feet, stay right on PCT
53.7	Mill Creek Trail #755, elevation 4,400 feet, stay left on PCT
54.0	East Creek Trail #756, elevation 4,400 feet, stay left on PCT
65.1	Cutthroat Creek Trail #483, elevation 6,800 feet, stay right on PCT
70.1	Rainy Pass, elevation 4,800 feet

Above Granite Pass, with Liberty Bell in the distance

Suggested Camps Based on Different Trekking Itineraries

Night	15–20 mpd	10–15 mpd	10 mpd
One:	18 miles - near Lakeview Ridge	15 miles - Hopkins Lake	10 miles - before Castle Pass
Two:	34 miles - near Windy Pass	29+ miles - below Devils Backbone	20+ miles - near Rock Creek Trail
Three:	54+ miles - Methow River Camp	44+ miles - beneath Tatie Peak	29+ miles - below Devils Backbone
Four:		60+ miles - Snowy Lakes Creek	39 miles - near Harts Pass
Five:			51+ miles - Methow Valley
Six:			60+ miles - Snowy Lakes Creek

The High Pasayten Traverse

Osceola, Carru, and Lago Peaks from Buckskin Ridge

Difficulty:	Strenuous
Distance:	48 miles
Elevation gain/loss:	12,600 feet gain; 16,800 feet loss
Best season:	Early July through mid-October; late July is the best time for flowers and late-September for fall colors.
Recommended itinerary:	3 days (15–20 miles per day)
Water availability:	Generally good, except water is unavailable from the major stream crossing at 5,600 feet elevation beneath Pistol Pass until reaching the Eureka Creek–Lost River confluence, a distance of about 7 miles.
Logistics:	The Buckskin Ridge and Monument Creek Trailheads are 14 miles and 4,500 feet elevation apart. Either use two vehicles, dropping one at the Monument

Creek Trailhead or contact Mountain Transporter, 509-996-8294, if you need to have your vehicle moved from the Buckskin Ridge Trailhead to Monument Creek Trailhead. Camping options are very limited once you begin the climb from Monument Creek toward Pistol Pass until reaching the Lost River Valley. Traveling to the trailhead vicinity the day before is recommended, as it is a 5-hour drive from west-side metropolitan areas. Several campgrounds are on the road to Harts Pass, including at the pass; lodging is also available in Mazama or Winthrop.

Jurisdictions: Pasayten Wilderness, 509-996-4000. Wilderness permits are required for travel in the Pasayten Wilderness. The permits are typically self-issued at trailheads.

Maps: Green Trails: Washington Pass, Pasayten Peak, Billy Goat Mountain, and Mazama

Trail location: Drive Interstate 5 to Burlington and take exit 230. Turn east and follow State Route 20 about 120 miles to near milepost 179. Turn left and drive 0.5 mile to the tiny community of Mazama. At the intersection by the Mazama Country Inn, turn left on Lost River Road, driving approximately 7 miles (just beyond the bridge crossing of the Lost River) to the Monument Creek Trailhead, elevation 2,400 feet. Leave one vehicle here and continue on Lost River Road (becomes Forest Service Road 5400) to Harts Pass, 12 miles from the Monument Creek Trailhead. At Harts Pass, turn right and follow Road 600 about 1.7 miles toward Slate Peak and the on-road parking at Slate Pass and the Buckskin Ridge Trailhead, elevation 6,900 feet.

Straddling the Cascade Crest in the northernmost reaches of Washington, the Pasayten Wilderness contains 530,000 acres of the most lonesome and wild land in the state. This classic trek savors the Pasayten bounty just east of the crest, from high meadows to pine forests. You will be challenged by either the heat of a summer day or the bite of a chill wind pouring through mountain passes from peaks high above. Although the scenery is splendid enough to pull your eyes from the path beneath your feet, carefully choose the proper path at trail junctions leading to places you've never heard of, for that is the ultimate attraction of the Pasayten—you can get lost out there!

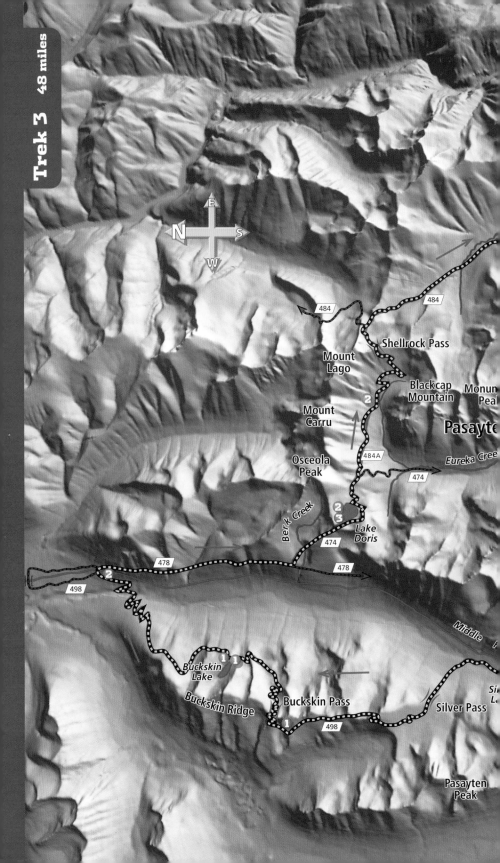

N
E
W
S

484

484

Shellrock Pass

Mount
Lago

Blackcap
Mountain

Monun
Pea

Mount
Carru

2

Pasayte

Osceola
Peak

484A

Eureka Cree

474

Berk Creek

2
3

474

Lake
Doris

478

478

2

498

Middle

Buckskin
Lake

1 1

Buckskin Ridge

Buckskin Pass

Silver Pass

Si
L

1

498

Pasayten
Peak

Monument Creek

Lost River

Pistol
Peaks

484

tol
ss

**4 3
5**

Eureka Creek

Lost River Road

Monument Creek
Trailhead **T**

Wilderness

Robinson
Mountain

Robinson Creek

Road 5400

yten River

575

478A

498

Road 600

T

Slate Pass

Harts
Pass

Slate
Peak

Road 700

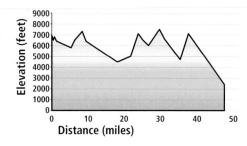

DAY ONE
13 miles   3,800 feet gain

Starting high means immediately walking through enchanting meadows and flower fields of lupine, daisies, heather, asters, and lilies. Views quickly turn from Silver Star Peak to Robinson Mountain and peaks to the north and east. The trail drops several hundred feet and then undulates with the terrain between 6,200 and 6,500 feet elevation. In 1.5 miles stay left past a trail junction leading down into the Pasayten Valley. A great break or lunch spot is Silver Lake, a long 5 miles into the trek. Silver Lake is a short distance (100+ yards) from the main trail and is reached via an obvious, though unsigned, way trail.

Beyond the steady ascent to Silver Pass the tread becomes more rugged. Descend several hundred feet and then quickly regain the elevation just lost. Traverse rocky, flowery meadows at 6,800 feet above the sweeping West Fork Pasayten River Valley. The view west to the Cascade Crest, just across the valley, is captivating. After descending into a small basin, begin climbing the switchbacks toward Buckskin Pass, 800 feet above. Exchanging meadows for rock outcroppings and dense alpine vegetation, reach the airy pass, elevation 7,300 feet. The "pass" is more like a ridge crossing, a rocky, alpine ridge at that. Achieving the pass brings a feeling of satisfaction that is akin to having climbed a mountain.

Descend scree-covered slopes eastward and start the traverse at 6,400 feet elevation toward the lake, 1 mile distant. Enter forest, step across an ample stream, and soon stand on the shore of Buckskin Lake. The forested shoreline of the lake gives way to a beautiful meadow cirque, forming a semicircle of green behind the calm waters.

DAY TWO   16 miles   4,000 feet gain

Day two is filled with challenge and excitement, including a river ford, two more visits to alpine lakes, and an evening in one of the most remote settings in the wilderness, the headwaters of Eureka Creek. After crossing the outlet stream of Buckskin Lake, come to a rudimentary, unsigned trail junction. Although the left, or uphill, trail looks to be more used, the proper choice is the right-hand trail, which, after descending about 50 feet in elevation, abruptly begins to traverse climactic alpine meadows.

Marvel at the beautiful high country of steep meadows and expansive views across the valley to Osceola, Carru, and Lago, the three mountains you will camp beneath at the end of this day. Down valley toward Canada the deep pine forests of the Pasayten Valley stretch endlessly, ridge after ridge melding into the distance.

Meadows above the Pasayten River

Eventually reach the end of Buckskin Ridge, give up your views on high, and began to descend switchbacks to the toe of the ridge near the Pasayten River. Descend through cool pine forests into the gentle valley below. While the trail bed itself is in good condition, there are numerous blow downs to scramble over or around. After passing the irksome blow downs, arrive at an unmarked and unmapped trail junction within sight of the Pasayten River. In a very short distance, the right-hand trail leads to a nice camp by the river and an ideal fording location. Robinson Creek Trail is easily reached on constructed trail once you are across the ford. The current and the slippery stones require a modest amount of care in order to avoid an impromptu bath. If the water level is high and the ford unsafe, then follow the Buckskin Ridge Trail north along the river for 2 miles, crossing the river on a bridge and then immediately turning right on the Robinson Creek Trail. After gaining the Robinson Creek Trail, head south (up valley) along the Middle Fork Pasayten River. Gently ascend, still in the shade of lodgepole pine trees. Shortly after crossing Berk Creek, reach a camp and junction with the Eureka Creek Trail #474. Turn left on the Eureka Creek Trail, immediately facing a climb from 5,000 feet to over 7,000 feet elevation. At 6,500 feet elevation, enjoy the respite of Freds Lake before climbing on to Lake Doris.

Steadily gain the initial 1,200 feet of elevation on open slopes interspersed with the welcome shade of ponderosa pine trees before completing the ascending traverse toward Freds Lake. The outlet stream, spilling down through a chasm of rock, is the first indication the lake is near. On a sunny day, the chilly water offers a refreshing break from the toil. Ascend the expansive alpine basin, climbing to the pass above Freds Lake, elevation 7,100 feet. Unlike Freds Lake, Lake Doris sits off the trail a few hundred yards toward Osceola Peak. From the pass, walk a short distance until just before the main trail switchbacks down a steep slope. At that point, head north on a way trail toward Osceola Peak. Travel is easy across this open terrain and within 5 minutes or so scramble down a slope directly to the lake.

Lake Doris is a perfect place to languish in the sun. Eat lunch, nap, swim, and hike the gentle rocky slopes of Osceola Peak. When you must leave, getting back on the main trail from Lake Doris is easy. Rather than retracing your steps and climbing above the lake, descend and pick up the trail below the aforementioned steep switchbacks. Traversing the headwaters of Eureka Creek is breathtaking. The deep, curving valley itself is rugged and beautiful. To the south, Mount Robinson dominates the skyline. To the north, you are literally standing on the slopes of Mounts Carru and Lago. The fact that you are deep in seldom-visited wilderness is self-evident. The trail is readily followed, but thin, certainly not a thoroughfare of any sort.

Soon reach the sketchy junction with the Shellrock Pass Trail #484A. Instead of staying on the Eureka Creek Trail, contour left on the Shellrock Pass Trail and continue the gently descending traverse into the very headwaters of Eureka Creek. Cross several small streams, providing ample opportunity to replace the liquid that soaks your clothes and drips from your skin. After descending to 5,800 feet, immediately begin climbing again. At 6,000 feet elevation, cross Eureka Creek for the first time. Beyond the stream crossing, the tread becomes very thin in the grassy, rocky upper valley. Follow rock cairns and stretches of trail. Even with little or no tread, the going is very easy along the gentle open valley floor. At 6,400 feet, the cairns lead back across Eureka Creek, where constructed trail climbs directly up toward Shellrock Pass. Here, near where the scree slopes turn to meadow beneath Mount Lago, is terrain level enough to set up camp. An old fire ring indicates the presence of hardy hikers or horseback hunters from decades past.

DAY THREE   19 miles   4,800 feet gain

Day three is the most diverse, physically challenging, and rewarding day of the trek. It can be made shorter by camping at the confluence of Eureka Creek and the Lost River, saving an easy 4-mile hike and drive home for the last day. This would be mandatory for nearly any party that chooses to camp at Lake Doris on the second night instead of hiking into the Eureka Creek headwaters.

In less than 1 hour ascend to Shellrock Pass, soaking up the nearby views of Blackcap Mountain and Monument Peak. Shellrock Pass is the divide between the wild valley of Eureka Creek and the even wilder valley of Monument Creek, which can't be accessed without a minimum of 12 very rugged miles of hiking and climbing up and over a 7,000-foot pass.

Descend the rocky terrain east of Shellrock Pass, turning right at the junction with Monument Creek Trail #484. Cross streams and hike through meadows and forests. Cross the destruction of uncleared avalanche swaths and walk through silent subalpine meadows. In time, ford beautiful Monument Creek, dancing across rocks in a vain effort to keep your feet dry. Soon come upon the ruins of a prospector's cabin, the folly of such a venture exceeded only by the imagination and courage of the prospector himself. Fill your water bottles upon crossing the stream near 5,600 feet elevation. There is little chance of finding water again until reaching the confluence of Eureka Creek and the Lost River. On a hot afternoon, 2 to 3 quarts of water will be necessary to see you through this stretch. Climb steadily with Pistol Peaks looming above and providing a measuring stick of sorts. Completing the climb, arrive at Pistol Pass, elevation 7,100 feet, the fourth and last pass over 7,000 feet.

Begin the winding, traversing descent toward the obvious prowlike ridge that thrusts into the sky from footings in the Lost River Canyon. There is enough uphill in the "traverse" that at times you might believe the trail is climbing Pistol Peaks instead of descending toward the valley. Cross rock gullies and traverse around

Crossing Monument Creek

corners, eventually reaching the top of the prowlike divide at 6,300 feet elevation.

Struggle on, likely hot and thirsty, trying to conserve water on the dry, steep-sided slopes. Minimal trail maintenance ensures the downhill grind to the inviting streams below is a strenuous adventure. Plan on climbing over logs, searching out the trail amongst blow downs, and scratching through the brush, all to cover what amounts to 5 downhill miles. What should take 90 minutes may take double that. Hot and frustrated, cross the sturdy bridge over Eureka Creek and soak up the long desired and refreshing liquid. Nearby is a lovely, cool camp at the confluence with the Lost River. Staying here leaves a short 4-mile morning walk to the trailhead, reducing the day to 15 miles from 19.

Trail Summary and Mileage Estimates

0.0	Buckskin Ridge Trail #498 at Slate Pass, elevation 6,900 feet
0.4	Slate Pass Trail #478A, elevation 6,500 feet, stay left on Trail #498
1.3	Whistler Trail #575, elevation 6,400 feet, stay left on Trail #498
18.0	Way trail to Pasayten River ford, elevation 4,500 feet, turn right and descend to ford
18.3	Robinson Creek Trail #478, elevation 4,500 feet, turn right on Trail #478
21.8	Eureka Creek Trail #474, elevation 5,000 feet, turn left on Trail #474
25.2	Shellrock Pass Trail #484A, elevation 6,500 feet, stay left on Trail #484A
31.1	Monument Creek Trail #484, elevation 6,600 feet, turn right on Trail #484
47.5	Monument Creek Trailhead, elevation 2,400 feet

Kids swimming in Lake Doris

Suggested Camps Based on Different Trekking Itineraries

Night	15–20 mpd	10–15 mpd	10 mpd
One:	13+ miles - Buckskin Lake	13+ miles - Buckskin Lake	10 miles - beneath Buckskin Pass
Two:	28+ miles - Eureka Creek		
	headwaters	24 miles - Lake Doris	18+ miles - Pasayten River ford
Three:	43 miles - Lost River	34 miles - Monument Creek ford	24+ miles - Lake Doris
Four:		43 miles - Lost River	34 miles - Monument Creek ford
Five:			43 miles - Lost River

The Devils Loop

Ross Lake from East Bank Trail

Difficulty:	Easier
Distance:	43 miles
Elevation gain:	9,200 feet
Best season:	Mid-July through mid-October. If periodic snow crossing aren't bothersome, much of this high country is snow-free in early July. Brilliant foliage and ripe blueberries dominate the fall season.
Recommended itinerary:	3 days (10–15+ miles per day)
Water availability:	Carry a minimum of 2 quarts liquid forward from each on-trail water source. Don't count on finding water between the North Fork Devils Creek until beyond Devils Dome unless you drop from Devils Pass 0.5 mile to Devils Pass Shelter. If camping at Skyline Camp, plan on carrying water from Devils Pass areas unless snow patches are evident and small

streams are running. If you end up waterless at Skyline Camp, go over the top of Devils Dome and into the basin beyond where water is plentiful.

Logistics: Boaters, who are sometimes a bit noisier than hikers, use camps along Ross Lake. Boaters are usually very generous and have better food. Be nice and they'll probably share.

Jurisdictions: Pasayten Wilderness, 509-996-4000; North Cascades National Park, 360-856-5700. The trek initially traverses the Pasayten Wilderness before transitioning into the Ross Lake National Recreation Area (managed by the Park Service). Self-issue wilderness permits are available at the trailhead for treks in the Pasayten Wilderness. However, a backcountry permit obtained from the Park Service is required in order to camp along the shores of Ross Lake.

Maps: Green Trails: Mt. Logan, Jack Mountain, Ross Lake, and Diablo Dam

Trail location: Drive Interstate 5 to Burlington and take exit 230. Turn east and follow State Route 20 until past milepost 141. Turn left into the Canyon Creek parking area and trailhead, elevation 1,900 feet.

The Devils Loop that circumnavigates Jack Mountain, the most visible 9,000-foot peak in the North Cascades, will thrill you with its splendid vistas of Cascade spires and Pasayten highlands, wilderness, solitude, and accomplishment.

DAY ONE   11 miles   5,200 feet gain

Leave Canyon Creek Trailhead and within a few hundred yards cross Granite Creek on a sturdy bridge. Staying left at the junction with Canyon Creek Trail, proceed toward Canyon Creek. Carefully stride over Canyon Creek on a foot log. If crossing in the early morning, the cold air, damp slimy log, and ice-cold consequences of a slip will abruptly clear your sleepy mind. Upon crossing the log, turn right on the Jackita Ridge Trail #738. After a couple hundred yards, the trail turns sharply uphill, entering a series of long switchbacks that whisk you near timberline in about 4 miles and 3,400 feet of elevation gain. Enjoy ever-expanding views up Canyon Creek gorge and beyond as you measure upward progress against the opposite hillside. At the junction with the Crater Mountain Trail #746, elevation 5,300 feet, stay to the right and enter the dewy, boggy meadows of McMillan Park. On the gentle descent, the views to nearby peaks and the meadow slopes of Devils Park foretell of the beauty to come.

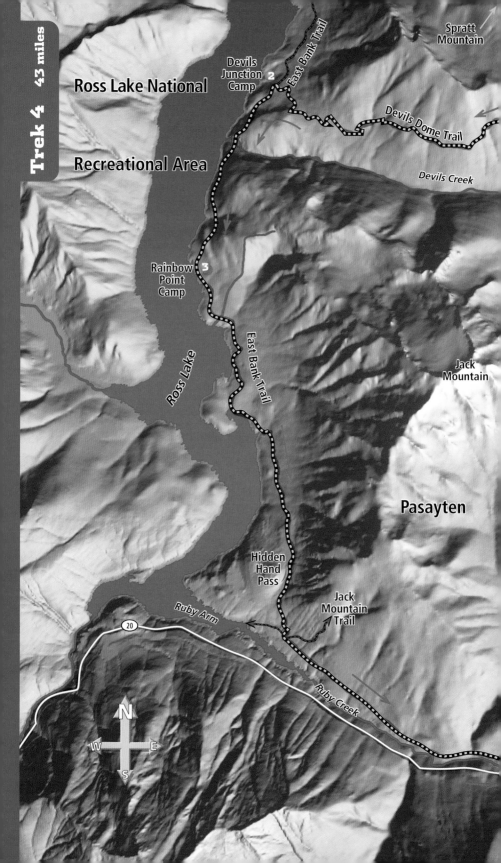

Ross Lake National

Recreational Area

Spratt
Mountain

Devils
Junction **2**
Camp

East Bank Trail

Devils Dome Trail

Devils Creek

Rainbow **3**
Point
Camp

East Bank Trail

Jack
Mountain

Ross Lake

Pasayten

Hidden
Hand
Pass

Jack
Mountain
Trail

Ruby Arm

20

Ruby Creek

N
W   E
S

Devils
Dome

2

Skyline
Camp

Devils Creek

752

North Fork Devils Creek

Devils
Pass

752

1

Jackita Ridge

738

Jerry
Lakes

Wilderness

Devils Park

1

Crater
Mountain

Crater
Lake

746

McMillan Park

738

Canyon Creek

Canyon
Creek
Trailhead

36

754

T

20

Granite Creek

Meadows of Devils Park

After crossing Nickol Creek, climb 1,000 feet into the open meadows of Devils Park. Rest for a while, maybe even enjoy lunch at Devils Shelter, hopefully also enjoying the view of deer grazing the rich meadows all around. When you resume your trek, traverse on trail through the upper reaches of Devils Park for 2 miles, climbing to 6,800 feet elevation on the very shoulder of Jackita Ridge. All around, lupine meadows cover the ground in purple waves. Below stands the shelter nestled in a grove of alpine firs. Beyond are the deep valleys of Canyon and Granite Creeks, and farther beyond rise the great peaks of Ragged Ridge, Black, and Goode. Just beyond the reach of your fingertips stands icy Jack Mountain; its serrated ridges and glistening glaciers rising into the sky above Devils Creek.

Force yourself to move on, crossing a rocky divide and descending the trail through steep scree into a small basin. Winding through the rocky basin, cross a minor divide and discover an even lovelier basin with a flowing stream and camp, elevation 5,800 feet. Savor this lovely camp and while away the afternoon with friendly conversation and stunning views in all directions.

DAY TWO 16 miles 3,000 feet gain

Upon leaving camp, complete a gently rising traverse across the slopes ahead, passing over a ridge crest at 6,300 feet elevation before descending into the North Fork of Devils Creek. In the creek bottom, avalanche snow may cover the trail, but the path so closely parallels the stream that routefinding is not an issue. Fill your water bottles prior to leaving the stream, as you may not see water again until beyond Devils Dome, about 8 miles ahead.

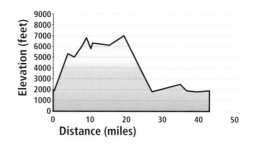

Continue climbing adjacent to the stream, seemingly headed toward the low point in Jackita Ridge called Anacortes Crossing. The route, however, does not utilize the crossing. Instead, stay left at the junction with this rarely used route and continue along the Jackita Ridge Trail #738. Now gently traverse for miles along or near the top of Devils Ridge. The meadows are lovely, even when peek-a-boo clouds cling to the ridge. Across the valley rises the ever-present form of Jack Mountain. Wind your way through Skyline Camp, a perfect spot except for the lack of a dependable water source, and continue on toward Devils Dome. Meadows give way to stone as you climb the rocky but secure path to the dome, at 6,982 feet elevation, the high point of your trek. Pause to rest and reflect on the beautiful scenery and wild country that envelops you.

Jack Mountain from Skyline Camp

Thirst will likely drive you from the fabulous vantage point of Devils Dome. Descend sharply and soon find yourself amidst the boulders, meadows, and streams in the sparkling basin just west of the dome. After stopping for water, cross through Dry Creek Pass and literally scamper down the hill to Ross Lake, 4,000 feet below. The path winds and traverses down open hillsides before entering forests above the lake. After your rapid descent, reach the junction with the East Bank Trail, elevation 1,800 feet. Follow the signs to the camp at Devils Landing, directly on the shores of Ross Lake.

DAY THREE 16 miles 1,000 feet gain

Unlike the first day's trek, which included a stern climb, and the second day's trek, which was dominated by the dizzying descent of more than 5,000 feet, the third and final trekking day is a gentle walk often near the lakeshore and always with pleasing scenery all around.

From your lakeshore camp, regain the East Bank Trail by turning right, south, and after trekking a mile or more cross the broad suspension bridge over the Devils Creek outlet. Look down the fjordlike cut as the tall cliffs of the narrow canyon dive deeply beneath the water's surface. For 3 miles, walk along the shore of breathtaking Ross Lake, at times just a short dive above the inviting water. The views across the lake to Pumpkin Mountain, the blue lake water, the spires of Mount Prophet, and the Colonial Peak group rising prominently in the distance are spectacular.

Revel in the shoreline vista and take some time to dabble your toes in the water or perhaps go for a full body rush! Nudge yourself onward. Beyond Rainbow Point Camp the tread moves into the forest a few feet, and amidst the fir trees and vine maples gradually begin the 800-foot climb to Hidden Hand Pass. Although the grade is gentle and the distance short, your tired legs will feel the incline. Once through the pass, descend toward Ruby Arm, the extension of Ross Lake up into the Ruby Creek Valley.

Upon reaching the three-way junction that includes the trail up Little Jack Mountain (a sharp left turn), make a gentle left turn and walk upstream along Ruby Arm, away from Ross Lake. In 2 miles, reach the Ruby Creek Trail junction. Just above and on the opposite side of Ruby Creek, SR 20 winds through the mountains. Continue along on the Ruby Creek Trail, always in sight of the roiling water of Ruby Creek. In 3.5 miles, cross Canyon Creek and Granite Creek, returning to the Canyon Creek Trailhead, having completed the loop named for the devil.

Trail Summary and Mileage Estimates

0.0	Canyon Creek Trailhead #754, elevation 1,900 feet
0.2	Jackita Ridge Trail #738, elevation 1,900 feet, stay left on Trail #738
0.3	Ruby Creek Trail, elevation 1,900 feet, stay right on Trail #738
4.0	Crater Mountain Trail #746, elevation 5,300 feet, stay right on Trail #738
13.3	Anacortes Crossing Trail, elevation 6,200 feet, stay left on Trail #738
15.3	Devils Ridge Trail #752, elevation 6,100 feet (at Devils Pass), stay left on Trail #752
27.1	East Bank Trail, elevation 1,800 feet, turn left on East Bank Trail
36.7	Jack Mountain Trail, elevation 1,900 feet, angle left on East Bank Trail
39.5	Ruby Creek Trail, elevation 1,800 feet, stay left on Ruby Creek Trail
43.0	Canyon Creek Trailhead, elevation 1,900 feet

Descending the basin beyond Devils Dome

Suggested Camps Based on Different Trekking Itineraries

Night	15–20 mpd	10–15 mpd	10 mpd
One:	20+ miles - Beyond Devils Dome	11 miles - near Jackita Ridge	8 miles - Devils Park Shelter
Two:		27 miles - Devils Junction Camp	18+ miles - Skyline Camp
Three:			30+ miles - Rainbow Point Camp

The Classic Passes— North

Little Beaver Valley from Whatcom Pass

Difficulty:	Easier
Distance:	52 miles
Elevation gain:	12,000 feet
Best season:	Mid-July through September
Recommended itinerary:	3 or 4 days (15+ miles per day plus a day for exploration)
Water availability:	Water is abundant throughout the trek.
Logistics:	The 4-day itinerary as recommended includes a day for roaming the obligatory high-country side trips near Whatcom Pass, entailing 2 nights at Whatcom Camp. Other itineraries can be modified to provide more time for exploration by adding a night's camp at Whatcom Camp. If Whatcom Camp is completely reserved, the

Tapto Lakes cross-country zone is an alternative. The obligatory side-trip mileage is factored into the trek, adding 2 miles to the on-trail distance to Whatcom Pass (Hannegan Peak side trip) and 4+ miles to the on-trail distance between Whatcom Pass and the next camp on each itinerary (Whatcom Pass side trips). The trek finishes 150+ road miles from the start, requiring a drop-off and pickup or a day's worth of logistical gymnastics.

Jurisdictions: North Cascades National Park, 360-856-5700. Backcountry permits are required. Because it is not convenient to access Park Service ranger stations en route to the trailhead, permits can be obtained at the Forest Service ranger station in Glacier, 360-599-2714.

Maps: Green Trails: Mt. Shuksan, Mt. Challenger, Ross Lake, and Diablo Dam

Trail location: Drive Interstate 5 to Bellingham and take exit 255. Turn east and follow State Route 542 up the Nooksack Valley until past milepost 46. Turn left on Forest Service Road 32 (Hannegan Road; could be labeled Road 402) and drive about 6 miles to the road end and trailhead, elevation 3,100 feet. For the return home, drive I-5 to Burlington and take exit 230. Turn east and follow SR 20 up the Skagit Valley to beyond milepost 134. Park at the Ross Dam/Lake access parking lot and trailhead, elevation 2,100 feet.

This trek is reminiscent of mountain travel as it was for Native Americans, hunters, prospectors, and explorers generations ago, while providing some of Washington's most spectacular trailside views. This cross-range trek over Hannegan, Whatcom, and Beaver Passes is the defining trek in the northern park region, providing up-close views into the Picket Range of North Cascades National Park, without question the most spectacular mountainous region in Washington.

DAY ONE   19 miles   6,000 feet gain
The first challenge you will face is getting a ride to the trailhead, getting picked up at trek's end, or both. Hardcore adventurers need hardcore supporters.

Starting beside Ruth Creek, the trail gradually ascends away from the creek, traversing the curving valley slope toward Ruth Mountain. Reaching subalpine terrain by a lovely creek, the tread switchbacks and climbs abruptly to Hannegan Pass, elevation 5,100 feet, 4+ miles from the trailhead.

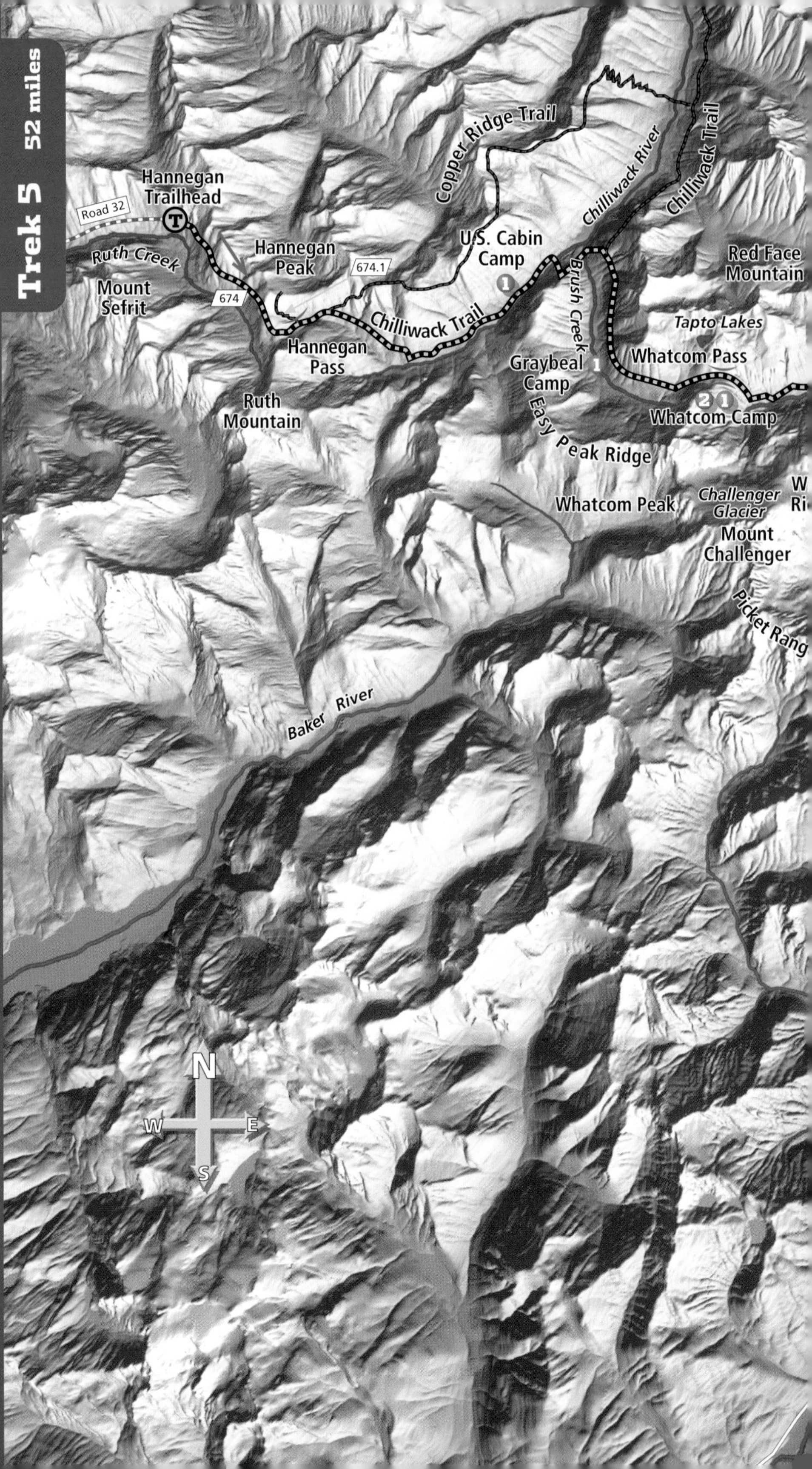

Road 32

Hannegan
Trailhead

(T)

Ruth Creek

Mount
Sefrit

674

Hannegan
Peak

674.1

Copper Ridge Trail

U.S. Cabin
Camp

(1)

Chilliwack River

Chilliwack Trail

Chilliwack Trail

Hannegan Pass

Ruth
Mountain

Chilliwack Trail

Brush Creek

Graybeal
Camp

Easy Peak Ridge

Whatcom Peak

Tapto Lakes

Red Face
Mountain

Whatcom Pass

1

Whatcom Camp

2 1

Challenger
Glacier

W
Ri

Mount
Challenger

Picket Rang

Baker River

N
W   E
S

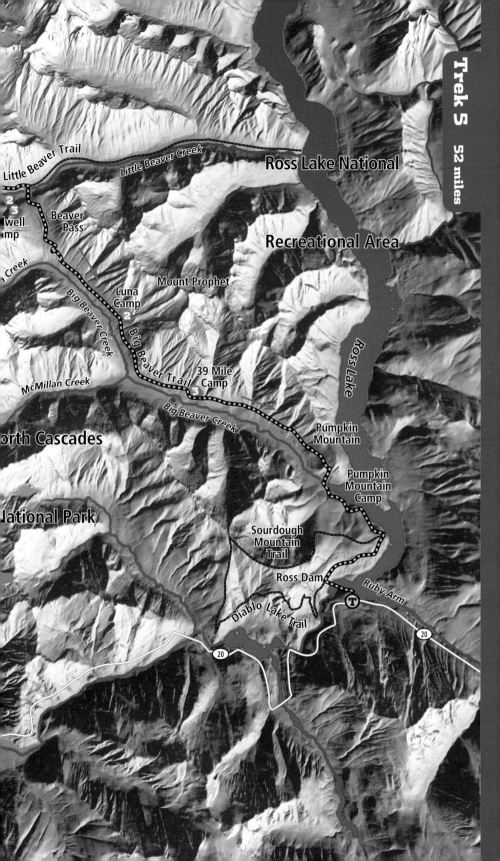

Little Beaver Trail

Little Beaver Creek

Ross Lake National

Little Beaver

2
3

dwell
mp

Beaver
Pass

Recreational Area

Creek

Big Beaver Creek

Mount Prophet

Luna
Camp
2

Big Beaver Trail

Ross Lake

McMillan Creek

39 Mile
Camp
3

Big Beaver Creek

orth Cascades

Pumpkin
Mountain

Pumpkin
Mountain
Camp

lational Park

Sourdough
Mountain
Trail

Ross Dam

Ruby Arm

Diablo Lake Trail

T

20

20

Obligatory side trip 1. Stash your backpack at the pass and climb north (left) on the Hannegan Peak Trail, leading upward 1,000 feet in 1 mile to the summit of meadowed Hannegan Peak, a marvelous regional viewpoint for Mounts Shuksan and Baker as well as nearby Copper Ridge.

Following tread or descending gentle snow into the basin, readily pick up the Chilliwack River Trail and soon arrive at the Copper Ridge Trail junction. Stay right and immerse yourself deep in the old-growth giants along the Chilliwack River, some reaching to 200 feet in height. The moss-laden trail feels like an ancient pathway, which it is. Used by Native Americans for untold centuries, this very path was hiked by trappers, traders, prospectors, and, ultimately, road builders, who eyed the terrain from an entirely different perspective. Try as they might, the road builders failed to pave this part of the landscape, and as a result, decaying cedar puncheon protects your feet from the muck of marshy terrain instead of asphalt. Mist often hangs above the racing waters of the Chilliwack, a beautiful broad streambed with moss-covered shoreline boulders melding into the slippery cobbles of the river channel. Giant fir, cedar, and hemlock shade the riverbank, intertwined with huckleberries, vine maples, and alders, further enhanced by ferns, trillium, and other adornments growing just inches from the rich soil. For miles the scene is intensely vegetated and breathtaking in both complexity and beauty.

Hike past U.S. Cabin (a camp) and soon reach a very unusual feature of the route. Encounter a single-person cable car, spanning a chasm above the roaring water. Not much explanation is necessary, just get in the tipsy car and pull yourself across using the rope provided. Blind faith will serve you better at this point than a questioning mind. One at a time, follow the instructions and arrive safely across the river. Continuing downstream, pass the river ford access trail and arrive at the Brush Creek Trail junction, elevation 2,600 feet, 14 miles from the trailhead. Turn right on Brush Creek Trail and begin the ascent to Whatcom Pass. The Brush Creek Trail ascends at valley grade for 2 miles. Beyond Graybeal Camp, the trail climbs several hundred feet before resuming its up-valley traverse deeply beneath the sheer rock face of Whatcom Peak and Easy Ridge. As you round a corner into the basin beneath Whatcom Pass, the trail resumes a switchbacking profile.

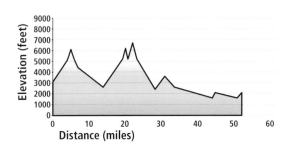

Crossing patches of snow (seasonal) and jumping creeklets, follow tread steadily uphill to arrive at Whatcom Camp, 19 miles from the trailhead (which includes the obligatory jaunt up Hannegan Peak). A few hours up to a full

Trekking along the Chilliwack River Trail

day can be spent exploring the scenic and obligatory side trips near Whatcom Pass that are described as part of day two.

DAY TWO   16+ miles   4,000 feet gain

From Whatcom Camp, arise in the predawn and in a couple of minutes arrive at the splendor of Whatcom Pass, elevation 5,200 feet. Beyond the Little Beaver Valley rise the stark sheer towers of Hozomeen Mountain. To the right is the gleaming ice of Challenger Glacier, tumbling from the airy rock summit over polished and glistening rock slabs into the valley floor. Directly above stands Whatcom Peak, a steep snow and rock ridge leading directly from Whatcom Pass to the summit—for climbers only!

Obligatory side trip 2. Take the time to hike up the way trail heading south on the ridge out of Whatcom Pass toward Whatcom Peak. The views of Challenger Glacier, Whatcom Peak, and the surrounding glory grow with each step. Turn around when time or terrain dictates. Maximum of 1.5 miles round trip and 1,000 feet elevation gain.

Obligatory side trip 3. Turn north on way trails leading out of Whatcom Pass and head sharply uphill toward Tapto Lakes, shimmering jewels set in a meadow basin with expansive views. If you are doing this jaunt early in the morning, take in the sunrise to the east and the dawn of day bursting forth over the Cascade Range with ridge after serrated ridge filling the scene in every direction. Maximum of 2.5 miles round trip and 1,500 feet elevation gain.

Stunned by the scenery, finally break camp and trek over Whatcom Pass before descending on steep switchbacks into the headwaters of Little Beaver Creek. The descent into the Little Beaver is very abrupt. The tread drops swiftly via switchbacks down gravelly slopes amidst rock outcroppings. Soon reach the wild valley floor, with glaciers hanging just above. Waterfalls roar at a deafening decibel, spilling from high Picket ridges over cliffs into the valley. Pick your way through the avalanche debris and brushy vegetation, enthralled by the unbridled powers of nature all around. Near Twin Rocks Camp enter deep forests once again, hiking adjacent to the rowdy stream until reaching the Big Beaver Trail junction, elevation 2,400 feet, 6+ miles from Whatcom Camp. Turn right on the Big Beaver Trail, crossing the swift deep waters of the Little Beaver on a sturdy new bridge, your trek a bit more than half completed.

Begin the gentle climb toward Beaver Pass, 1,200 feet above. Finally, the gentle overlapping switchbacks produce results and you will enter the broad saddle of Beaver Pass. For nearly 1 mile the trail neither rises nor drops perceptibly. After passing Beaver Pass Camp, the trail descends adjacent to the flat wild valley of Luna Creek. Strain your neck to see the Picket summits above and beyond the green jungle that confronts you.

Recommended side trip 1. From Beaver Pass Camp, trek up the trail-less sidehill to the east (behind camp), climbing several hundred feet to seek an opening in the vegetative canopy providing a view into the spectacularly wild reality of Luna Cirque. It is impossible to exaggerate the stunning beauty of Luna Cirque, certainly one of the most magnificent views in the Cascades, what with Challenger, Crooked Thumb, Ghost, Phantom, and Fury forming a wall of mountains that define the cirque. Looking down, the wild valleys of the Pickets offer some of the most unvisited land in the world—their jungles as impenetrable as those of the Amazon.

Fortunately, the Big Beaver Trail ushers you through the climactic old-growth forest in speedy comfort. On broad tread, travel easily along the valley floor to the earthy comfort of Luna Camp.

DAY THREE   16+ miles   2,000 feet gain

Day three (or four if you spent a day rambling at Whatcom Pass) is a day to revel in unrivaled old-growth beauty. With occasional glimpses of high peaks, descend past impenetrable McMillan Creek into the lower Big Beaver Valley, famous for its

Mount Challenger from Whatcom Pass

gigantic old-growth western red cedar trees as well as that for a generation the City of Seattle threatened to flood the valley by raising Ross Dam in order to generate more hydroelectric power. By now the Big Beaver runs slow, deep, and broad, more a river than a stream. The old-growth fir and cedar trees are staggeringly immense. The marshes, bogs, and beaver ponds are captivating, lush with flora from ferns to fireweed. After walking nearly 10 flat miles through the most glorious old-growth valley in Washington, reach Ross Lake. Unless you are camping or desire a swim, turn right, immediately crossing the Big Beaver on a substantial bridge. Past Pumpkin Mountain Camp, climb sharply above Ross Lake and wind past two lovely streams before undulating several hundred feet above the shoreline. The view down through open trees and rock outcroppings to the shimmering water is oh so inviting! In an hour, pass the "backside" Sourdough Mountain Trail junction. Rounding a broad curve, descend toward the lake, walking just above the highly desirable Ross Lake Resort, headed for Ross Dam. Finally, walk across the dam itself.

Ross Dam, 540 feet high, was the last and tallest of the three hydroelectric projects constructed by Seattle City Light in the formerly deep wild canyon of the Skagit River. Entire towns, such as Concrete and Cement City, were established and flourished providing the cement necessary for construction of the dams on the Skagit River and its Baker River tributary. Completed in the mid-1940s, the resulting Ross Lake and its highly valued recreational amenities were recognized with the establishment of the Ross Lake National Recreation Area in 1968. Finishing on the uphill, hunker down and climb the last mile to the trailhead adjacent to SR 20.

Trail Summary and Mileage Estimates

0.0	Hannegan Pass Trailhead, elevation 3,100 feet
4.0	Hannegan Pass, elevation 5,100 feet and junction with Hannegan Peak Trail
	(side trip 1, 2 miles round trip)
6.0	Return to Hannegan Pass, turn left (east) on Chilliwack River Trail
7.0	Copper Ridge Trail, elevation 4,400 feet, stay right on Chilliwack River Trail
12.6	Cable car crossing of the Chilliwack River
14.0	Junction with Brush Creek Trail, elevation 2,600 feet, turn right on Brush Creek Trail
19.4	Whatcom Pass, elevation 5,200 feet and junction with obligatory side trips 2 and 3
	(4 miles round trip)
23.4	Return to Whatcom Pass, head east on Little Beaver Trail
28.4	Junction with Big Beaver Trail, elevation 2,400 feet, turn right on Big Beaver Trail
31.0	Beaver Pass, elevation 3,600 feet
44.8	Ross Lake, elevation 1,600 feet, stay right on Big Beaver Trail
48.0	Sourdough Mountain Trail, elevation 2,100 feet, stay left on Big Beaver Trail
52.2	Happy Flats, Ross Lake/Dam Trailhead, elevation 2,100 feet

Note: The obligatory side trips are included in the mileage and elevation estimates.

Beaver ponds in Big Beaver Valley

Suggested Camps Based on Different Trekking Itineraries

Night	15–20 mpd	10–15 mpd	10 mpd
One:	19 miles - Whatcom Camp	16 miles - Graybeal Camp	10 miles - U.S. Cabin Camp
Two:	35+ miles - Luna Camp	29 miles - Stillwell Camp	19 miles - Whatcom Camp
Three:		40 miles - 39 Mile Camp	29 miles - Stillwell Camp
Four:			40 miles - 39 Mile Camp

TREK 6

The Classic Passes—South

Mount Buckner from upper Park Creek

Difficulty:	Strenuous
Distance:	55 miles
Elevation gain:	13,500 feet
Best season:	Late July through September, early August is best for flowers
Recommended itinerary:	4 days (15–20 miles per day, including side trips and general wandering)
Water availability:	Water is abundant throughout the trek.
Logistics:	You will enjoy the trek more if you don't complete the hike through Cascade Pass on a weekend, as this popular area is a little too crowded for maximum enjoyment. There will likely be snow on slopes leading to both Easy and Park Creek Passes through

mid-August. Just pick your way up or around the snow. The descents from both passes are on sunny slopes and will be snow-free even if the approaches aren't. For any itinerary, using Pelton Basin Camp for an overnight stay will afford you the time and energy to explore both Sahale Arm and the fabulous yet rarely completed off-trail ramble to the Trapper Lake overlook. Also, note the trek is completed 70+ road miles from where you start, requiring two vehicles, a drop-off and pickup, or a day's worth of logistical gymnastics.

Jurisdictions: North Cascades National Park, 360-856-5700. In addition to a backcountry permit, a Buckner cross-country zone permit is required for camping in Horseshoe Basin.

Maps: Green Trails: Diablo Dam, Mt. Logan, Cascade Pass, and McGregor Mountain

Trail location: Drive Interstate 5 to Burlington and take exit 230. Turn east and follow State Route 20 beyond milepost 151 to the Easy Pass parking area and trailhead, elevation 3,700 feet. For the return trip, follow SR 20 from Burlington approximately 45 miles to the community of Marblemount. Beyond milepost 106, continue straight ahead across the Skagit River (SR 20 turns 90 degrees left at this junction) and drive the Cascade River Road 22 miles to the road end at the Cascade Pass Trailhead, elevation 3,600 feet.

This fabulous journey over Easy, Park Creek, and Cascade Passes is the defining trek in the southern park section. Each of the passes is a classic in its own right. Upper Fisher Creek Basin, Horseshoe Basin, and the panorama from Sahale Arm add seasoning to this outdoor feast. Take the trek and discover why this adventure is such a significant North Cascades experience.

DAY ONE   13 miles   3,300 feet gain

After crossing the foot log over Granite Creek (a bridge is planned), a mere 150 yards from the car, you quickly transition to the wilderness reality. The crystal water splashes over golden granitic boulders, creating a beguiling golden hue. Think twice before fording the stream instead of searching out a log crossing because this creek is always running fast and is often deep. Once on the other side, settle into a pace and climb steadily through the fir-dominated old-growth forest. In seemingly only

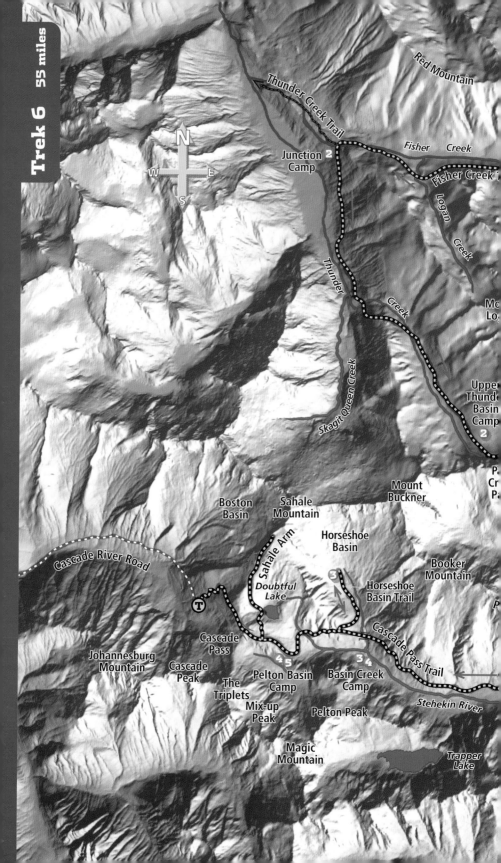

Red Mountain

Thunder Creek Trail

Fisher   Creek

Junction
Camp **2**

Fisher Creek

Logan   Creek

Thunder

Mo
Lo

Creek

Skagit Queen Creek

Uppe
Thund
Basin
Camp **2**

P
Cr
Pa

Boston
Basin

Sahale
Mountain

Mount
Buckner

Cascade River Road

Sahale Arm

Horseshoe
Basin

Booker
Mountain

Doubtful
Lake

3

Horseshoe
Basin Trail

T

Cascade Pass Trail

P

Cascade
Pass

4 5

3 4

Johannesburg
Mountain

Cascade
Peak

Pelton Basin
Camp

Basin Creek
Camp

The
Triplets

Mix-up
Peak

Pelton Peak

Stehekin River

Magic
Mountain

Trapper
Lake

Granite

T Easy Pass Trailhead

741

Easy Pass Creek

Mesahchie Peak

Ragged

Fisher Creek Trail

Easy Pass

Ridge

Creek

20

Cosho Camp

1 1

Easy Pass

1

Fisher Camp

Fisher

Creek

Mount Arriva

Fisher Peak

North Cascades

National Park

Goode Mountain

uckner Camp

2 3

Goode

Ridge

k
Ridge

Park Creek

hekin River

Stehekin Road

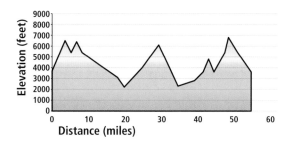

minutes, gain more than 1,000 feet in elevation and break into subalpine, avalanche-induced meadows beneath Graybeard Peak. The impressive scene envelops you. High above the meadows, rock and snow lead to the narrow gap of Easy Pass. By no means easy, the pass represents the only trail-accessed break in the mountainous wall east of Thunder Creek, from SR 20 to the Stehekin Valley. The pass stands out as a beacon, drawing you onward. The subalpine vegetation blossoms into multitudinous flower species, including tiger lilies, heather, cow parsnip, and monkey flower, as the trail traverses and then climbs through the basin. Streams are abundant and the basin rings with the musical sound of falling water. Climb switchbacks through the scree or snow to the pass, elevation 6,500 feet, 3.5 miles from the trailhead.

Enjoy the amazing view of mountains near and far. Nearby Fisher Peak, Mount Arriva, and Mesahchie Peak dominate the scene before you. Down valley, the bulky shoulders of Mount Logan and Thunder Peak fill the sky. Behind you across the Granite Creek Valley stand Tower Mountain, Golden Horn, and Mount Hardy. Flower fields dominate the foreground view, stretching from high above the pass down more than 1,500 feet into the valley floor of Fisher Creek.

The path traverses then switchbacks into the valley. The descent is breathtaking, as the view seems to turn from wide angle to telephoto. Features in the valley, seemingly insignificant when viewed from high above, grow as you descend. At the very foot of the switchbacks, near where the trail begins to turn downstream a short distance before Fisher Camp, lies an unmarked trail. The unmarked trail turns left, leading through alpine firs and meadows into remote upper Fisher Creek Basin.

Obligatory side trip 1. Dropping your pack and taking lunch with you, turn left on the boot-built trail. The sketchy tread becomes unnecessary in the open upper valley, approximately 1.5 miles long with 1,000+ feet of elevation gain. Merely walk through the meadows and boulders, always near the stream. The valley abounds with scenic vistas up valley to Fisher, Graybeard, and Arches Peaks or down valley to the spines of Ragged Ridge. Opportunities to enjoy lunch or just savor the solitude are everywhere. The farthest turnaround point is a knoll in the upper valley, from where the stream springs forth.

Once back on the constructed trail, the gentle forest walk down Fisher Creek seems effortless. Hike for several miles very near the stream until reaching Cosho Camp.

Park Creek

DAY TWO   17 miles   4,500 feet gain

From Cosho Camp, cross over Fisher Creek and continue down valley. Water is abundant as you continually encounter torrents streaming from the high country to the valley floor. Leaving Fisher Creek for a time, rejoin it near the intersection with the Thunder Creek Trail, elevation 3,100 feet, 5+ miles from Cosho Camp. Soak up the view across the Thunder Creek Valley from your perch 1,000 feet above the valley floor.

Turn left, heading up valley on the Thunder Creek Trail toward Park Creek Pass. Even though you are heading "up" valley, the trail in fact descends 1,000 feet before reaching Thunder Creek and beginning the steady climb to Park Creek Pass, more than 4,000 feet above. Climb steeply through the ever-diminishing stature of the old-growth forest as you strive for timberline vistas, crossing Thunder Creek once and then again before reaching Thunder Basin Camp, elevation 4,900 feet.

From Thunder Basin climb steadily with ever-expanding views into the upper basin of Thunder Creek. Climbing higher, reach the snowy profile of Park Creek Pass, elevation 6,100 feet. If the trail is lost in snow near the pass, realize that the trail does not pass through the low point of the divide, which is a perennial snow

Waterfalls of Horseshoe Basin

slope. Instead, it crosses through boulders on the east (left) side of the pass, about 20 feet above the snow. As you transition through the pass, stop to photograph the east face of Mount Booker, a cliff of Skagit gneiss 3,000 feet tall and nearly a mile wide. The meadows near the pass offer hours' worth of exploration, with always stunning views of the dominating spires of Mount Buckner and the steep ice of Buckner Glacier. Continue on to Buckner Camp, with the camp itself providing the final impressive view of Mounts Booker and Buckner rising high above Park Creek.

DAY THREE   13+ miles   2,600 feet gain
From Buckner Camp leave the open upper Park Creek Valley. Descend in the pleasant old-growth forest, dominated by ancient fir trees, for several miles, finally crossing classically beautiful Park Creek on a sturdy footbridge, passing by a small camp adjacent to the stream. Moving along, gently descend the remaining 2 miles to Park Creek Camp and Stehekin Road, 5 miles from Buckner Camp. Portions of Stehekin Road were washed away by floods during the winter of 1995–96. As the road is open to just upstream from Park Creek, turn right and walk the 4+ miles to its former end at Cottonwood Camp. The walk along the old road in tree-filtered sunlight, accompanied by the sound of water splashing and rumbling toward Lake Chelan, is delightful. Periodically walk newly brushed trail or a flagged route through the bushes in places where the road was swallowed whole by the raging waters.

Arriving at Cottonwood Camp, transition to trail and climb steadily up the valley through talus slopes with views to Trapper, Pelton, Glory, Magic, Mix-up, and other crowning Cascade peaks. After passing Basin Creek Camp, cross Basin Creek on a small suspension bridge and climb a series of long switchbacks to the Horseshoe Basin Trail junction.

Obligatory side trip 2. Treat yourself to one of the most wondrous trail views in all of Washington. Turn right and walk the broad trail, originally created as a road in the 1940s to truck ore from the Black Warrior Mine down to Lake Chelan, after original plans to construct a road via Cascade Pass never materialized. The road lasted less than five years before it was destroyed by snow slides. Climb 1,200 feet in 1.5 miles to reach far into the basin, with its dozen or more cascading waterfalls and wild views. Basin Creek, boulder-strewn meadows ablaze with fireweed, the waterfalls, and the great cirque of peaks beyond combine to create a vista nothing short of unforgettable.

Camp here in the Buckner cross-country zone, alone but for the roar of water careening over cliffs and the neck-straining views to mountaintops in every direction. While roaming the basin, seek out the considerable evidence of mining activities that were initiated in this wildly rugged and remote basin, which was worked extensively by miners throughout the 1890s into the mid-1900s.

Particularly active mining activities were associated with the Black Warrior and

Davenport mining claims, operating in lower and upper Horseshoe Basin, respectively. Mining activities occurred in fits and starts for more than fifty years, ending about 1950. Miners attempting to work year-round in this harsh environment lived with their mining operations and quarters buried beneath feet of snow for protection against life-threatening snow avalanches, as they chased elusive mineral veins, including gold, silver, and copper deposits, through ridges and into valleys extending from Cascade Pass to Thunder Creek.

DAY FOUR   12 miles   3,100 feet gain

Leaving Horseshoe Basin, descend back to the main trail, turn right, and continue your steady ascent to historic Cascade Pass, a path used through the centuries by all inhabitants of the Northwest. The pass was likely the primary Native American trade route linking inland and coastal tribes. Alexander Ross was arguably the first European to cross from the Stehekin to Skagit Valley via Cascade Pass, a journey first chronicled in 1855. Cascade Pass was traveled extensively from the late 1800s through the early 1900s by miners and associates moving goods and ore to and from the mines on either side of the divide. After the final "rush" of the 1940s and after all threats of further road building ceased, the trail to Cascade Pass and beyond became an avenue for hikers and climbers seeking the beauty and adventure lost in modern living.

Cross the spectacular tumbling waterfall of Doubtful Creek before climbing the switchbacks through deep brush. Upon reaching Pelton Basin Camp, you are again presented with a delightful off-trail opportunity.

Recommended side trip 1. If time allows, the 1.5-mile off-trail scramble to the viewpoint ridge above Trapper Lake ranks as an unforgettable visual experience. Descend into Pelton Basin and ford the stream, the Stehekin River actually. This ford may require hip-deep wading in gently flowing water. If the water crossing seems unappealing, hike up valley in talus and meadow until a more desirable crossing can be made. Once across the water, walk gentle alpine slopes southeast, around the northeast shoulder of Pelton Peak. Then ascend on game trails or boot-built tread to the narrow ridge crest east of Pelton Peak, elevation 5,600 feet.

The view of glacier-fed aqua-colored Trapper Lake is stunning. Vast in size, the broad lake fills the basin beneath the sheer towers of both Glory and Trapper Mountains. The ice and rock towers of Hurry-up and Pelton Peaks and Magic Mountain rise starkly above. Across the valley are Sahale Mountain, Ripsaw Ridge, and Mounts Booker and Buckner. Down the gorgeous green valley of the Stehekin rises McGregor Mountain, yet another 8,000-foot climax viewpoint over the land.

Return to the trail and traverse alpine greenery and talus slopes before finally climbing to Cascade Pass. A few feet before the pass is the junction with the trail to Sahale Arm, and like Horseshoe Basin it is an absolute necessity to witness with your own eyes.

Obligatory side trip 3. Stash your pack in bushes nearby, turn right, and follow the narrow tread sharply uphill, gaining 1,000 feet in less than 1 mile. Then walk the gently rising meadow ridge at least another mile, with spectacular regional views in all directions. Easily ascend the gentle meadowed ridge, with new views west to the sharp rock pyramid of Forbidden Peak, the sheer tower of Mount Torment, and the vast snow ridges of Eldorado Peak. To the south, see the peaks of the fabled Ptarmigan Traverse all the way to Glacier Peak and beyond.

The entire Cascade Pass region is a match for the beauty and grandeur of Europe's famous Alps. This same comparison holds true for the crowds of casual hikers who complete the pilgrimage each weekend. With the trek nearly complete, descend back to Cascade Pass and greet a steady stream of hikers as you near the trailhead and your journey's end.

Trail Summary and Mileage Estimates

0.0	Easy Pass Trailhead, elevation 3,700 feet
5.2	Junction with way trail to upper Fisher Creek Basin (3 miles round trip)
8.2	Regain Fisher Creek Trail, turning left (down valley)
17.8	Thunder Creek Trail, elevation 3,100 feet, turn left on Thunder Creek Trail
34.5	Stehekin Road, elevation 2,300 feet, turn right on Stehekin Road
39.0	Regain historic Cascade Pass Trail at Cottonwood Camp, elevation 2,800 feet
41.4	Horseshoe Basin Trail, elevation 3,600 feet (3 miles round trip)
44.4	Regain Cascade Pass Trail, turning right (up valley)
47.4	Sahale Arm Trail, elevation 5,400 feet (3.5 miles round trip)
51.0	Regain Cascade Pass Trail at Cascade Pass, turn right
54.7	Cascade Pass Trailhead, elevation 3,600 feet

Note: The obligatory side trips are included in the mileage and elevation estimates. The recommended side trip to the Trapper Lake overlook adds 3 miles and 1,200 feet elevation gain to the trek.

Suggested Camps Based on Different Trekking Itineraries

Night	15–20 mpd	10–15 mpd	10 mpd
One:	13+ miles - Cosho Camp	13+ miles - Cosho Camp	9 miles - Fisher Camp
Two:	30+ miles - Buckner Camp	25+ miles - Upper Thunder Basin Camp	18+ miles - Junction Camp
Three:	43+ miles - Horseshoe Basin	40+ miles - Basin Creek Camp	30+ miles - Buckner Camp
Four:		46 miles - Pelton Basin Camp	40+ miles - Basin Creek Camp
Five:			46 miles - Pelton Basin Camp

The Pacific Crest Trail:
Rainy Pass to Stevens Pass

Pacific Crest Trail sign atop Fire Creek Pass

Difficulty:	Most strenuous
Distance:	124 miles
Elevation gain:	24,500 feet
Best season:	Late July through September; early to mid-August is best for flowers.
Recommended itinerary:	7 days (15–20 miles per day)
Water availability:	Other than as noted, water is abundant. Water can be scarce from Cady Ridge south to Janus Lake, a distance of 20 miles. Leave Lake Sally Ann with at least 2 quarts of liquid and fill up at every opportunity. Water scarcity affects the location of camps for night six of the recommended itinerary and nights seven through nine for the alternate itinerary. While you may discover and even select other camps, water is not guaranteed to be available.

Logistics: Expect snow crossings near Fire Creek Pass and on either side of Red Pass until mid-August. The crossings can be steep and familiarity with snow travel is helpful. Often it is possible to traverse above or below uncomfortable snow crossings with little inconvenience. The trek ends about 200 road miles from the start, requiring a drop-off and pickup or use of public transportation. On the return trip, it may be possible to use commercial bus service from Stevens Pass back to the Seattle area. Contact Greyhound, 206-628-5508 (Seattle), or *www.greyhound.com,* or try Mountain Transporter, 509-996-8294.

Jurisdictions: Glacier Peak Wilderness, 360-436-1155, and North Cascades National Park, 360-856-5700. Backcountry permits are not required for travel in the Glacier Peak Wilderness and adjoining wilderness areas. However, as described, both itineraries require a permit for the first night's camp in the Lake Chelan National Recreation Area (High Bridge Camp, Bridge Creek Camp, or any other camp in the North Cascades National Park/Lake Chelan National Recreation Area complex).

Maps: Green Trails: Washington Pass, Stehekin, McGregor Mountain, Holden, Glacier Peak, and Benchmark Mountain

Trail location: Drive Interstate 5 to Burlington and take exit 230. Turn east and follow State Route 20 to either just beyond milepost 157 at Rainy Pass or near milepost 159 at the Bridge Creek Trailhead, as the PCT parallels SR 20 for 2 miles before descending Bridge Creek. Either park in the parking lot on the right side of Rainy Pass and pick up the trail a few feet off the highway, elevation 4,800 feet, or drive 2 miles east on SR 20 to the well-signed parking lot for the Bridge Creek Trail (PCT South), elevation 4,400 feet. Pick up the trail directly across the road. (Purists walk from Rainy Pass.) For the return trip, drive I-5 to Everett and take exit 194. Travel east on U.S. Highway 2 to beyond milepost 64. Upon reaching Stevens Pass, the trailhead is on the north (left side) of the road behind an A-frame building, elevation approximately 4,000 feet.

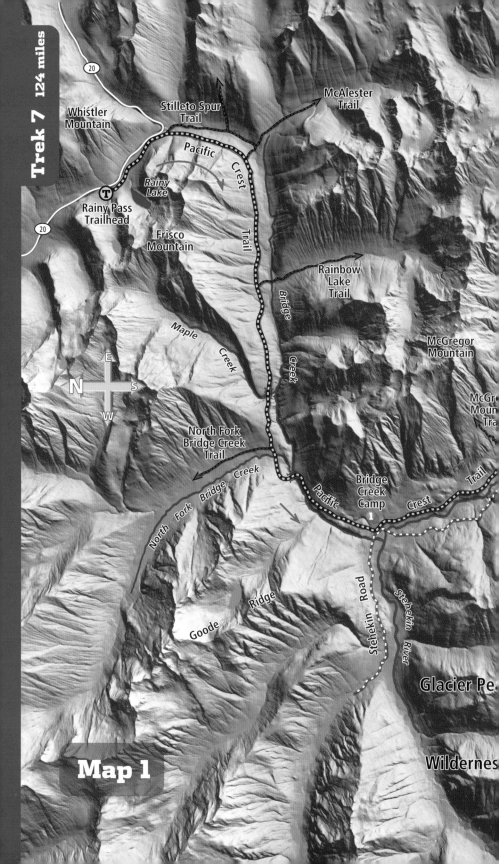

(20)

Whistler
Mountain

Stilleto Spur
Trail

Pacific

McAlester
Trail

Crest

T

Rainy
Lake

Rainy Pass
Trailhead

(20)

Frisco
Mountain

Trail

Rainbow
Lake
Trail

Bridge

Maple

McGregor
Mountain

Creek

Creek

McGr
Moun
Tra

N E S W

North Fork
Bridge Creek
Trail

Creek

Bridge

Pacific

Bridge
Creek
Camp
1

Crest

Trail

North Fork

Stehekin Road

Stehekin River

Goode

Ridge

Glacier Pe

Map 1

Wilderness

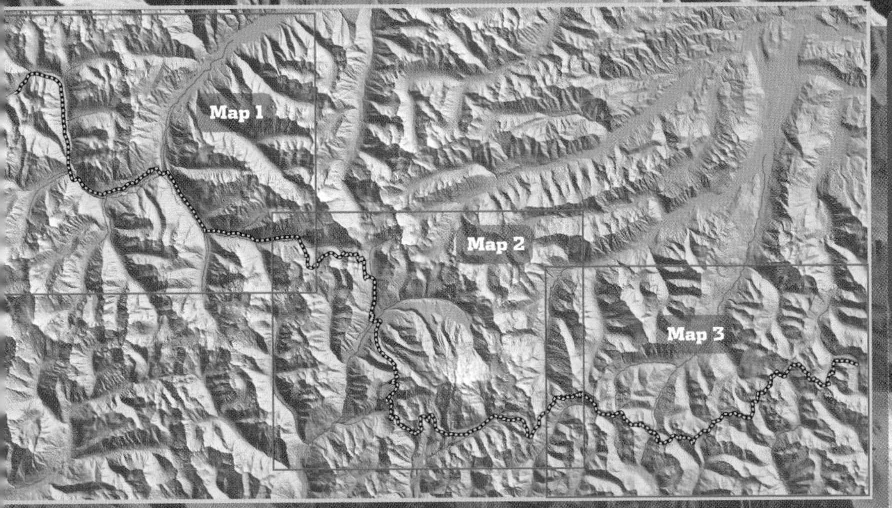

Map 1

Map 2

Map 3

Trek 7 overview

Glacier Peak

High Bridge
Camp

Wilderness

Stehekin Road

2000

e Gorge Trail

Agnes

Creek

1242

Cedar
Camp

2

1239

2000

Agnes   Creek

2000

South   Fork   Agnes   Creek

1272

West Fork Agnes Creek

2000

Spruce

Creek

Agnes
Mountain

Bannock
Mountain

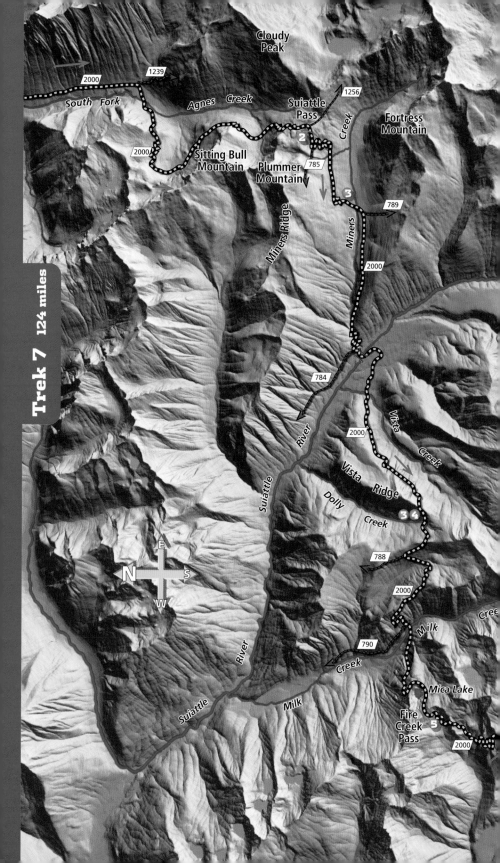

Map 2

Trek 7 124 miles

Glacier Peak

Wilderness

Glacier
Peak

White

River

Indian
Head
Peak

1507

2000

5

2000

River

White
Mountain

White
Pass

Sauk

River

2000

White Chuck
Cinder Cone

6

Portal
Peak

649

North

Fork

Chuck

2000

Red
Pass

643.1

White

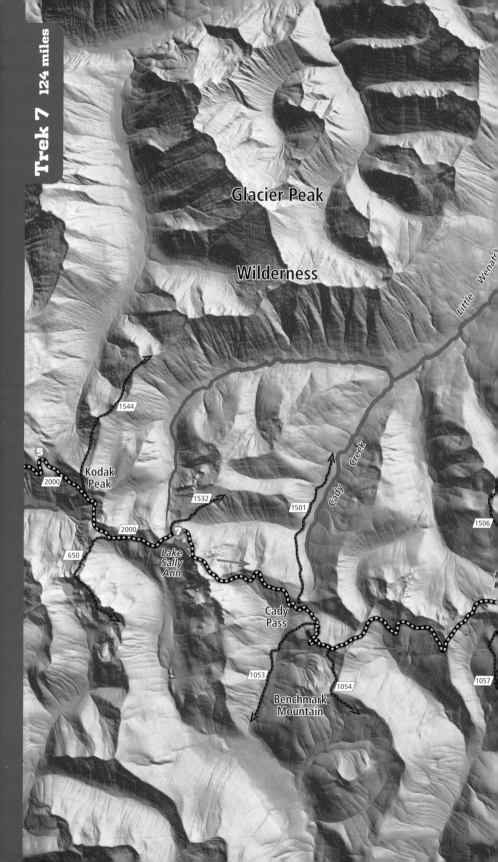

Glacier Peak

Wilderness

Little Wenat...

1544

5

2000

Kodak
Peak

1532

1501

Cady

Creek

1506

2000

650

7

Lake
Sally
Ann

Cady
Pass

1053

1054

1057

Benchmark
Mountain

N
E
W
S

1590

Lake Janus

Union Gap

Lichtenberg Mountain

Lake Valhalla

9

Mount McCausland

Glasses Lake

~ather ~ake

Grizzly Peak

T

2

Rapid River

Map 3

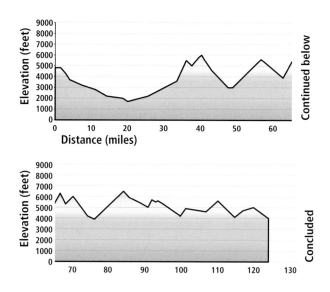

The Pacific Crest Trail through the Glacier Peak Wilderness is the signature trek for experiencing the crest of the Cascade Mountains with all its diversity. Arguably the most beautiful and one of the most challenging sections of the entire PCT, this trek will introduce you to the allure and demands experienced by true long-distance hikers.

DAY ONE   20 miles   1,500 feet elevation gain

Wave good-bye to family or friends, hoist your backpack, leave Rainy Pass on the PCT, and begin paralleling SR 20 as the trail descends toward Bridge Creek. Gently descend through fir and hemlock forests for 1.5 miles until intersecting a short side trail leading out to the highway and a major parking area. This alternate start saves the aforementioned 1.5-mile walk but is completely unacceptable to a purist! Stay to the right upon reaching the alternate trailhead access and stay to the right again several minutes later upon reaching the Stiletto Spur Trail. Now firmly entrenched on the PCT, away from the distraction of the highway, enjoy forested beauty, roaring streams, and views to high peaks and rugged valleys. The gently descending trail through subalpine meadows and open forests makes for lovely, yet quick walking. Pass the junction with McAlester Creek Trail, staying to the right. A few miles later again stay to the right upon reaching the South Fork Bridge Creek Trail junction.

Through Washington and Oregon, much of the inspiration for the route we now call the PCT owes a debt of gratitude to Forest Service Supervisor Fred Cleator, who in the late 1920s to 1930s inspired development of the "Cascade Crest Trail" through Washington and completion of the "Skyline Trail" through Oregon. To this day the rustic trail sign at Fire Creek Pass on the shoulder of Glacier Peak bears the "Cascade Crest" name.

Onward toward the Stehekin River winds the narrow tread, with views across the valley to the Ptarmigan Traverse peaks, including Mounts Spider and Formidable. Enjoy a break upon reaching the small suspension bridge crossing lively Maple Creek, 10 miles from Rainy Pass. While this day is long at 20 miles, the saving grace is that the trail generally descends all the way to the Stehekin Valley, preserving your muscles if not your feet.

Soon reach the North Fork Bridge Creek Trail junction. Stay left on the PCT, switchbacking downward to the sturdy bridge crossing the combined flows of Bridge Creek and all its tributaries, a mighty torrent of icy chill moving as a crystal liquid. Stop to behold the inspiring beauty of the confluence, as the North Fork Bridge Creek roars into a frothy union with Bridge Creek. After walking a couple more miles in the likely hot lower valley, reach Stehekin Road, elevation 2,200 feet, 14+ miles from Rainy Pass. Walk the short distance along Stehekin Road just until the PCT starts to drift into the woods to the left. Now you have the choice of following the road or the PCT. The road is one-lane wide, rarely traveled, and offers better views of the Stehekin River than the trail does. Having walked both the trail and the road, I prefer the road. The objective of both routes is to reach High Bridge Camp and the Agnes Creek Valley.

To follow the PCT, stay on the trail as it edges left into the woods, winding down valley and crossing several splashy torrents en route. Stay right at the McGregor Mountain Trail junction and just beyond view marshy but pretty Coon Lake, one of the very few subalpine lakes in the North Cascades. Soon turn right again, rejoining Stehekin Road at High Bridge Camp, a Park Service outpost and shuttle stop if nothing else. Walk across High Bridge, a well-named bridge spanning the Stehekin River that roars through the impressive chasm below. Climbing one switchback on the road itself, reach Agnes Creek and the PCT south. Just a few feet up the road is High Bridge Camp, 20 miles from your beginning at Rainy Pass.

DAY TWO   20+ miles   5,300 feet gain

Upon rousing yourself and preparing for the day's journey, do not mistake the adjacent Agnes Gorge Trail with the Agnes Creek Trail (PCT South). The Gorge Trail is a pleasing and spectacular dead-end 2.5-mile walk along the wrong side of Agnes Creek, with no hope of crossing back over to the PCT. Leave High Bridge Camp and Stehekin Road, reentering forest near Agnes Creek and beginning the 20-mile sojourn through the beautiful valley.

Drop slightly to the crossing of raging Agnes Creek, contained in a deep narrow gorge as it rockets down the narrow canyon into the Stehekin River. After crossing the stream on a sturdy bridge, ascend several hundred feet before walking alongside the more gently rolling water. Travel deeper and deeper into the wilderness,

Crossing Agnes Creek on a foot log

in 5.5 miles crossing Pass Creek and reaching Fivemile Camp. Almost immediately thereafter reach the West Fork Agnes Creek Trail junction. Stay left, having no interest in the jungle-like brush of the West Fork. The valley is classically beautiful, the trail never far from the stream. Pass Swamp Creek and Cedar Camps before reaching Hemlock Camp, 13 miles from Stehekin Road. Upon leaving Hemlock Camp turn right at the trail junction representing both the old and new versions of PCT tread. Although the old tread makes more logistical sense than the new, cross lovely Agnes Creek on a worn log and bid the stream good-bye.

Leaving the cool protection of the shadowy valley, ascend and traverse muggy, sun-drenched (hopefully) subalpine slopes. Climbing to 5,500 feet elevation beneath Sitting Bull Mountain, you are rewarded with lovely meadows and expansive views down Agnes Creek and across the valley to incomparable Bonanza Peak. The tread picks along, dropping into a basin at 5,000 feet elevation before ascending and traversing beneath Plummer Mountain into Suiattle Pass, elevation 6,000 feet, 20 miles from Fivemile Camp. Moving through the pass, immediately descend through alpine firs laced with blueberry plants and heather. Find camp in the subalpine terrain 0.5 mile from the pass.

DAY THREE 15 miles 3,400 feet gain

Upon leaving camp, in a short distance reach the junction with the Miners Ridge Trail #785. Stay left and descend deeper into the Suiattle Valley. Upon reaching the glassy, slow-moving waters of Miners Creek, flowing from remote Fortress Mountain, stop for a break and luxuriate in the quiet beauty of the scene. Your thoughts may well be dominated by the reality of the pending 3,400-foot climb to Vista Ridge. On a sunny day, walk through the patchwork sunlight splaying magical designs in the ancient old-growth forest. Staying right at the junction with Middle Ridge Trail #789, descend steadily toward the muddy Suiattle itself. Reach the banks of the Suiattle River at the junction with the Suiattle River Trail #784. Turn left, walking out onto the boulder-strewn riverbank and across the sturdy Skyline Bridge. View the mighty, muddy Suiattle, very different from the crystal-hued waters of your hike thus far. Draining the immense east side of Glacier Peak, including glaciers named Chocolate and Dusty, the filthy but pure water reminds me of the Carbon River spewing forth from Mount Rainier.

The broad Suiattle Valley continues to enthrall. For more than 2 miles wind awestruck through the old-growth giants, gawking in amazement at the girth and height of old-growth cedars and firs. After crossing Gamma and Vista Creeks, finally begin the daunting ascent. The tread takes its time, languishing uphill, scarcely switchbacking until over 4,500 feet elevation. Above 5,000 feet elevation climb through lavish meadows on gentle switchbacks, each one taking you closer to Vista Ridge. Finally, cross over the divide at 5,500 feet elevation and traverse into the headwaters of Dolly Creek. Camp here amidst the splendor. To the north rises Miners Ridge with Dome Peak peering over its shoulder. To the east, through Suiattle Pass, rises Bonanza Peak. Down valley, the mighty Suiattle flows for miles bound by high peaks and ridges too numerous to name.

DAY FOUR 17+ miles 3,500 feet gain

Arise from the slumber of the weary, and in the crisp air of early morning view Dome Peak more clearly across the broad, magnificent Suiattle as you begin the day's trek. In season, the lupine are hip deep. Stumble upon grazing deer while viewing the icy thrust of Glacier Peak just above. For an hour or more meander the alpine headwaters of Dolly and Milk Creeks, passing the side trail to Grassy Point. Then, crossing a divide at 5,600 feet, descend gentle switchbacks toward Milk Creek itself. As you lose elevation, look across the valley to Fire Creek Pass, rising ever higher above you as the loss continues. Immediately after crossing Milk Creek, you will begin climbing right back uphill 2,500 feet to Fire Creek Pass.

At the base of the descent, turn left at the junction with Milk Creek Trail #790 and immediately cross the stream on a sturdy bridge. In intermittent forest and subalpine vegetation, climb the gentle, interminable switchbacks toward Mica Lake. Climb through dry open forest into sunny meadows, the views and hues of alpine vegetation steadily improving. Meadows the colors of a painter's palette, volcanic rock, and ice blue liquid merge in the glacial cirque of incomparable Mica Lake. Resume your uphill trek, likely crossing a short but steep stretch of snow, to reach the broad, flat, glorious meadow of Fire Creek Pass. Rest, recuperate, snack, sun, and enjoy the views in all directions. When finally ready, or forced to by schedule, descend into the basin west of the pass. Continue your alpine circumnavigation, with Glacier Peak rising above and all the while surrounded by flower meadows, for an hour or two until selecting a scenic campsite with abundant vistas near Pumice or Glacier Creeks.

DAY FIVE   18+ miles   4,300 feet gain

Begin the winding descent toward the White Chuck Valley far below. Temporarily abandoning the high country, within 2 miles stay left at the junction with Kennedy Ridge Trail #639. Switchbacking down to the boulder and log hop of muddy Kennedy Creek, continue in forest on more gentle tread, crossing Sitkum Creek on a log before reaching the junction with Upper White Chuck River Trail #643.1, 3+ miles from camp. Stay left and begin walking up the valley, famous for its hot spring in the lower valley and luxurious meadows and dramatic views of Glacier Peak in the upper valley.

The first milestone within the upper valley is crossing the screaming White Chuck torrent, on a good bridge, thankfully. The roaring river will send shivers down your spine. Next, ascend past a lovely stream and waterfall descending as a foaming white ribbon into the White Chuck River below. Steeply climb through forest into the gentle meadows of the upper valley. The White Chuck now spills down a series of waterfalls interspersed with meadows and alpine firs. Likely find patchy snow interspersed with meadows as you round the bend beneath the cinder cone, a volcanic remnant from eons ago. Rising as a rust-colored mound 200 feet above the surrounding meadows, the cinder cone is in fact the remnant of a "younger" and certainly smaller volcano than Glacier Peak, but nonetheless a volcano that distributed its lava and volcanic materials throughout the greater White Chuck area. Finally, ascend the upper basin toward Red Pass, climbing through the meadow cirque ringing with myriad splashing streams, then continue up snow patches and across scree slopes. Reach dramatic Red Pass, a narrow cleft opening to the broad meadow ridges that stretch nearly to Stevens Pass. Back over your shoulder, the view of Glacier Peak above the White Chuck Valley dominates the scene. Across the Sauk Valley to the south rise Sloan Peak and the Monte Cristo group: Cadet, Foggy, Kyes, Monte Cristo, and Columbia.

From Red Pass, traverse the steep, flower-strewn slopes of White Mountain toward White Pass. Until late August there are intermittent steep snow patches both on the open slopes and in the stream courses. Exercise caution, traversing above or below snow patches if the crossings appear perilous. Stay left at the junc-

Meadow traverse through Glacier Creek Basin

tion with the North Fork Sauk River Trail #649. Soon reach the glorious meadow saddle of White Pass, elevation 5,900 feet. In sheer alpine bliss, contour in meadows past the White River Trail before descending to a timberline camp at Indian Pass, elevation 5,000 feet. Find water in small creeklets above Indian Pass on the slopes of Indian Head Peak.

DAY SIX   15 miles   3,000 feet gain
You've earned a day of leisure in the lovely meadows of the crest. From Indian Pass climb several hundred feet back to meadows and stay there for miles. There are nearly a dozen trail junctions between Indian Pass and the camp at Pear Lake, nearly one per mile. Keep your map handy but remember your route basically stays on the spine of the Cascades all day. On a clear day the forward view reveals Mount Rainier and Mount Stuart, while back over your shoulder rises the still dominating

form of Glacier Peak. There are no big climbs or descents, nothing more than several hundred feet at once, but the dips and peaks of the trail still amount to 3,000 feet of gain. Trek through scenic meadow after meadow to the shores of lovely Lake Sally Ann. Take time to lunch and perhaps swim in the cool yet inviting water. Beyond the lake, descend into forests at Cady Pass before climbing back into meadows at Benchmark Mountain. Stay left, high on the ridge crest on newly constructed tread beyond Saddle Gap. For the first time, other hikers may join you, for the innumerable valley trails connecting to the crest make for splendid walking. Descend slightly to the subalpine beauty of Pear Lake, elevation 4,900 feet, and camp here. Note there is likely no on-trail water source from Pear Lake until Lake Janus, nearly 9 miles away.

DAY SEVEN   18 miles   3,500 feet gain

From Pear Lake transition into a day of subalpine splendor after spending the last several days above timberline. Enjoy vistas not only of Pear Lake but also Peach Lake and Top Lake as you descend into forests at Wenatchee Pass. In the pass, stay right at the Top Lake Trail junction and trek steadily up the crest and literally right over the top of 5,600-foot Grizzly Peak. Heather and Glasses Lakes are shining jewels in the forested greenery east of your top-of-the-world perch. Still on the mountainous spine, finally leave the crest as you descend to marshy, but very pretty, Lake Janus, the first on-trail water source since Pear Lake. Water becomes more available thereafter, as the trail no longer tracks with the true crest of the Cascades, instead traversing slopes with drainage courses aplenty.

Reflecting on the magnificence of your soon-to-be-completed journey, contour and climb through Union Gap, staying right at the Smith Brook Trail #1590 and traversing east-side slopes just beneath the crest. The last site to anticipate is Lake Valhalla, a very popular destination hike via Smith Brook Trail or even from Stevens Pass along the PCT. Crossing a divide emanating from Mount McCausland, descend into the lovely cirque of Valhalla, enjoying the intense blue of the water amidst subalpine greenery, majestic firs, and sheer rock outcroppings. Contouring about in subalpine forest, sweep around several corners until Stevens Pass Highway (US 2) comes into view. Walk the gentle grade toward the trek's end in the pass.

Trail Summary and Mileage Estimates

0.0	PCT #2000 South at Rainy Pass, elevation 4,800 feet
1.5	Bridge Creek Trail, elevation 4,400 feet, stay right on PCT #2000
2.3	Stiletto Spur Trail, elevation 4,300 feet, stay right on PCT
5.0	McAlester Creek Trail, elevation 3,700 feet, stay right on PCT
7.5	South Fork Bridge Creek Trail, elevation 3,200 feet, stay right on PCT
11.2	North Fork Bridge Creek Trail, elevation 2,800 feet, stay left on PCT
14.3	Stehekin Road, elevation 2,200 feet, turn left and follow road/PCT

18.8	McGregor Mountain Trail, elevation 2,000 feet, stay right on PCT
20.1	Agnes Creek Trail at High Bridge, elevation 1,700 feet, walk the road across the bridge and up one switchback to the Agnes Creek Trail (PCT south)
25.6	West Fork Agnes Creek Trail, elevation 2,200 feet, stay left on PCT
33.6	Upper Agnes Creek Trail, elevation 3,600 feet, turn right on PCT
39.5	Railroad Creek Trail, elevation 5,800 feet, stay right on PCT
40.3	Cloudy Pass way trail at Suiattle Pass, elevation 6,000 feet, turn right on PCT
41.2	Miners Ridge Trail #785, elevation 5,500 feet, stay left on PCT
43.0	Middle Ridge Trail #789, elevation 4,600 feet, stay right on PCT
47.5	Suiattle River Trail #784, elevation 3,000 feet, stay left on PCT
48.7	Upper Suiattle River Trail #798, elevation 3,000 feet, stay right on PCT
56.7	Grassy Point Trail #788, elevation 5,600 feet, stay left on PCT
62.7	Milk Creek Trail #790, elevation 3,900 feet, stay left on PCT
74.2	Kennedy Ridge Trail #639, elevation 4,200 feet, stay left on PCT
76.2	Upper White Chuck Trail #643.1, elevation 3,900 feet, stay left on PCT
85.9	North Fork Sauk River Trail #649, elevation 5,900 feet, stay left on PCT
88.9	White River Trail #1507, elevation 5,400 feet, stay right on PCT
90.9	Indian Creek Trail #1502, elevation 5,000 feet, stay right on PCT
92.0	Bryant Peak Trail #1544, elevation 5,700 feet, stay right on PCT
93.0	Little Wenatchee River Trail #1525, elevation 5,500 feet, stay right on PCT
93.7	Skykomish River Trail #1051, elevation 5,600 feet, stay left on PCT
95.1	Cady Ridge Trail #1532, elevation 5,300 feet, stay right on PCT
99.4	Cady Creek Trail #1501, elevation 4,300 feet, stay right on PCT
99.7	Pass Creek Trail #1053, elevation 4,200 feet, stay left on PCT
101.3	West Cady Ridge Trail #1054, elevation 4,900 feet, stay left on PCT
106.7	Top Lake Trail #1506, elevation 4,600 feet, stay right on PCT
116.9	Smith Brook Trail #1590, elevation 4,700 feet, stay right on PCT
124.1	Stevens Pass, elevation 4,000 feet

Suggested Camps Based on Different Trekking Itineraries

Night	15–20 mpd	10–15 mpd	10 mpd—not feasible
One:	20 miles - High Bridge Camp	14+ miles - Bridge Creek Camp	
Two:	40+ miles - beneath Suiattle Pass	30+ miles - Cedar Camp	
Three:	56 miles - Dolly-Vista Camp	44 miles - near Miners Creek	
Four:	73+ miles - Glacier Creek Basin	56 miles - Dolly-Vista Camp	
Five:	91 miles - Indian Pass	68 miles - beyond Fire Creek Pass	
Six:	106 miles - near Pear Lake	82 miles - upper White Chuck Basin	
Seven:		95+ miles - near Lake Sally Ann	
Eight:		106 miles - near Pear Lake	
Nine:		115 miles - near Lake Janus	

TREK 8

The Rainbow Paths to Stehekin

Rainbow Lake and Rainbow Pass

Difficulty:	Easier
Distance:	43 miles
Elevation gain:	9,900 feet
Best season:	Mid-July through mid-October
Recommended itinerary:	3 or 5 days (each itinerary allows 1 day in Stehekin)
Water availability:	Good throughout the trek
Logistics:	No challenging logistics. Both the treks into and out of Stehekin join Stehekin Road about 0.7 mile from the Stehekin Pastry Company or 2.6 miles from Stehekin Landing. Utilize the lower valley shuttle, walk to the bakery and ask for a ride to the landing, or just wave down a vehicle and ask for a ride. In

Stehekin, everyone is a local. Shuttle service in the lower valley is available for the trip between the trailhead and Stehekin. Down-valley service is generally provided at 3:30 P.M. and 6:30 P.M., while up-valley service is generally provided at 8:15 A.M. and 11:15 A.M. Shuttle service may not be available after October 1. Lodging is available at or near Stehekin Landing, or camp at Purple Point Campground (at the landing) or other camps in the valley that are reachable by shuttle. There is also a restaurant and small store at the landing. Contact Stehekin Lodge, 509-682-4494; Silver Bay Inn, 509-682-2212; or visit *www.stehekinvalley.com.*

Jurisdictions: Most of the trek and all of the recommended campsites are within either the North Cascades National Park or Lake Chelan National Recreation Area, 360-856-5700. A backcountry permit is required if you stay overnight along the way to Stehekin, and camping reservations are required at Purple Point Campground and all other campsites.

Maps: Green Trails: Washington Pass, Stehekin, and McGregor Mountain

Trail location: Drive Interstate 5 to Burlington and take exit 230. Turn east and follow State Route 20 to near milepost 159 at the Bridge Creek Trailhead, also marked as the PCT South, elevation 4,400 feet. Pick up the trail directly across the road.

Stehekin is a historical settlement on the northwest end of Lake Chelan, deep within the heart of the North Cascades, Glacier Peak, and Lake Chelan–Sawtooth Wilderness complex. On the route used by Native Americans to traverse back and forth between the coastal regions and eastern Washington, Stehekin became an outpost for trappers, traders, miners, and ultimately a few homesteaders. In the early 1900s tourism flourished and the elegant Fields Hotel drew an international clientele that arrived by steam-powered vessels churning up lake. Accessible only by boat, float plane, or trail, Stehekin's natural beauty, touch of civilized ambience, and wilderness access create a unique trekking experience. Because of the possibility of lodging and prepared meals in Stehekin, this trek can be backpacked with tents, bags, and stoves or traveled light and quick, relying on civilization for the comforts of home. Visit Stehekin once and you will return again and again.

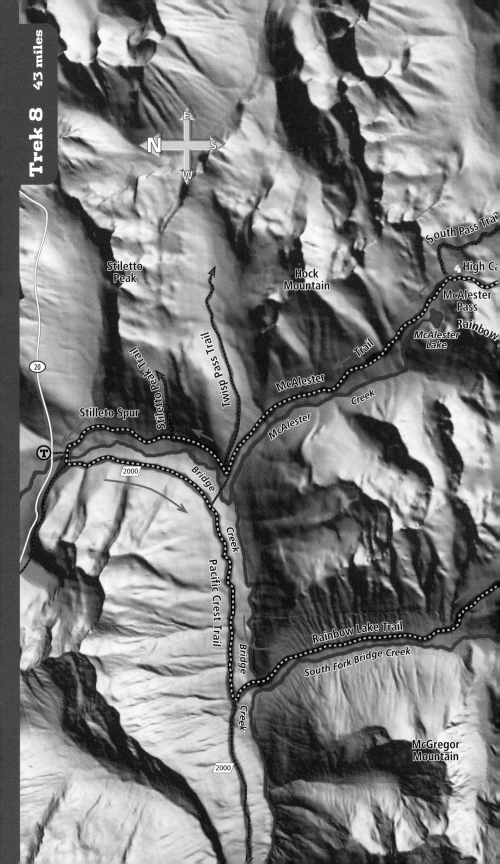

N E S W

Stiletto
Peak

Hock
Mountain

South Pass Trail

4 High Ca

McAlester
Pass

Rainbow

McAlester
Lake

Trail

McAlester

Creek

McAlester

Stiletto Spur

Stilleto Peak Trail

Twisp Pass Trail

T

20

2000

Bridge

Creek

Pacific Crest Trail

Bridge

Creek

Rainbow Lake Trail

South Fork Bridge Creek

McGregor
Mountain

2000

Reynolds
Peak

Purple
Mountain

McAlester
Mountain

Boulder Creek

North Cascades Stehekin Lodge   1-2
Purple Point Camp   2-3

Boulder Creek Trail

Stehekin Road

Lake
Chelan

Rainbow   Creek   Trail

Rainbow

Creek

Rainbow Lake Trail

North   Fork

Rainbow Loop Trail

Stehekin   River

wan
untain

inbow
ke
mp 1

Rainbow
Lake

nbow
'ass

Lake Chelan

National Recreational Area

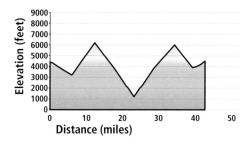

DAY ONE

23+ miles   3,700 feet gain

Take the Pacific Crest Trail along Bridge Creek, elevation 4,400 feet. Trending gently downhill, never far from the stream, hike past the relics of a prospector's cabin. Stay right at the McAlester Creek Trail junction and continue near the rolling rapids of Bridge Creek. Reach the junction with the Rainbow Lake Trail, which accesses Rainbow Lake via South Fork Bridge Creek and Rainbow Pass. Turn left on the Rainbow Lake Trail, 6 miles from the trailhead and cross the roiling waters of Bridge Creek on a sturdy log.

Abruptly gain 400 feet of elevation, then settle into the up-valley grade. The subalpine meadows and open forests are captivating with views growing toward McGregor and Bowan Mountains towering above. From the sparse but reliable tread and the absence of any human effect in the valley, it will be obvious your chosen path is rarely traveled and that solitude will reign. The valley becomes more beautiful as the trail rises steadily higher, passing through timberline and into lovely, lush green meadows sprinkled with alpine color. Ahead a waterfall stream shimmers over rocks and through the flowers. The trail transitions to switchbacks through talus slopes and snow patches. With views growing ever more expansive, reach the saddle of Rainbow Pass, elevation 6,200 feet, 12.3 miles from the trailhead. Stop for lunch in an area sprinkled with large larch trees and surrounded by boundless views; look forward toward peaks of the Sawtooth Range and backward to Cascade landmarks Black, Corteo, and McGregor Mountains.

Descending from the pass, round a corner and greet Rainbow Lake, a splendid alpine pool tucked closely beneath Rainbow Pass. As the trail swings away from the pass, the large lake looms closely below. Beyond Rainbow Lake, after walking through open forest you will break out into spectacular Rainbow Meadows, a 1-mile-long walk through the most splendid alpine flowers imaginable—lupine, paintbrush, tiger lilies, shooting star, bistort, daisies, and asters to name a few.

The trail drifts away from North Fork Rainbow Creek leaving you baking in the sun on a hot afternoon. Finally, switchback sharply down into the main canyon of Rainbow Creek and ford the biting cold water. Enjoy a break in the damp gravel and shade next to the stream. Upon leaving the ford, immediately reach the junction with Rainbow Creek Trail and turn right, heading downhill toward Stehekin. Traverse with ups and downs in the canyon of Rainbow Creek. In 1 mile, cross back over the stream on a suspension bridge and enter the shade of stately pine trees towering more than 100 feet above. With more ups and downs, contour through both sun-drenched slopes and shady respites as the trail pulls away from

Looking south from the head of Lake Chelan

Rainbow Creek, plunging sharply down the canyon. Leaving the narrow valley and gaining a staggering view of impressive Lake Chelan, descend the facing slope 800 feet and reach the Rainbow Loop Trail junction. Turn left, immediately crossing Rainbow Creek on a sturdy bridge. A few minutes later, stay right at the Boulder Creek Trail junction, headed for Stehekin. Breaking out onto an open knoll, gaze down toward Lake Chelan and civilization directly below. Descend the final distance to the Stehekin Road. If your arrival coincides with the shuttle schedule, ride the shuttle to Stehekin. If not, turn left and walk the Stehekin Road 2.6 miles to the Stehekin Landing and services. Accepting a ride is an alternative to walking the road.

A stay in Stehekin can vary from a day to a week or more. First there is the pleasure of simply enjoying the beautiful aspects of the natural setting and the usually sunny weather. Bikes are available for rent, enabling you to explore the lower and upper valleys by pedal power. Rainbow Falls, the log cabin school, the historic Buckner Orchard, and the lovely valley from Harlequin Bridge to High Bridge and on even to Bridge Creek are essential explorations. There are also a multitude of day-hiking options from the mellow Rainbow Loop Trail to the demanding hikes up to Purple Pass and McGregor Mountain.

Antique truck at Buckner Orchard

DAY TWO   19+ miles   6,200 feet gain

Riding the lower valley shuttle to the bakery and beyond, start day two by turning right on the lower terminus of the Rainbow Loop Trail, elevation 1,200 feet. This tread will be familiar to your feet, as the first 5.5 miles retrace the route into Stehekin. After climbing several hundred feet, reach the open hillside with wonderful views of Lake Chelan and the surrounding mountains. After crossing Rainbow Creek on a sturdy bridge, turn right, leaving the Rainbow Loop Trail in favor of the Rainbow Creek Trail. After quickly gaining 800 feet, contour through the steep pine-forested slopes above the stream. Enjoy once again reaching Rainbow Creek at Rainbow Ford Camp. Contrary to the name of the camp, the stream is in fact crossed on a suspension bridge.

Sometimes contouring, sometimes switchbacking, the trail climbs steadily. Pass the junction with the Rainbow Lake Trail and proceed on toward McAlester Pass. Hiking past Bowan Camp you really do ford Rainbow Creek and proceed beyond to subalpine meadows. For more than 1 mile, walk the open boulder-strewn valley, the lovely stream always nearby. Gradually ascend Rainbow Valley, leaving the stream and switchbacking up the sidehill at 5,000 feet elevation. With every step the views grow, down valley to peaks above Lake Chelan, nearby to McAlester Mountain and South Pass. Reaching 6,000 feet elevation, the trail contours into the flowery meadows of McAlester Pass, one of the most beautiful and lesser-visited passes in the Cascades.

Walk straight past the trail junction with South Pass and drop over the ridge toward McAlester Creek. Passing lovely McAlester Lake, descend deeply into the wild valley. After 4 miles, reach the Twisp Pass Trail, just short of Bridge Creek and opposite the PCT, elevation 3,900 feet. Turn right and immediately stay left at the junction with the Stiletto Spur Trail. Moving on, pass the Stiletto Peak Trail and finally the Copper Creek Trail, each approximately 1 mile apart. Beyond Copper Creek Trail, cross State Creek and rejoin the PCT. Turning right, traverse the final familiar mile back to Bridge Creek Trailhead, likely completing your journey as the sky turns pale blue and the high ridges cast shadows upon the valley.

Trail Summary and Mileage Estimates

0.0	Bridge Creek Trailhead for PCT #2000 South, elevation 4,400 feet
0.8	Stiletto Spur Trail, elevation 4,300 feet, stay right on PCT
3.5	McAlester Creek Trail, elevation 3,700 feet, stay right on PCT
6.0	Rainbow Lake Trail, elevation 3,200 feet, turn left on Rainbow Lake Trail
12.3	Rainbow Pass, elevation 6,200 feet
17.8	Rainbow Creek Trail, elevation 3,800 feet, turn right on Rainbow Creek Trail
21.0	Rainbow Loop Trail, elevation 2,200 feet, turn left on Rainbow Loop Trail
21.6	Boulder Creek Trail, elevation 2,000 feet, stay right on Rainbow Loop Trail
23.2	Stehekin Road, elevation 1,200 feet, 2.6 miles from Stehekin
RETURN TRIP	
23.2	Rainbow Loop Trail, elevation 1,200 feet
24.8	Boulder Creek Trail, elevation 2,000 feet, stay left on Rainbow Loop Trail
25.4	Rainbow Creek Trail, elevation 2,200 feet, turn right on Rainbow Creek Trail
28.6	Rainbow Lake Trail, elevation 3,800 feet, stay right on Rainbow Creek Trail
34.3	South Pass Trail, elevation 6,000 feet, stay left on McAlester Creek Trail
39.2	Twisp Pass Trail, elevation 3,900 feet, turn right on Twisp Pass Trail
39.3	Stiletto Spur Trail, elevation 3,900 feet, stay left on Stiletto Spur Trail
40.3	Stiletto Peak Trail, elevation 4,000 feet, stay left on Stiletto Spur Trail
41.5	Copper Creek Trail, elevation 4,200 feet, stay left on Stiletto Spur Trail
41.8	PCT, elevation 4,300 feet, turn right on PCT
42.6	Bridge Creek Trailhead, elevation 4,400 feet

Note: Distances presume you catch a shuttle ride or hitch a ride for the 2.6 miles of road to travel between the trailhead and Stehekin Landing.

Suggested Camps Based on Different Trekking Itineraries

Night	20+ mpd	10–15 mpd	10 mpd—not necessary
One:	23 miles - Stehekin Landing	13 miles - Rainbow Lake Camp	
Two:	23 miles - Stehekin Landing	23 miles - Stehekin Landing	
Three:		23 miles - Stehekin Landing	
Four:		34 miles - McAlester Pass Camp	

TREK 9

The Sawtooth–Lake Chelan Traverse

Oval Lakes from Chelan Summit

Difficulty:	Very strenuous
Distance:	86 miles
Elevation gain:	20,400 feet
Best season:	Mid-July through mid-October
Recommended itinerary:	6 days (15–20 miles per day, plus 1 day in Stehekin)
Water availability:	Generally adequate. Upon leaving Boulder Creek carry at least 2 quarts of liquid and fill up at every on-trail water source for the remainder of the trek.
Logistics:	The trek ends at War Creek, about 10 road miles from the beginning at South Creek. Either stash a bicycle to expedite retrieval of your vehicle or have Mountain Transporter move your vehicle from South Creek to War Creek Trailhead, 509-996-8294. The

trek offers "east side" weather, often dry when the Cascades are wet and chilly. In mid-July don't be shocked to find the upper Rainbow Creek Valley all or partially snow covered from winter's accumulation and avalanche debris. Don't panic; the trail parallels the stream, so merely travel the path of least resistance until tread is found at about 4,800 feet elevation. As with Trek 8, Trek 9 includes a visit to Stehekin. See Trek 8 for details.

Jurisdictions: Lake Chelan–Sawtooth Wilderness, 509-996-4000; North Cascades National Park, 360-856-5700. Permits are not required for trekking or camping in the Lake Chelan–Sawtooth Wilderness, but they are required within the Lake Chelan National Recreation Area administered by the National Park Service.

Maps: Green Trails: Stehekin, Buttermilk Butte, Prince Creek, and Lucerne

Trail location: Drive State Route 20 beyond Winthrop to the town of Twisp, turning west onto Twisp River Road beyond milepost 201. Continue on Twisp River Road about 22 miles to the South Creek Trailhead, elevation 3,100 feet. If you are leaving a bicycle or vehicle at War Creek Trailhead for your return home, leave Twisp River Road at about 15 miles, turn left, cross the Twisp River, and then turn right on Forest Service Road 4430. Within 1 mile, turn left on War Creek Road 100 and reach the trailhead in 1 long mile.

The Sawtooth–Lake Chelan Traverse boasts the most varied terrain of any trek in Washington, rising from pine forests through numerous daunting passes touching nearly 7,500 feet elevation before plummeting to 1,100 feet along the shores of Lake Chelan. The trek offers a lakeshore pilgrimage, the splendor of Stehekin, and the wild beauty of the Chelan-Sawtooth summits, with a return via dramatic Purple Pass.

DAY ONE   16+ miles   3,800 feet gain

Leaving the South Creek Trail, immediately cross the Twisp River on a sturdy bridge and after a sharp climb settle into a valley-grade walk above South Creek. Staying right at the trail junction with Louis Lake at about 4,800 feet elevation, encounter the first water since leaving the Twisp River. Fill up before contouring into lovely meadows, ever more beautiful as you approach South Pass, elevation

Road 4420

Road 44

Road 100

T

War Creek

Road 4430

409

408

Road 4440

Twisp River

T

428

Reynolds Peak

408

South Creek

W. Cre Pa

Lake Juanita

279

Juanita Lake Camp

401

Boulder Creek Trail

Rennie Camp 2

Boulder Creek

Purple

Mosquito Lake

McAlester Mountain

Purple Point Campground

South Pass

McAlester Pass

1 High Camp

Rainbow Ford Camp

Rainbow Bridge Camp

1

Rainbow Creek Trail

1

McAlester Trail

Rainbow Lake Trail

Rainbow Creek

Rainbow Loop Trail

Bowan Mountain

1259.1

1254

1255.2

Middle Fork

Star
Peak

3 4

1249

411

Surprise
Lake

Prince

Finney
Peak

Creek

East Fork

1255

Gray
Peak

1259E

1248

Prince
Creek
Camp

5
3

1259B

attle
untain

Lake Chelan–Sawtooth

259

1248.1

Wilderness

1247

Blue
rouse
asin
amp

Meadow
Creek
Camp 4

Fish Creek

1248

Moore
Point
Camp 6

Lake Chelan

hekin
ding

N
E
S
W

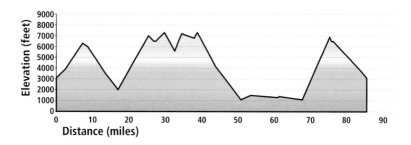

6,300 feet. Savor the nearby views of seldom-seen peaks like McAlester, Bowan, and Crescent. Below, the graceful curve of Rainbow Creek descends toward Lake Chelan.

After savoring the gentle alpine stroll into McAlester Pass, turn left on the Rainbow Creek Trail and, after 1 mile of walking through glorious fields of paintbrush, lupine, valerian, and arnica, switchback down into the Rainbow Creek Valley. The route parallels the stream for a long mile, often through avalanche snow remnants and broken trees, before reaching bare ground and defined tread. Ford the rowdy stream and continue down valley. Stay left at the junction with Rainbow Lake Trail, descending into the afternoon shadows as the valley narrows.

Cross the foaming froth of Rainbow Creek once again, this time on a suspension bridge, then settle into an undulating traverse before descending in open pine forests to the junction with the Rainbow Loop Trail. Turn left, and after crossing Rainbow Creek a third time, find camp near the stream before it plummets over cliffs as spectacular Rainbow Falls.

DAY TWO 15 miles 5,600 feet gain

Day two includes the second-most daunting climb of the trek, but remains a mere warm-up to the demands of climbing to Purple Pass. Just a few minutes beyond Rainbow Bridge Camp, turn left on the Boulder Creek Trail, elevation 2,000 feet, reaching for the highlands and adventure.

Facing a steady climb to 7,000 feet elevation, with continual ups and downs thereafter, amble gently upward. Pass a decent camp with water at Rennie Creek, and gradually ascend into alpine terrain. Splashing across delightful Boulder Creek for the first time near Reynolds Camp, switchback onto the lovely meadow divide beyond and traverse toward the Sawtooth crest. (For the remainder of the trek it is wise to fill up 2 or more quarts of water when you come to an on-trail water source.) Far below spy the blue-green waters of Chelan and the Stehekin Valley. Impressive Reynolds Peak rises nearby. Reaching the beautiful divide, views grow as you look down the Twisp Valley and beyond into eastern Washington.

Upon reaching War Creek Pass and Trail #408, stay right and shortly thereafter cross a ridge into the basin of tiny Juanita Lake and reach a junction with the

Purple Creek Trail. Stay left on what is now the Chelan Summit Trail #1259 and steadily traverse before ascending to the 7,300-foot saddle demarking the Lake Chelan National Recreation Area and the Chelan-Sawtooth Wilderness. Laze in the sun, your day nearly complete, staring ahead deep into the wilderness and savoring the beauty in every direction. Descending from the saddle, cross the bubbling source of Fish Creek and find camp in the meadows and forest near Blue Grouse Basin.

DAY THREE   20 miles   2,800 feet gain
Day three traces the Chelan summit ridges for 11 miles before plummeting down the valley of Prince Creek to reach a camp along the shores of Lake Chelan. Descend briefly into subalpine forest, staying left at the junction with North Fork Fish Creek Trail #1248.1. Climb to over 7,000 feet elevation and cross a ridge accessing the high, alpine basin beneath Gray Peak and the tiny basin of Tuckaway Lake just above the trail. Firmly tracking with the Chelan summits, pass trail junctions leading uphill to Eagle Pass, Tuckaway Lake, and then Fish Creek Pass, while passing the trail descending into the East Fork Fish Creek.

Meandering through one alpine basin after another, trek along between 6,500 and 7,200 feet elevation. Looking north, trace the spine of the Sawtooths back to their origin near Silver Star Peak. Reaching the final high pass, the 7,300-foot divide between Star Peak and Baldy Mountain, revel in the beauty around you, from distant views of Jack and Crater Mountains to nearby Star Peak and down into the rugged canyon of Prince Creek. Looking south, peer over the Navarre Peaks and down onto Lake Chelan. Finally moving along, saunter through gentle meadows, soon reaching the junction with Surprise Lake Trail #1249. Stay left at the junction with Surprise Lake Trail and leave the high country, soon turning right on Prince Creek Trail #1254.

The valley of Prince Creek is narrow and rugged, bound by high cliffs all around. Always near the stream, the crashing water is deafening in early summer when Prince Creek runs full with snowmelt. Splash across the Middle Fork of Prince Creek, pass the Middle Fork Trail junction, and continue straight down the valley. After crossing Prince Creek on a sturdy bridge, climb and then traverse through high cliffs above the narrow canyon, baking in the sun as Lake Chelan beckons. Finally, the valley of Prince Creek yields and the trail gently descends 1,000 feet to the inviting waters of Lake Chelan. Find camp near the lake and enjoy a refreshing, renewing swim.

DAY FOUR   17 miles   2,200 feet gain
As impressive as the highlands are, the lakeshore is no less enchanting. Amble along the lake on the Chelan Lakeshore Trail #1247 toward Stehekin, taking in the views of the cold blue water shimmering in the breeze and the majestic peaks.

Lady of the Lake leaving Prince Creek

Directly across the valley rise the high peaks of the Entiat Mountains, Cardinal, and Saska. Ahead, the lake extends farther than your eyes can see. After a couple of miles, leave the lakeshore and gently ascend, descend, and traverse the cliffy terrain several hundred feet above the lake.

Stop for water at Meadow Creek and continue forward, reaching the Moore Point Trail junction, 10+ miles from Prince Creek. Stay to the right, crossing Fish Creek and in a few minutes reach the Fish Creek Trail junction. Stay left on the Lakeshore Trail, climbing high above the lakeshore along Hunts Bluff, with panoramic views down to Moore Point and out to peaks spanning the horizon from Mount Buckner to Mount Fernow. The trail returns to the water's edge at Flick Creek Camp, an idyllic lakeshore retreat with a dock and a shelter. Relax here for a while before finishing the walk along the lakeshore to Stehekin. With prior arrangements, you can treat yourself to a stay in the North Cascades Lodge.

DAY FIVE   no miles   no elevation gain
Enjoy a restful day immersed in the delights of Stehekin as described in Trek 8.

DAY SIX   18 miles   6,000 feet gain
One final challenge must be surmounted before the Chelan-Sawtooth Range is known completely. Directly above Stehekin, high on the summit ridge of the Chelan Mountains, stands Purple Pass, the gateway back into the Chelan-Sawtooth Wilderness and the return route to civilization via War Creek. The elevation gain

Purple Pass Trail

from Stehekin to Purple Pass is 5,800 feet, one of the longest continuous uphill climbs in the Cascades and the most demanding single climb among all the treks.

Start the day on Purple Creek Trail. Switchback steadily uphill through open forests, crossing Purple Creek at 2,700 feet elevation. The stream is likely your first and only water source on the ascent, so top off your water bottles. The terrain transitions from open forests to dry rocky hillsides. Higher, gain the prow of a ridge descending from the summits still high above you. Views down to the lake are staggering, the boats motoring on the lake look like toys. Continuously ascending, traverse a steep hillside and finally switchback into the narrow profile of Purple Pass, elevation 6,900 feet. Rest and savor the panorama: Dome, Bonanza, Glacier Peak, the Ptarmigan Traverse peaks, Mount Goode, the craggy profile of Cascade Pass and Sahale Arm, and Mount Logan. Few mountain summit views rival that from Purple Pass. Pause for lunch in the meadows near tiny Lake Juanita.

Beyond Lake Juanita reach the Chelan Summit Trail #1259 once again. Turn left and in just a few minutes reach War Creek Pass and the War Creek Trail #408 junction. War Creek, an ancient trade route used by Native Americans, is so named as the location of an ancient battle between coastal and inland-based tribes. Turn right on this historic route and in a short mile leave alpine meadows for shady pine forests and swaths of avalanche greenery. Descending the valley, enjoy periodic sparkling streams, the first abundant water since early in the trek. Pass an old cabin maintained by the Forest Service, then the junction with South Fork War Creek Trail befor reaching the trailhead and journey's end.

Chelan summits Gray, Courtney, and Star

Trail Summary and Mileage Estimates

0.0	South Creek Trail #401, elevation 3,100 feet
2.5	Louis Lake Trail #428, elevation 3,900 feet, stay right on Trail #401
8.7	Rainbow Creek/McAlester Creek Trail, elevation 6,000 feet, turn left on Rainbow Creek Trail
13.4	Rainbow Lake Trail, elevation 3,600 feet, stay left on Rainbow Creek Trail
16.6	Rainbow Loop Trail, elevation 2,200 feet, turn left on Rainbow Loop Trail
17.0	Boulder Creek Trail, elevation 2,000 feet, turn left on Boulder Creek Trail
26.8	War Creek Trail #408, elevation 6,500 feet, stay right on Chelan Summit Trail #1259
27.3	Purple Creek Trail, elevation 6,500 feet, stay left on Trail #1259
32.5	North Fork Fish Creek Trail #1248.1, elevation 5,600 feet, stay left on Trail #1259
33.5	Eagle Pass Trail #1259B, elevation 6,500 feet, stay right on Trail #1259
36.0	Tuckaway Lake Trail #1259E, elevation 7,000 feet, stay right on Trail #1259
37.7	East Fork Fish Creek Trail #1248, elevation 6,800 feet, stay left on Trail #1259
37.9	Fish Creek Pass Trail #1259, elevation 6,800 feet, stay right on Trail #1259
39.7	Surprise Lake Trail #1249, elevation 6,700 feet, stay left on Trail #1259
41.5	Prince Creek Trail #1254, elevation 5,600 feet, turn right on Trail #1254
43.7	Middle Fork Prince Creek Trail #1255.2, elevation 4,200 feet, stay right on now Trail #1255
50.8	Chelan Lakeshore Trail #1247, elevation 1,100 feet, turn right on Trail #1247
61.0	Moore Point Trail #1247A, elevation 1,300 feet, stay right on Trail #1247
61.4	Fish Creek Trail #1248, elevation 1,400 feet, stay left on Trail #1247
67.8	Stehekin, elevation 1,100 feet, find Purple Creek Trail behind North Cascades Lodge
75.8	Chelan Summit Trail #1259, elevation 6,500 feet, turn left on Trail #1259
76.3	War Creek Trail #408, elevation 6,500 feet, turn right on Trail #408
84.1	South Fork War Creek Trail #409, elevation 3,700 feet, stay left on Trail #408
85.6	War Creek Trailhead, elevation 3,100 feet

Suggested Camps Based on Different Trekking Itineraries

Night	15–20 mpd	10–15 mpd	10 mpd
One:	16+ miles - Rainbow Bridge Camp	14+ miles - Rainbow Ford Camp	9 miles - McAlester Pass Camp
Two:	31+ miles - Blue Grouse Basin	27 miles - Lake Juanita	21 miles - Rennie Creek Camp
Three:	51 miles - Prince Creek Camp	41 miles - past Surprise Lake Trail	31+ miles - Blue Grouse Basin
Four:	68 miles - Stehekin	58 miles - Meadow Creek Camp	41 miles - past Surprise Lake Trail
Five:	Stehekin - night two	68 miles - Stehekin	51 miles - Prince Creek Camp
Six:		Stehekin - night two	61+ miles - Moore Point Camp
Seven:		76 miles - Lake Juanita	68 miles - Stehekin
Eight:			Stehekin - night two
Nine:			76 miles - Lake Juanita

TREK 10

Across the Great Cascades and Back

Upper Lyman Basin

Difficulty:	Easier
Distance:	47 miles
Elevation gain:	11,000 feet
Best season:	Mid-July through September
Recommended itinerary:	6 days (less than 10 miles per day; last day 15 miles)
Water availability:	Plentiful except for ascent to Miners Ridge
Logistics:	This hike begins at the Suiattle River Trailhead and ends at the Cascade Pass Trailhead, approximately 60 miles apart. You will need two cars or a drop-off and pickup. For information on accommodations in Holden Village write to Registrar, Holden Village, Chelan, WA 98816, or visit *www.holdenvillage.com*. For information on the *Lady of the Lake* boat schedule

on Lake Chelan, contact 509-682-4584. If you have a choice, always take the faster boat. For information on Stehekin, including accommodations, permits, and the trailhead bus/van shuttle schedule/reservations, contact the National Park Service, 360-856-5700. From Stehekin, if you want to start hiking earlier in the day than the shuttle schedule allows, take the late-afternoon shuttle to the trailhead the day before restarting your hike. In 1995–96, the Stehekin Road was washed out above High Bridge. As of 2002, the road had been reopened to beyond Flat Creek. The mileage description in this guide assumes you begin hiking near Flat Creek, adding about 3 miles to the trek. The narrow road is pleasant walking, often very near the river (hence the washouts). For more information on the Stehekin Valley, see Trek 8.

Jurisdictions: Glacier Peak Wilderness, 360-436-1155; North Cascades National Park Complex, 360-856-5700. Permits are not required for overnight stays in the Glacier Peak Wilderness. Permits are required for overnight stays in the Lake Chelan National Recreation Area and the North Cascades National Park. A permit for camping at Purple Point Campground, Cottonwood Camp, or Basin Camp can be obtained from the visitor center in Stehekin or the North Cascades National Park Complex Ranger Station in Marblemount.

Maps: Green Trails: Glacier Peak, Holden, Lucerne, Cascade Pass, and McGregor Mountain

Trail Location: Drive Interstate 5 to exit 208. Turn east and follow State Route 530 about 5 miles through Arlington and 26 miles to Darrington. Beyond milepost 49, in Darrington, turn left and continue on SR 530 past milepost 56 until just beyond the bridge crossing of the Sauk River. Turn right on Suiattle River Road and follow it about 24 miles to its end at the Suiattle River Trailhead, elevation 1,800 feet. You can also reach Suiattle River Road by leaving I-5 at Burlington, exit 230, and following SR 20 beyond milepost 97 to Rockport. At Rockport, turn right and follow SR 530 beyond milepost 57 to Suiattle River Road. For the return trip, drive I-5 to exit 230. Follow SR 20 east

Cascade River Road

Doubtful
Lake

Horseshoe
Basin

Johannesburg
Mountain

Cascade
Pass

Booker
Mountain

Park Creek Trail

Mix-up
Peak

Stehekin

6
5

River

Basin Creek
Camp

Magic
Mountain

Glory
Mountain
Shuttle Stop

Glacier Peak

Wilderness

N
W · E
S

Agnes

Creek

Suiattle
River
Road

T

Sulphur
Mountain

Canyon Creek

784

Image
Lake

785.3

Plummer
Mountain

2000

Clo
P

Cloudy
Pass

Miners Ridge

1

2
1

785

2
3

Suiattle

1

795

1256A

River

784

Suiattle
Pass

2000

Lyman
Falls

Ly
L

Chiw
Mou

Pacific Crest Trail

McGregor
Mountain

Reynolds
Peak

Stehekin

River

Stehekin

Rainbow Creek Trail

Road

Stehekin
3 4 5

Lady of the Lake

anza
eak

1256

Boat Ride

Lake Chelan

Holden

Railroad **2 3 4**

Creek

Road 8301

Lucerne

art
ke

Domke
Lake

mbell
untain

Holden Village:
From here, travel by
bus to Lucerne and
boat to Stehekin.

for about 45 miles to Marblemount. Beyond milepost 106, continue straight ahead across the Skagit River (SR 20 turns 90 degrees left at this junction) and drive 22 miles on Cascade River Road to the road end at the Cascade Pass Trailhead, elevation 3,600 feet.

This classic adventure over Suiattle and Cloudy Passes to the remote village of Holden, only to return via the alpine splendor of Cascade Pass, is Washington's most unique trekking experience.

DAY ONE   8 miles   600 feet gain

The Glacier Peak Wilderness is a cornerstone of the protected wilderness core extending from Stevens Pass to the Canadian border. Created in 1964, the wilderness includes nearly 600,000 acres of pristine old-growth forested valleys, unspoiled streams and rivers, astounding meadows of flowers and berries, varied wildlife, and snow-clad spires straining for the blue sky above. When coupled with the Lake Chelan National Recreation Area and the North Cascades National Park, more than a million acres of natural bounty are yours to view and enjoy.

Glacier Peak from Suiattle Valley

Start up the Suiattle River Trail #784, elevation 1,800 feet, into the Glacier Peak Wilderness. Your destination is a camping spot along Canyon Creek, about 8 miles up the trail. This fairly flat and easy segment of the trek can readily be completed in a single afternoon. Reach camp near

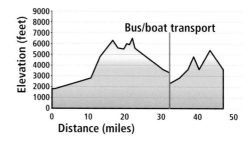

Canyon Creek, which is filled with water as clear as glass, tumbling over boulders on its way down from the high mountains.

DAY TWO   8.5 miles   4,000 feet elevation gain

Day two is the sternest of the trek. From Canyon Creek, continue more than 3 miles to the trail junction at the base of the climb toward Miners Ridge and Image Lake. Turn left on Miners Ridge Trail #785 and begin the ascent toward the alpine treasures above. Reaching the junction with Miners Cabin Trail #795, at 4,800 feet elevation, stay left on the continuing ascent toward Miners Ridge. The whistling of curious marmots and the temptation of sweet blueberries may distract you from your labor. At the crest of Miners Ridge, turn right and come to Image Lake in 1 mile. Glacier Peak, the namesake of the wilderness, fills the tiny lake with its reflection. Camp just beyond the lake, which provides a base for an afternoon's or even a day's roaming. Wander back along Miners Ridge toward the former fire lookout, explore the basin of Image Lake, venture toward Canyon Lake on seldom-visited tread, or scramble the ridge of Plummer Mountain.

DAY THREE   7 miles   2,000 feet gain

Leaving Image Lake, stay right at the junction with Canyon Lake Trail #797 and continue toward Suiattle Pass. Continue on Trail #785 until joining the Pacific Crest Trail #2000 about 1 mile below Suiattle Pass. Turn left on the PCT and ascend 1 gentle mile to the pass, elevation 6,000 feet. At the pass, take the Cloudy Pass Hikers Trail #1279, the narrow footpath descending and traversing meadow and talus slopes, until joining the Railroad Creek Trail #1256 a short distance below Cloudy Pass. Turn right at this junction and immediately climb to the pass, elevation 6,500 feet.

The view from Cloudy Pass is nothing short of spectacular. To the east and 1,000 feet below lies aqua-colored Lyman Lake, made green by rock dust ground from solid stone by the Lyman Glacier. Above the Lyman Glacier rise Dumbbell and Chiwawa Mountains, separated by the icy saddle of Spider Gap. To the north the view is dominated immediately by Cloudy Peak, giving way to the immense rock mass of Bonanza Peak. At 9,511 feet tall, Bonanza Peak is the highest

Meadow reflected in Image Lake

nonvolcanic peak in Washington; its glacier-clad granitic spires a stark contrast to the rounded domes of Washington's taller volcanic summits. To the west, through the gap of Suiattle Pass, rises Glacier Peak. From the pass gently descend through parklands 1.5 miles to camp near Lyman Lake. Much like Image Lake Basin, Lyman Basin provides several opportunities for exploring. Walk the near lakeshore to the falls spilling into the lake from upper Lyman Basin. To visit upper Lyman Basin itself, cross the roaring Lyman Lake outlet stream on a sturdy log and in 1 long mile reach the upper basin, which extends all the way to Spider Gap at 7,100 feet.

DAY FOUR   9 miles   200 feet elevation gain

Leaving Lyman Lake, the trail descends and traverses down rocky, brushy slopes beneath Cloudy, North Star, and finally Bonanza Peak on its route toward Hart Lake and lower Railroad Creek. Once across Isella Creek, you are roughly halfway to Holden Village. From a knoll, you can see down the valley of Railroad Creek to the mine tailings near Holden, reminders of the village's early days as a mining town, before it began its current life as a wilderness retreat.

Holden has the appearance and feeling of a rustic alpine village. The high peaks of the Cascades flare up to the blue sky. The sound of Railroad Creek, its water boiling over rocks on the way to Lake Chelan, is always present. Trimmed lawns and colorful flowers are everywhere. Town amenities include the library, a pottery shop, a weaving shop, a recreation center (with pool tables and bowling [pins set by hand]), an ice cream parlor, a coffee shop, and a general store, gift shop, post office, and souvenir stand all in one.

In Holden, merchants don't accept *any* credit cards. They will, however, accept cash or personal checks. So when hiking to Holden, carry the "Eleven Essentials": the first ten plus some cash and five or six checks. Holden has a price matrix that varies from adult to child and for length of stay. The price for children is lower than for adults and the per-day price decreases as your stay lengthens. The per-day cost includes lodging, three meals, and access to many free amenities—bowling, library, pool tables, childcare programs—virtually all program offerings. Holden is a bargain!

DAY FIVE   no miles   no elevation gain

Day five is a day of leisure. In fact, spend a few days in Holden if possible, for there is much to do and not do. On the recommended itinerary, day five is the transition day for traveling by bus, then boat, to Stehekin.

Board the Holden bus for the 40-minute ride to Lucerne. In Lucerne, board the *Lady II,* the express boat, for the 1-hour ride to Stehekin, an outpost of civilization on the remote end of Lake Chelan that is accessible only by boat, plane, or trail. The road to Lucerne follows the steady but gentle valley of Railroad Creek until reaching the slopes directly above Lake Chelan. Reaching from the deserts of eastern Washington back into the mountains of the North Cascades, the water flowing into Lake Chelan comes from many of the most remote ridges and valleys in the Cascade Range. Not surprisingly, the water is clean, clear, deep, and cold.

While the bus grinds down the switchbacks to the lake far below, the volunteer driver describes the rich mining history of the Railroad Creek area. Beginning in 1887, James Holden staked claims and attempted to develop a successful mining venture at his namesake's town site for nearly thirty years. Decades passed, but only when the Howe Sound Company spent ten years developing roads, facilities, and worker housing could the mining efforts really take hold in the late 1930s. Holden thrived as a successful mining venture until 1957, when dropping mineral prices, increasing costs, and diminishing production drove the mine to closure and the town's transition to a wilderness retreat in the early 1960s.

Linking with the boat, find yourself en route up lake to Stehekin. Stehekin lacks several of the attributes Holden has, but offers a few things Holden doesn't.

Stehekin has a restaurant, hotel, and a world-class bakery. There are also bed and breakfasts in the lower valley, private residences, and a few dude ranches. Because the Stehekin Valley lies in the Lake Chelan National Recreation Area, the National Park Service manages a visitor center and a campground in the area. You can rent bikes to ride to the bakery and many other interesting and beautiful locations in the valley. The rich history of Stehekin and the delights of the valley are worthy of days of exploration. More information on Stehekin can be found in Trek 8.

DAY SIX 15 miles 4,200 feet gain

If your itinerary allows, spend a day or more in the Stehekin Valley. When leaving Stehekin, realize the regular shuttle service will not deposit you at the Cascade Pass Trailhead until about 10 A.M. If you desire an earlier start, or want to break the last day into two, ride the afternoon shuttle leaving Stehekin at 2:15 P.M. and arrive at the trailhead about 4:15 P.M. This itinerary will allow time to hike either the 2.7 miles to Cottonwood Camp or an additional 1 mile to Basin Creek Camp. This itinerary also moderates the last day of trekking as described and provides ample opportunity for the obligatory side trip into Horseshoe Basin.

The shuttle bus makes a stop at Rainbow Falls, allowing time to admire the alluring ribbon of water as it cascades into two tempting pools. About 10:00 A.M., arrive at the road end and the new Cascade Pass Trailhead. Trek up valley, reaching the Horseshoe Basin Trail in 5 miles.

Obligatory side trip 1. The gentle uphill mile or so from the Cascade Pass Trail into Horseshoe Basin offers one of the most spectacular views in all of Washington. A dozen or more powerful waterfalls plummet nearly 1,500 feet, fed by the high snow slopes beneath Ripsaw Ridge. The subalpine fireweed and other flowers of the lower basin provide a colorful and delicate contrast to the raging falls. The deeply carved basin, literally shaped like a horseshoe, offers the opportunity to poke around mining relics while enjoying expansive views toward Glory and Trapper Peaks. The trail into the basin was established during mining days as a mine-to-market road.

Back on the trail to Cascade Pass, soon cross the stair-step falls of Doubtful Creek. Past the falls, climb steadily on switchbacks through dense subalpine vegetation. After gaining nearly 1,000 feet from the stream crossing, contour above Pelton Basin and break into the expansive meadow and talus slopes beneath Cascade Pass. Contour and climb the remaining 500 feet to the most visited alpine pass in the North Cascades National Park. The six thousand annual visitors willing to make the 7.5-mile round-trip hike can't be fooled—Cascade Pass provides as dramatic a view as that of El Capitan in Yosemite National Park or Mount Rainier from Paradise in Mount Rainier National Park. Descend long switchbacks to the trek's end at the Cascade Pass Trailhead.

Trail Summary and Mileage Estimates

0.0	Suiattle River Trail #784, elevation 1,800 feet
0.8	Milk Creek Trail #790, elevation 1,800 feet, stay left on Trail #784
10.8	Miners Ridge Trail #785, elevation 2,800 feet, turn left on Trail #785
13.3	Miners Cabin Trail #795, elevation 4,800 feet, stay left on Trail #785
16.8	Canyon Lake Trail #797, elevation 6,300 feet, stay right on Trail #785
18.2	Miners Cabin Trail #795, elevation 5,600 feet, stay left on Trail #785
19.8	PCT #2000, elevation 5,500 feet, turn left on PCT
20.6	Suiattle–Cloudy Pass Trail #1279, elevation 6,000 feet, turn right on Trail #1279
21.3	Railroad Creek Trail #1256, elevation 5,900 feet, turn right on Trail #1256
22.8	Lyman Lake Spur Trail #1256A, elevation 5,600 feet, stay left on Trail #1256
23.1	Lyman Falls Spur Trail #1256B, elevation 5,500 feet, stay left on Trail #1256
30.4	Holden Lake Trail #1251, elevation 3,600 feet, stay right on Trail #1256
32.3	Holden Village

Bus transportation to Lucerne on Lake Chelan

Boat transportation to Stehekin on Lake Chelan

Bus/van transportation to Cascade Pass Trail (likely near Flat Creek)

32.3	Cascade Pass Trailhead at road end, elevation 2,300 feet
35.0	Cottonwood Camp and end of Stehekin Road prior to washouts in 1995–96
37.4	Horseshoe Basin Trail, elevation 3,600 feet, turn right and take side trip to basin
40.4	Cascade Pass Trail, elevation 3,600 feet, turn right and continue to Cascade Pass
43.4	Sahale Arm Trail, elevation 5,400 feet, stay left on Cascade Pass Trail
47.1	Cascade Pass Trailhead, elevation 3,600 feet

Suggested Camps Based on Different Trekking Itineraries

Night	15–20 mpd	10–15 mpd	10 mpd
One:	16+ miles - Image Lake	13+ miles - junction Trail #795	7+ miles - Canyon Creek
Two:	32+ miles - Holden Village	23+ miles - Lyman Lake	16+ miles - Image Lake
Three:	32+ miles - Stehekin	32+ miles - Holden Village	23+ miles - Lyman Lake
Four:		32+ miles - Stehekin	32+ miles - Holden Village
Five:		36 miles - Basin Creek Camp	32+ miles - Stehekin
Six:			36 miles - Basin Creek Camp

Glacier Peak—
The Wilderness Trail

Triad Lake and Clark Mountain

Difficulty:	Most strenuous
Distance:	91 miles
Elevation gain:	18,900 feet
Best season:	Late July through early September
Recommended itinerary:	6 days (15–20 miles per day)
Water availability:	Good except for the climb to Image Lake
Logistics:	Expect a snow crossing near High Pass at all times of year. Expect snow crossings between White and Red Passes, plus upper White Chuck Valley, and at Fire Creek Pass until late August. Carry an ice ax and know its use. The off-trail route segment between High Pass and the Napeequa Valley is straightforward, but does require the ability to interpret a

map and visually determine a route when no trail exists. Prior to late July, the Napeequa River ford can be challenging, particularly late in the day. As of 1996, there was no trail junction sign at the Napeequa ford (no sign of a trail junction either).

Jurisdictions: Glacier Peak Wilderness, 360-436-1155. Backcountry permits are not currently required.

Maps: Green Trails: Glacier Peak and Holden

Trail location: Drive Interstate 5 to exit 208. Turn east and follow State Route 530 about 5 miles through Arlington and an additional 26 miles to Darrington. Beyond milepost 49 in Darrington, turn left and continue following SR 530 past milepost 56 until just beyond the bridge crossing the Sauk River. Turn right on Suiattle River Road and drive about 24 miles to road end at the Suiattle River Trailhead, elevation 1,800 feet. You can also reach Suiattle River Road by leaving I-5 at Burlington, exit 230, and following SR 20 beyond milepost 97 to Rockport. At Rockport, turn right and follow SR 530 beyond milepost 57 to Suiattle River Road.

The Wilderness Trail is actually my name for a combination of several trails and one nontrail segment circumnavigating Glacier Peak. The route around Glacier Peak is the most splendid of the wild country. For 91 miles you will climb, descend, traverse, and stand in awe of the wilderness scene around you. You will gain and lose approximately 18,900 feet of elevation. The Wilderness Trail is real wilderness—remote, pristine, lonesome—providing all the beauty and experiences that draw people to the mountains.

DAY ONE   16+ miles   4,500 feet gain

The first dramatic trekking day delivers you through the Suiattle Valley to spectacular Image Lake for a late afternoon of relaxation as well as unforgettable sunset and sunrise photographic opportunities. Begin on the Suiattle River Trail #784, elevation 1,800 feet. Upon reaching the junction with the Miners Ridge Trail #785, elevation 2,800 feet, about 11 miles from the Suiattle River Road, turn left and begin climbing steadily to alpine nirvana above. After gaining 2,000 feet elevation through old-growth forest dominated by firs, reach another junction. Stay left on Trail #785, and continue climbing toward Miners Ridge. Breaking through timberline and into the glorious expanse of meadows and views that have made the ridge famous, finally stand atop Miners Ridge, elevation 6,000 feet. Turning right,

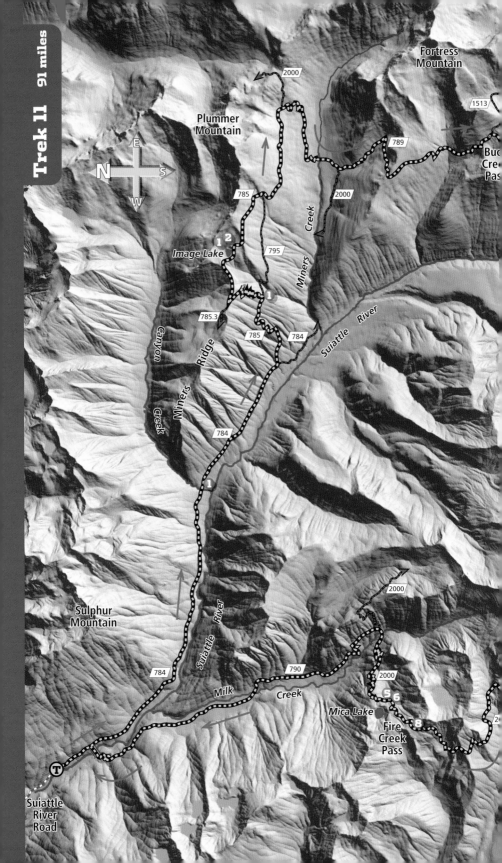

Fortress
Mountain

1513

2000

789

Buc
Cre
Pas

785

Plummer
Mountain

N
E
S
W

2
1
Image Lake

795

Miners   Creek

2000

1

785.3

785

784

Canyon

Miners   Ridge

Creek

Suiattle   River

784

1

2000

Sulphur
Mountain

Suiattle   River

784

2000

Milk   Creek

790

S 6

Mica Lake

8

Fire
Creek
Pass

2

T

Suiattle
River
Road

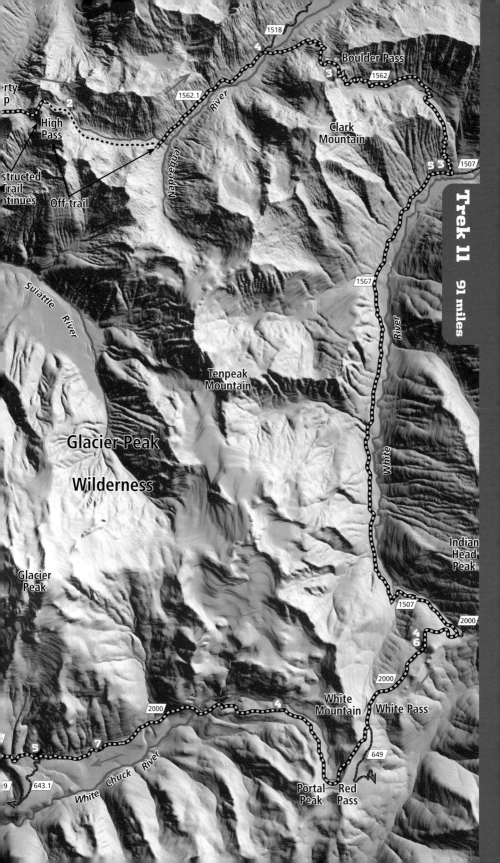

1518

4

Boulder Pass

3

1562

1562.1

Napeequa River

rty
p

2

High
Pass

structed
Trail
ntinues

Off-trail

Clark
Mountain

5 3

1507

Suiattle River

1507

White River

Tenpeak
Mountain

Glacier Peak

Wilderness

Indian
Head
Peak

Glacier
Peak

1507

2000

4
6

2000

White
Mountain

White Pass

2000

4

7

5

7

White Chuck River

649

9

643.1

Portal
Peak

Red
Pass

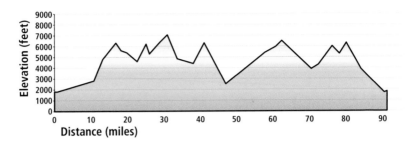

away from the ridge-top lookout, arrive at Image Lake in a short mile. The lake resides in a small meadowed cirque at 6,100 feet elevation, 16.5 miles from the Suiattle River Trailhead. Find camp just beyond the lake amongst alpine firs and bushes.

Glacier Peak rises dramatically behind alpine firs near the outlet stream of the lake. Developed over nearly a million years of geologic time, Glacier Peak's 10,541-foot summit was shaped and carved by lava flow, eruption, and glaciation. Every feature of this trek, from the slopes of Glacier Peak, Clark Mountain, and Dome Peak to the mighty Suiattle River Valley, elegant Miners Ridge, and the grandeur of High Pass, owes its origin to the grinding and sculpting of ice.

DAY TWO   15 miles   4,600 feet gain

Day two begins with the sublime traverse toward Suiattle Pass and ends with the incomparable meadow traverse from Buck Creek Pass to High Pass. Quickly climb above Image Lake, staying to the right on Trail #785 upon reaching the Canyon Lake Trail junction. Trek onward through beautiful meadows beneath Plummer Mountain, merging with Trail #795, which bypasses Miners Ridge, and continuing on toward Suiattle Pass.

Enjoy a break and a brief soaking as you rock-hop the chilly stream that descends as a waterfall from the slopes of Plummer Mountain. Beyond, reach the junction with the Pacific Crest Trail #2000, elevation 5,500 feet, 3 miles from Image Lake. Turn right on the PCT and descend toward the forests of Miners Creek. Savor the downward path in shade and the subalpine meadows near Miners Creek, which flows quietly along the gentle valley floor.

In less than 1 mile from Miners Creek, reach the junction with the Buck Creek Pass Trail #789. Turn left, leaving the PCT in favor of Middle Ridge and then Buck Creek Pass. Trek ever upward near a rushing stream, then through an alpine basin before traversing to the crest of the ridge. Nearing the crest of Middle Ridge, new views northeast toward Bonanza Peak will steal your momentum. Enjoy a brief respite at the ridge crest, elevation 6,200 feet, before immediately descending 900 feet only to once again climb above timberline.

Traverse through meadows toward the Flower Dome and on to Buck Creek Pass. Photographically, this area should be visited in the morning hours when the light from the east illuminates Glacier Peak like a displayed jewel.

Awash in wildflowers near High Pass

From the area of the Flower Dome, the trail gets a bit confusing because there are a few unofficial paths to consider. In addition, the main trail crosses Buck Creek Pass at about 100 feet elevation above and left of the pass itself. As you approach the pass on the main trail, look down 100 feet into the pass. See your route of choice, the obvious tread heading south and uphill out of Buck Creek Pass toward Liberty Cap. Simply descend a boot-built trail into Buck Creek Pass proper and walk through meadows on similarly built trails until intersecting the obvious constructed trail that climbs toward Liberty Cap. If you have any doubt where to walk, just walk to the low point in the saddle of Buck Creek Pass and head south, staying exactly on top of the ridge crest, indeed the Cascade Crest, until the afore-mentioned obvious tread is reached.

On the uphill climb out of Buck Creek Pass, elevation 5,800 feet, hike toward High Pass. Reach the flat, grassy meadow at 6,400 feet on the ridge crest just beyond Liberty Cap. In all directions are views of peaks made famous through hiking and climbing literature: Glacier, Dome, Sinister, Bonanza, Fortress, Chiwawa, and Maude. Continue on the tread as it switchbacks and then holds to the ridge. At about 6,800 feet elevation, the tread crosses to the east side of the ridge and continues to rise gently as you move toward High Pass. The spectacular form of Clark Mountain rises beyond High Pass from the opposite side of the Napeequa Valley.

Climb higher, finally running out of trail atop a gentle knoll, elevation 7,050 feet, a short distance from High Pass. Descend gentle snow and gravel slopes for 200 feet into a small, shallow basin beneath the pass. Walk across the basin and then ascend diagonally over moderately steep snow for about 150 feet to reach High Pass. The view downward across icy Triad Lake toward Glacier Peak is stark and awesome. Cliffs and spires, immersed in the dark of evening shadows, rise above the nearly ice-covered lake. Just out of reach across the gentle glacial curve of the Suiattle Valley spy the white ice of Glacier Peak. Looking south, see down into the Napeequa Valley, often compared to the fabled valley of Shangri-La because of its beauty and inaccessibility. Interestingly, in Nepali lingo "La" means a mountain pass, not a valley. Camp here amongst the splendor, or descend 300 feet to the lakelet in the basin toward the Napeequa.

DAY THREE   16+ miles   2,300 feet gain

Day three is a day of remote splendor and trekking challenges, including an off-trail route, a ford of the Napeequa River, and the climb to Boulder Pass.

Descend down to the stream pouring forth from the lakelet. As the stream drops off more steeply, traverse right on tread along a heather bench. From the far end of the bench, the tread descends sharply down a heathery rib, to the right of the stream originating from the lakelet and to the left of the stream coming from west of High Pass. The going is through meadows and choosing a route is easy. This is visual navigation using the path of least resistance. As the streams begin to converge, cross right and boulder-hop the stream on your right (west). At about 5,900 feet elevation, perhaps cross back over what is now one larger stream and continue descending along the left (east) side of the stream. Stay on whichever side of the stream looks better to you. There is tread here and there, but don't worry about having to follow a particular path. Your goal is to reach the beautiful flat meadow at 5,500 feet elevation on the west side of the stream at the lip of valley. In the summer of 1996, avalanche snow spanned the stream near this point, so it was easy to cross the natural snow bridge back over to the right (west) side of the stream. If you don't clearly see a snow bridge created by avalanche debris and the stream volume is high, consider staying right (west) of the stream, thereby avoiding a wet and scary crossing at the lip of the valley.

From the meadow at the lip of the side valley, the floor of the immense Napeequa Valley is surprisingly close. Only 600 feet of descent is required to reach the valley floor on constructed, if unmaintained, tread. The trick is to choose a route of descent that keeps you from becoming entangled in the dreadful-looking brush all around. Miraculously, such a route exists! From the meadow, find tread heading right (west). Although the tread does not drop immediately, stick with it. Soon it begins to turn and descend. Sometimes the tread moves horizontally, sometimes straight down, always avoiding the dense brush. Continue on, visually checking around to confirm the best path when in doubt. Nearing the floor of the valley, the tread again traverses right in deep grasses between groves of slide alder. Stay with the tread and soon you will be deposited, without a single scratch, on the bank of the stream descending from High Pass, near its confluence with the Napeequa River, elevation 4,900 feet. The descent from High Pass will take 1 to 3 hours.

The valley is wild and remote—a place visited by few. The river is clear and fast moving; the snow and glaciers of Clark Mountain hang just above the valley floor. The steep, high valley walls offer few, if any, paths out.

Find the tread of the Napeequa Valley Trail near the riverbank and easily descend the valley. The trail is not always easy to find through the grassy upper valley. However, each time a thicket of brush is reached, good tread materializes. Crossing the showery cascades of Louis Creek without getting wet is a tricky challenge, a break from straining to find the trail. The tread gets easier to follow and in the flat valley floor beyond Louis Creek, changes in elevation are gradual. Therefore it is easy to miss the trail junction leading to the river ford and then onward toward Boulder Pass. When traveling down valley, as you will be, the trail joins and fords the Napeequa River near 4,400 feet elevation, where the timber first reaches *all* the way down to the opposite riverbank.

Napeequa Valley

Fording the Napeequa will likely soak you to mid-thigh, typical for a mid-size Cascade stream. In uninspiring fashion the tread climbs to Boulder Pass. Flat, overlapping switchbacks deeply scar the meadows. The old and rational tread is still visible, a witness to the desecration that occurred when this route was slated to become a part of the PCT. In just a few hours, reach Boulder Pass and descend what seems like a long 6 miles into the valley, turning right on the White River Trail #1507. The trail up the White River Valley begins flat but is poorly maintained. Choose a camp near the trail junction, or within a couple of miles upstream near the river, or where a stream tumbles from Clark Mountain above.

DAY FOUR   15+ miles   4,000 feet gain

From an unglamorous beginning deep in the White River Valley, day four recovers to showcase the mesmerizing beauty of White and Red Passes, with the upper White Chuck splendor ultimately the day's goal. Early on the lack of trail maintenance may be aggravating and at times you may have to check your map to confirm the location of the trail.

For several miles, the trail is nearly flat, alternating between stands of beautiful old-growth timber and the dense brush of innumerable avalanche swaths. In its upper reaches, the White River must be crossed three times and in 1996 there was not a bridge remaining at any of the three crossings. The crossings are usually easy, but will soak your shoes just the same. After the first river crossing, the trail begins to gain some elevation. You will welcome the steeper tread and switchbacks beyond the third stream crossing. Finally, reach Little White Pass and turn right on the PCT #2000. From here on and for the remainder of the day, stunningly beautiful meadows, tumbling falls, and mountain vistas will destroy your pace and gobble your film.

Cross through White Pass and begin moving toward Red Pass beyond the North Fork Sauk River Trail #649 junction. Beware of one or more steep short snow crossings on this trail segment. Again an ice ax or extensive snow travel experience is very helpful. And remember there is no shame in dropping beneath or climbing around a scary snow patch.

The route to Red Pass and down the White Chuck Valley is splendid, a sublime experience on a trek filled with sublime experiences! Views of the Sauk River Valley and rugged peaks of the Monte Cristo group, capped by impressive Sloan Peak, are exchanged for meadows and foaming streams of the White Chuck Valley contrasted with the beauty of Glacier Peak in the background. Find camp here in the upper White Chuck Valley amidst the meadows, waterfalls, and alpine firs.

DAY FIVE   17 miles   3,000 feet gain

Day five is the only day of the trek spent closely on the slopes of Glacier Peak. As you move on from camp, the roaring White Chuck River will amaze you with its beauty and power, especially at the dramatic bridge crossing where the river roars through a narrow chasm. Beyond, the tread languishes in gentle forest. Past the junction with the Upper White Chuck River Trail #643.1, stay right on the PCT and after log- and rock-hopping first Sitkum Creek and then muddy Kennedy Creek, reach the junction with Kennedy Ridge Trail #639. Stay right on the PCT and begin ascending the wooded ridge toward the meadows and meandering terrain beneath the Scimitar and Kennedy Glaciers.

The north side of Glacier Peak is wildly rugged and scenic. Streams tumbling directly from the glaciers and snowfields on the mountain will cross your path. The flower meadows are among the best in the land, spanning thousands of feet in width and depth and offering shooting star, cow parsnip, bistort, tiger lilies, daisies, lupine, and paintbrush, while the views toward White Chuck Mountain and Mount Pugh above the green-mantled valley are overpowering. Savoring every step, bob and weave through meadows, across streams, and around ridges, eventually climbing 1,000 feet to the broad meadows and grandeur of rugged Fire Creek Pass, elevation 6,300 feet.

After relaxing and enjoying Fire Creek Pass, in just a few steps encounter a perennially tricky snow crossing. The slope is not very wide or long, but it is moderately steep and a slip will result in injury. Again, if you aren't sure, don't cross it. Instead, go beneath or around the slope. The crossing completed, descend through

Glacier Peak from above Kennedy Hot Springs

lupine fields and rock gardens toward the deep cirque of Mica Lake, finding camp near the outlet stream or just beyond. New views up to Glacier Peak and across the Suiattle Valley toward Dome Peak will add spice to the already flavorful views.

DAY SIX   10+ miles   500 feet gain

Finally, begin the last trekking day and it's an easy day at that. Tear yourself away from spectacular Mica Lake and then, on gentle trail, descend through subalpine vegetation and forest into the valley of Milk Creek. Cross Milk Creek, so named for the milky-colored water draining from Ptarmigan Glacier, on a very sturdy bridge. After crossing the stream, leave the PCT, turning left on the Milk Creek Trail #790. Then descend down the length of the valley, heavily vegetated and humid, nearly a jungle in appearance. The magnificent stands of old-growth forests offer shade and earthy beauty on a warm day.

After more than 8 miles of walking from Mica Lake, and within sight and sound of the roaring Suiattle River, the trail has one last trick to play. For more than 1.5 miles the tread contours in gentle ups and downs about 400 above the river. Finally, the tread relents and quickly descends to the large bridge spanning the mighty river. Within a hundred yards of the bridge crossing, reach the junction with the Suiattle River Trail. Turn left and, for 1 mile, retrace the route where your adventure began days before.

Trail Summary and Mileage Estimates

0.0	Suiattle Trail #784, elevation 1,800 feet
0.8	Milk Creek Trail #790, elevation 1,800 feet, stay left on Trail #784
10.8	Miners Ridge Trail #785, elevation 2,800 feet, turn left on Trail #785
13.3	Miners Cabin Trail #795, elevation 4,800 feet, stay left on Trail #785
16.8	Canyon Lake Trail #797, elevation 6,300 feet, stay right on Trail #785
18.2	Miners Cabin Trail #795, elevation 5,600 feet, stay left on Trail #785
19.8	PCT #2000, elevation 5,500 feet, turn right on PCT
22.6	Buck Creek Pass Trail #789, elevation 4,600 feet, turn left on Trail #789
27.6	High Pass Trail #1562.2, elevation 5,900 feet, turn right on Trail #1562.2
33.6	Napeequa River Trail #1562.1, elevation 4,900 feet, follow Trail #1562.1
38.0	Boulder Pass Trail #1562, elevation 4,400 feet, turn right on Trail #1562
47.0	White River Trail #1507, elevation 2,500 feet, turn right on Trail #1507
57.8	PCT #2000, elevation 5,400 feet, turn right on PCT
60.8	North Fork Sauk River Trail #649, elevation 5,900 feet, stay right on PCT
70.5	Upper White Chuck River Trail #643.1, elevation 3,900 feet, stay right on PCT
72.5	Kennedy Ridge Trail #639, elevation 4,300 feet, stay right on PCT
84.0	Milk Creek Trail #790, elevation 3,900 feet, turn left on Trail #790
90.5	Suiattle River Trail #784, elevation 1,700 feet, turn left on Trail #784
91.3	Suiattle River Trailhead, elevation 1,800 feet

Suggested Camps Based on Different Trekking Itineraries

Night	15–20 mpd	10–15 mpd	10 mpd
One:	16+ miles - Image Lake	13+ miles - junction Trail #795	7+ miles - Canyon Creek
Two:	31+ miles - near High Pass	28 miles - Buck Creek Pass	16+ miles - Image Lake
Three:	48 miles - near White River	41+ miles - near Boulder Pass	28 miles - Buck Creek Pass
Four:	63+ miles - White Chuck Valley	58 miles - before White Pass	38 miles - Napeequa ford
Five:	80+ miles - near Mica Lake	71 miles - Sitkum Creek	48 miles - near White River
Six:		80+ miles - near Mica Lake	58 miles - before White Pass
Seven:			68 miles - lower White Chuck
Eight:			79 miles - Fire Creek Pass

White Chuck Valley

TREK 12

The Flowered Ridges of Glacier Peak

Sloan Peak beyond wildflowers of the Cascade Crest

Difficulty:	Strenuous
Distance:	46 miles
Elevation gain:	12,600 feet
Best season:	Late July through mid-September
Recommended itinerary:	4 days (10–15 miles per day)
Water availability:	Okay except for climb from North Fork Sauk River until beneath Johnson Mountain. Leave the river with 3 quarts of liquid. Because water is intermittently unavailable on this ridge-top route, carry at least 1 quart at all times.
Logistics:	Stash a bike along North Fork Sauk Road at Lost Creek Ridge Trailhead or walk 4 miles to North Fork Sauk

River Trailhead at trek's end. Expect some steep snow crossings in gullies between White and Red Passes, and the upper White Chuck Valley, until late August. Carry an ice ax or be prepared to go above or below scary stretches of snow.

Jurisdictions: Glacier Peak Wilderness, 360-436-1155. Wilderness permits are not currently required.

Maps: Green Trails: Sloan Peak, Benchmark Mountain, and Glacier Peak

Trail location: Drive Interstate 5 to Arlington and take exit 208. Turn east and follow State Route 530 about 5 miles through Arlington and an additional 26 miles to Darrington. In Darrington, beyond milepost 49, turn right on the Mountain Loop Highway. Follow it 16 miles to North Fork Sauk Road 49. Turn left on North Fork Sauk Road, passing the Lost Creek Ridge Trailhead in approximately 3 miles and reaching the North Fork Sauk River Trailhead near Sloan Creek Campground in 4 more miles, elevation 2,100 feet.

Expect every aspect of this trek to be the best that backpacking offers. As with most ridges in Washington, Pilot and Lost Creek Ridges undulate every step of the way. While the Pacific Crest Trail may be a bit busy, the ridge segments provide solitude. Glacier Peak will command your attention for miles at a time. The recommended itinerary allows plenty of time for roaming the gentle peaks and high country and camping in idyllic alpine settings.

DAY ONE   11+ miles   4,800 feet gain

On this trek, you finish on the same road, but 4 miles from where you started. If possible, leave old bikes at the trek's end, the Lost Creek Ridge Trailhead. At a minimum, bikes offer a faster and different form of misery than walking a road at the end of a trek.

Quickly reach the junction with Pilot Ridge Trail #652, 1.9 miles up the North Fork Sauk River Trail. Turn right on Trail #652 and in a short distance reach the bank of the Sauk River. Although the stream can usually be forded where the path meets the gravel bank, a trail built by the boots of hikers seeking a drier and safer alternative leads upstream about 100 yards. In this distance, you are likely to find a nice log to use to cross over the stream, then just work your way back down the bank to where you started. Don't be tempted to turn uphill too soon, the official tread of the Pilot Ridge Trail begins directly opposite the bank where you first arrived.

Glacier
Peak

River

Chuck

2000

White

3

643.1

White Chuck River

643

Lake
Byrne

2

Glacier Peak

Camp
Lake

Wilderness

3

646

Red
Mountain

**Sloan Creek
Campground**

Lost Creek

Road 49

North Fork Sauk River

Round
Lake

T

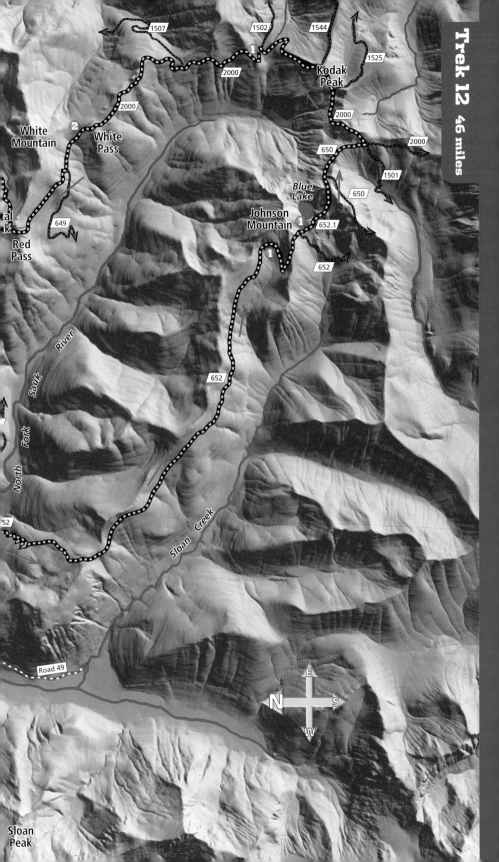

1507

1502

1544

1525

1

2000

Kodak
Peak

2000

2000

White
Mountain

2000

2

White
Pass

650

2000

Blue
Lake

1501

650

649

650

Johnson
Mountain

652.1

tal
k

Red
Pass

1

1

652

River

Sauk

652

North
Fork

Sloan   Creek

52

Road 49

N
E
W
S

Sloan
Peak

Pilot Ridge and Sloan Peak

The trail to the top of Pilot Ridge was built to climb, gaining 2,600 feet in less than 3 miles. Continue up the ridge, breaking into flowers at 5,300 feet elevation before dropping back to 5,000 feet. Then the sheer magnificence of Pilot Ridge begins to unfold with each step. Climb to meadows teaming with helebore, lupine, daisies, valerian, and arnica atop the ridge at 5,600 feet elevation, where you can see as far away as Mount Stuart and Mount Rainier to the south and Mount Baker to the north. With continual ups and downs, traverse Pilot Ridge and head across a meadow basin with water to the ridge on the southwest side of Johnson Mountain. As you traverse, the prominent trail leading left and up onto Johnson Mountain appears the more obvious path; however, stay to the right to continue on to a possible first night's camp.

Recommended side trip 1. If your itinerary allows, make the 30-minute side trip up Johnson Mountain. The view from the summit is a fantastic collage of peaks, meadows of the crest, and views of Blue Lakes.

Upon reaching the southwest ridge of Johnson Mountain and the unmarked trail junction with the Johnson Mountain Trail, elevation 6,100 feet, turn right. The Pilot Ridge Trail descends the ridge crest for about 0.3-mile. The trail then angles across meadows to the junction with the Blue Lake High Trail #652.1, between upper and lower Blue Lakes. Turn left, toward upper Blue Lake, which sits about 100 feet elevation higher than the trail junction. Find camp in the lake basin, 11+ miles from the trailhead (nearly 13 miles if you trekked up Johnson Mountain).

Meadows of aster, paintbrush, and lupine

DAY TWO 13 miles 2,800 feet gain

The second day of trekking is 100 percent alpine splendor spent roaming the ridge tops and alpine basins with constantly changing views of Glacier Peak at nearly every turn. Immediately after crossing the Blue Lake outlet stream, climb toward the narrow pass east of the lake. Likely cross a short stretch of snow and switchback on good but steep trail up to the pass, elevation 6,300 feet. Descend abruptly into the land of trail junctions at nearly every turn. Quickly reach the junction with the Bald Eagle Trail #650, turn left. In about 1 more mile, reach Dishpan Gap and the PCT #2000. Again turn left, this time onto the PCT. Now stay left at every trail junction until beyond White Pass, nearly 7 miles away.

Touch the trees of Indian Pass, at 5,000 feet your lowest elevation since first stepping on Pilot Ridge. However, the meadows aren't lost as the trail ascends gently but steadily toward Little White Pass, beyond to Reflection Pond, and then on to White Pass, elevation 5,900 feet. I have walked this segment of trail four times now, and the beauty of the meadows and Glacier Peak still stops me in my tracks. If your schedule and energy allow, from White Pass take time to scramble up White Mountain or traverse the gentle boot-built path east out of the pass into the incomparable beauty of streaming waterfalls and luxurious meadows of Foam Basin.

From White Pass, the beauty continues along the ascending and traversing trail leading toward Red Pass. In less than 1 mile from White Pass, reach the junction with the North Fork Sauk River Trail #649. Stay right on the PCT and continue the glorious traverse, soon reaching Red Pass, elevation 6,500 feet, and the awesome sight of the upper White Chuck River Basin. Before mid-August, anticipate some short, but steep, snow-covered gully or meadow crossings between White and Red Passes.

The trek down into the White Chuck Valley defies description. Start by descending moderate snow into the creek-filled meadow basin below. Glacier Peak is directly above. The trail winds gently through meadows, the White Chuck River spilling downward in a series of small waterfalls and rushing torrents. The upper valley is long and broad. Camp here and roam the alpine terrain that is just begging for private exploration for as long as your time allows.

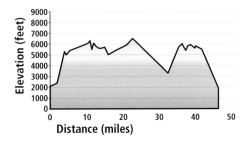

DAY THREE
11+ miles 3,000 feet gain

From camp, regain the trail as it roams down the valley. In time, old-growth timber is reached as the White Chuck roars out of sight below. After passing lacey waterfalls of tributary streams, the time comes to cross the White Chuck River itself. Fortunately, a sturdy new bridge makes crossing the river merely humbling and breathtaking instead of terrifying and life threatening. For within arms reach of the bridge, the entire river dumps over a waterfall in a chasm scarcely 6 feet wide.

Gentle trail in old growth continues beyond the crossing. There is camping throughout the White Chuck Valley and water is obviously abundant. After several gentle miles, reach a trail junction and turn left on the Upper White Chuck River Trail #643.1 toward Kennedy Hot Springs. Gentle, even rising at first, the trail drops several hundred feet in about 2 miles to the forested camp near the hot springs, elevation 3,300 feet. The appeal of the single small, murky hot-spring pool itself, popularized to the point of being overrun from a wilderness perspective, is certainly in the eyes of the beholder. If your muscles are sore and you have a few hours to spend before facing the climb to Lake Byrne and beyond, step in.

Turn left on Trail #774 and walk in front of the ranger's cabin toward the bridge crossing of the White Chuck River. After crossing the river, either continue walking a short distance to reach the hot spring pool itself or, resisting the urge, turn

Lake Byrne

right, a sign within 100 yards verifying you are on the path toward Lost Creek Ridge and Lake Byrne. In an extremely efficient manner the trail climbs directly through forests of massive old-growth firs, the deep patterns of richly carved bark a diversion from the heart-pounding effort, until breaking above timberline once again.

Beyond Lake Byrne, cross a broad plateau and descend down a couple of hundred feet to Camp Lake. Sloan Peak looms over the top of Lost Creek Ridge. Down the White Chuck Valley rises its mountain namesake, overshadowed by Mount Baker in the distance.

DAY FOUR   10+ miles   2,000 feet gain

From Camp Lake, begin the final long traverse of this trek along the rugged and beautiful expanse of Lost Creek Ridge. With continual ups and downs between 5,400 and 5,800 feet elevation, follow good tread just below the ridge crest on the north side. Dropping as low 5,400 feet, the tread climbs back to nearly 6,000 feet before crossing over to the south side of the ridge for good. Views across Lost Creek and the Sauk Valley to Sloan Peak and down the ridge to White Chuck Mountain are as enthralling as the meadow views and private basins.

Twilight over Lost Creek Ridge

With minor ups and downs the trail traverses irregular terrain at about 5,600 feet elevation, then climbs back to nearly 6,000 feet. Throughout this south-side traverse, stretches of snow may complicate your routefinding. Past the junction with Round Lake Trail #646.1 the traverse transitions to a steady descent. Head quickly down on good tread, one final descent through the magnificent old-growth forests. Soon reach the trailhead 46 miles from the trek's beginning, but you aren't done.

Retrieve the bikes you stashed a few days ago and pedal your way to the North Fork Sauk River Trailhead or be prepared to hike the last 4 miles on the roadbed.

Trail Summary and Mileage Estimates

0.0	North Fork Sauk River Trail #649, elevation 2,100 feet
1.9	Pilot Ridge Trail #652, elevation 2,400 feet, turn right on Trail #652
10.4	Johnson Mountain Trail (unsigned), elevation 6,100 feet, stay right on Trail #652
11.4	Blue Lake High Trail #652.1, elevation 5,500 feet, turn left on Trail #652.1
12.5	Bald Eagle Trail #650, elevation 5,800 feet, turn left on Trail #650
13.3	PCT #2000, elevation 5,600 feet, turn left on PCT
14.0	Little Wenatchee River Trail #1525, elevation 5,600 feet, stay left on PCT
14.9	Bryant Peak Trail #1544, elevation 5,700 feet, stay left on PCT
15.9	Indian Creek Trail #1502, elevation 5,000 feet, stay left on PCT
17.9	White River Trail #1507, elevation 5,400 feet, stay left on PCT
20.9	North Fork Sauk River Trail #649, elevation 5,900 feet, stay right on PCT
30.6	Upper White Chuck River Trail #643.1, elevation 3,900 feet, turn left on Trail #643.1
32.4	Lake Byrne Trail #774, elevation 3,300 feet, turn left on Trail #774
41.8	Round Lake Trail #646.1, elevation 5,500 feet, stay left on Trail #646
46.4	Lost Creek Ridge Trailhead, elevation 1,900 feet

Suggested Camps Based on Different Trekking Itineraries

Night	15–20 mpd	10–15 mpd	10 mpd
One:	16 miles - near Indian Pass	11+ miles - Upper Blue Lake	10 miles - near Johnson Mountain
Two:	35 miles - Lake Byrne	24+ miles - White Chuck Valley	20 miles - near White Pass
Three:		36 miles - Camp Lake	30 miles - near Sitkum Creek
Four:			40 miles - on Lost Creek Ridge

The Fabulous Icicle Divide

Upper Doelle Lake

Difficulty:	Very strenuous
Distance:	45 miles
Elevation gain/loss:	13,500 feet gain; 16,200 feet loss
Best season:	Late July through mid-October
Recommended itinerary:	3 days (15–20 miles per day)
Water availability:	Good to Doelle Lakes and just okay beyond. Leave on-trail water sources with 1 to 2 quarts liquid unless it is obvious that water will be readily available. From Cabin Creek to the Icicle Ridge Trailhead, a distance of 13 miles, there may only be one water source. Carry 3 quarts of liquid when leaving Cabin Creek.

Logistics:	The trailheads are approximately 35 miles apart, so use of two vehicles is recommended. It is possible to travel via bus from Seattle to a drop-off at Stevens Pass and catch scheduled bus service from Leavenworth back to Seattle. Contact Greyhound, 206-628-5508, or *www.greyhound.com*. Expect snow crossing in gulleys between Ladies Pass and Lake Edna until mid-August.
Jurisdictions:	Alpine Lakes Wilderness, 509-548-6977. Backcountry permits are required for overnight travel in the Alpine Lakes Wilderness. Inquire about use restrictions in the area of Lakes Mary and Margaret (which this trek passes above).
Maps:	Green Trails: Stevens Pass, Chiwaukum Mountain, and Leavenworth
Trail location:	Drive Interstate 5 to Everett. Take exit 194 and follow U.S. Highway 2 east beyond milepost 99. Turn right on Icicle Road. Drive 1.4 miles, turning right into the Icicle Ridge Trailhead and parking lot, elevation 1,200 feet. Leaving a vehicle at this point, return to US 2 and drive back beyond milepost 65 to Stevens Pass. Turn left (south) at the pass, winding into the upper parking lot and trailhead for the PCT #2000 (headed south), elevation 4,100 feet.

Nowhere in the Alpine Lakes region is there a trail as high, lonesome, rigorous, and outrageously beautiful as Icicle Ridge. This trek ranks step for step as one of Washington's most demanding and rewarding trekking challenges. Expect a trail that is never flat for more than a few strides. Keep your map available because you will often need to verify that the faint scuff before you is indeed the trail. Also expect to be a bit daunted by the loneliness encountered over most of this route. This trek has the potential to be one of the most profoundly beautiful and fulfilling of your outdoor experiences.

DAY ONE   17+ miles   6,100 feet gain

Starting at just over 4,000 feet elevation at Stevens Pass on the Pacific Crest Trail #2000, the goal of day one is to reach marvelous upper Florence Lake, an idyllic ending to what is a demanding day. Easily traverse up through the Stevens Pass ski area and over the ridge into Mill Creek. There are substantial powerlines to cross beneath, along with crossing the gravel service road, but the PCT #2000 is continuous and easy to follow as it descends to about 4,500 feet elevation. The trail

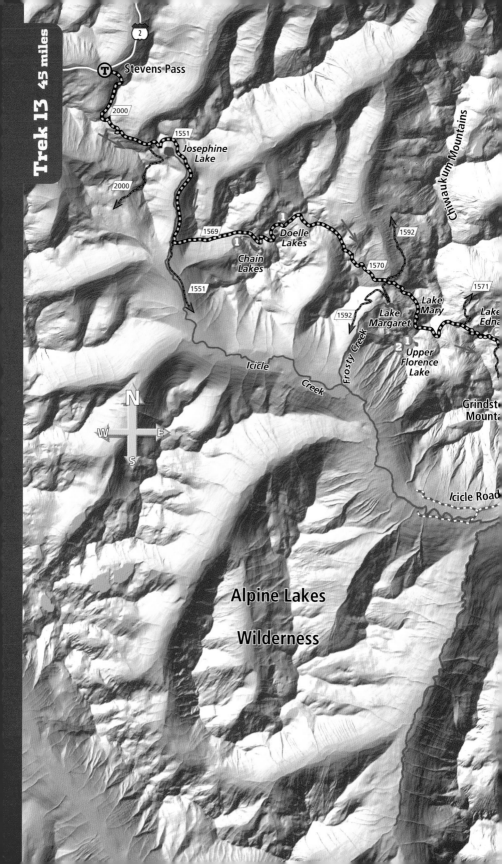

Stevens Pass

2

2000

1551

Josephine Lake

2000

1569

Doelle Lakes

Chain Lakes

1551

1592

1570

Lake Mary

1571

Lake Edna

Chiwaukum Mountains

1592

Frosty Creek

Lake Margaret

Upper Florence Lake

Icicle

Creek

Grindstone Mountain

Icicle Road

N
W   E
S

Alpine Lakes

Wilderness

Big Jim
Mountain

1575

3 2

Lake
Augusta

1577

1570

Icicle

Ridge

Cabin

3

Creek

1579

Icicle

Wenatchee

River

Leavenworth

2

Icicle

Creek

Icicle Road

Ridge

1570

T

Mount
Cashmere

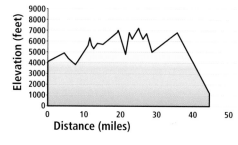

then traverses past Lake Susan Jane before climbing to the junction with the Icicle Creek Trail #1551, elevation 4,900 feet, 4.5 miles from Stevens Pass.

Turn left on the Icicle Creek Trail, circling above and then down to the shore of Josephine Lake. The descent continues, in forest, past Whitepine Creek Trail #1582 and on to the junction with the Chain Lakes Trail #1569, elevation 3,800 feet, 7.6 miles from Stevens Pass. Turn left on the Chain Lakes Trail, immediately cross Icicle Creek, and climb to 4,900 feet before enjoying the ascending flower-laden traverse to the first of the Chain Lakes, elevation 5,600 feet. This lake is passed along the right shoreline. Beyond the first lake there are several boot-built trails that are easily confused with the main trail. The proper trail crosses the outlet stream of the second lake and traverses, then climbs, above the shoreline and through a pass, elevation 6,300 feet. The pass and descending slopes above Doelle Lakes offer expansive views of summits as near as Glacier Peak and as distant as Mount Baker. The trail reaches upper Doelle Lake, then traverses clockwise to the outlet stream. Continue descending to the outlet stream of lower Doelle Lake at 5,600 feet, about 12 miles from Stevens Pass.

Cross the stream and descend on thin but followable tread, this meager offering being the beginning of Icicle Ridge Trail #1570. Recrossing the outlet stream in a short distance, survey the countryside toward Frosty Pass, 3 miles distant. Although seemingly abandoned, the trail is marked by boot prints as it descends toward the obvious flat, marshy meadow at 5,300 feet elevation, where tread ceases temporarily. Curving around the left edge of the meadow, easily regain the trail in about 150 yards, where it enters a wooded area of scrub evergreens and deciduous trees. Back on the track, the trail traverses at about 5,300 feet elevation for nearly 1 mile before climbing to a ridge saddle at 5,500 feet elevation. Now officially standing atop the elegant divide of Icicle Ridge, ascend tread directly up the ridge crest to 5,800 feet. Cross over the ridge and enjoy the expansive green slopes and waterfall-strewn vistas of Icicle Ridge. On even thinner tread, descend to 5,600 feet and then traversing with numerous small ups and downs, pick your way to Frosty Pass, elevation 5,700 feet, about 15 miles from Stevens Pass. As you traverse the slopes into Frosty Pass, the trail is hard to follow. Relax though, for if you don't see the trail in front of you, simply choose a course that follows the path of least resistance, holding to about 5,700 feet elevation; you can't miss Frosty Pass.

Trek through the junction with the Frosty-Wildhorse Trail #1592, remaining on the Icicle Ridge Trail. In striking meadows of green, with flowers of all colors and refreshing streams that chill with their clarity as much as their touch, climb high above Lake Margaret and Lake Mary. This is the most well-known portion of Icicle Ridge and the views from Mary Pass, at 6,800 feet elevation, are staggering in every direction. Admire Glacier Peak, the Stuart Range, Mount Daniel, the lakes below, and the ridge beyond. Through fields of lupine, phlox, monkey flowers, elephants head, and paintbrush, walk entranced along the undulating path, leaving the main trail and finding a very obvious route to upper Florence Lake and camp, 17+ miles from Stevens Pass.

Kristy Woodmansee and lunker trout

DAY TWO   9+ miles   3,700 feet gain
Don't let the distance of day two fool you, the camp at Lake Augusta will be a most welcome sight.

From Florence Lake climb back up to the main trail and enjoy the spectacular traverse through an open basin to Ladies Pass, elevation 6,800 feet. Stay right at the junction with Chiwaukum Creek Trail #1571, continuing on the Icicle Ridge Trail. The north-facing slopes beyond Ladies Pass may be a bit snowy. If so, cross the snow if you are comfortable or find an easier way above or below. Climb and traverse scree slopes amongst rock outcroppings and narrow gullies at about 7,000 feet elevation for 0.5 mile. Beyond, the trail drops abruptly to tiny yet beautiful Lake Edna, located on a meadow and slab-covered bench.

Continue descending from Lake Edna on a faint trail. Soon reach a junction that may be labeled "horse trail" (in reality the Icicle Ridge Trail). Take the horse trail, even if you have only two legs, no tail, and aren't excited about eating hay! Continue down on thin tread, which vanishes at the crossing of Lake Edna's outlet stream. Cross the stream and pick up the trail on the other side, a few feet below the crossing. The tread improves as it continues into the woods, dropping to the crossing of Index Creek at 4,800 feet elevation. At the junction with Index Creek Trail #1572, stay right on the Icicle Ridge Trail and immediately gain back all the elevation so recently lost. Although maps show no streams in the vicinity of the trail, depending on the timing of your trek the trail bed may double as a watercourse. The upper portion of the ascent leads through lush alpine meadows, culminating in a saddle at 6,700 feet elevation.

Beyond the saddle, descend abruptly into the small meadowed valley below. In season, the alpine flowers are so pretty the scene will be permanently imprinted in your retinas. The trail is very easy to lose, in fact, plan on losing it. The key to finding it is to realize the tread does not cross the stream immediately upon reaching the floor of the small valley. Instead, the trail contours a short distance above the stream, following the left bank downstream 0.25 mile until crossing the stream and climbing a short distance to poorly named Carter Lake, which is a swamp and frog pond. Near Carter Lake, stay right at the junction with Painter Creek Trail #1575 and begin a gradual winding ascent, first in meadows, then on scree slopes, to the 7,200-foot pass on the shoulder of Big Jim Mountain. Enjoy climactic distant views while looking down on beautiful Lake Augusta, 25 or more miles from Stevens Pass. Then move along to the lake and make camp amidst tree glades near the lake.

DAY THREE   18 miles   3,700 feet gain

The descending then rising traverse from Lake Augusta leads to the ridge-top junction with Hatchery Creek Trail #1577 at elevation 6,700 feet. Stay right on the Icicle Ridge Trail and descend the open spur ridge on faint tread to about 6,200 feet elevation. The tread is easily lost but can be found again because the trail stays on top of the rounded crest of the ridge. At about 6,200 feet elevation, the faint trail begins to switchback down into the Cabin Creek Valley. If you lose the trail, stop immediately and relocate the tread. Upon reaching the valley floor, walk the

Sky reflected in Lake Edna

parted-grass trail through slide alder to the well-established camp in the big timber. A short distance beyond, cross Cabin Creek on a footbridge. Then walk and log-hop the marsh to the wooded margin of the valley floor. To find the trail upward, walk downstream (left) along the margin of marsh and forest until the trail reappears after about 50 yards. The reward for finding your way on trail into the Cabin Creek Valley is a continuous climb on decent tread from 5,000 feet elevation to 6,800 feet elevation atop Icicle Ridge amid the panorama of the Enchantments, Stuart Range, and more. Atop the ridge, stay left at the junction with Fourth of July Creek Trail #1579.

Passing a trickle of water and an adequate camp, descend directly down the ridge toward Leavenworth. The destruction wrought by the fires of 1994 and 2001 is obvious, as you pass through a forest of silver snags silhouetted against the sky. Still, life is returning to the charred pine forest, with ground covers and lavender-colored fireweed growing abundantly. Looking directly into Leavenworth, the trail ceases switchbacking at the last moment and traverses the final mile away from town and toward the trek's end along Icicle Road.

Trail Summary and Mileage Estimates

0.0	PCT #2000 South, elevation 4,100 feet
4.5	Icicle Creek Trail #1551, elevation 4,900 feet, turn left on Trail #1551
5.6	Whitepine Creek Trail #1582, elevation 4,400 feet, stay right on Trail #1551
7.6	Chain Lakes Trail #1569, elevation 3,800 feet, turn left on Trail #1569
12.1	Transition to Icicle Ridge Trail #1570 at lower Doelle Lake, elevation 5,600 feet
15.1	Frosty-Wildhorse Trail #1592, elevation 5,700 feet, stay on Trail #1570
19.0	Chiwaukum Creek Trail #1571, elevation 6,800 feet, stay right on Trail #1570
21.3	Index Creek Trail #1572, elevation 4,800 feet, stay right on Trail #1570
23.1	Painter Creek Trail #1575, elevation 6,200 feet, stay right on Trail #1570
27.1	Hatchery Creek Trail #1577, elevation 6,700 feet, stay right on Trail #1570
35.6	Fourth of July Creek Trail #1579, elevation 6,800 feet, stay left on Trail #1570
44.6	Icicle Ridge Trailhead, elevation 1,200 feet

Suggested Camps Based on Different Trekking Itineraries

Night	15–20 mpd	10–15 mpd	10 mpd
One:	17+ miles - Florence Lake	12 miles - Doelle Lakes	10 miles - Chain Lakes
Two:	27 miles - Lake Augusta	20+ miles - Lake Edna	17+ miles - Florence Lake
Three:		31+ miles - Cabin Creek	27 miles - Lake Augusta
Four:			38 miles - Icicle Ridge

Note: Itineraries are complicated by the lack of water atop Icicle Ridge.

TREK 14

The Pacific Crest Trail:
Stevens Pass to Snoqualmie Pass

Spectacle Lake, Lemah Mountain, and Chimney Rock

Difficulty:	Strenuous
Distance:	71 miles
Elevation gain:	16,000 feet
Best season:	Mid-July through mid-October, with mid-September on better for fall colors
Recommended itinerary:	5 days (10–15 miles per day)
Water availability:	Generally good, except for the 8 to 9 miles from Waptus River to Lemah Creek via Escondido Ridge. Carry at least 2 quarts of liquid when leaving the Waptus River and refill at the stream en route to the ridge top.
Logistics:	The trailheads are more than 120 road miles apart,

so a drop-off and pickup or preplacement of a vehicle is required. It is possible to travel via bus from Seattle to a drop-off at Stevens Pass, and catch scheduled bus service from Snoqualmie Pass back to Seattle. Contact Greyhound, 206-628-5508, or *www.greyhound.com*. Snow crossings should not be an issue during the recommended season. If you are traveling earlier, be aware that the Kendall Catwalk is treacherous if snow covered.

Jurisdictions: Alpine Lakes Wilderness, 425-888-1421. Backcountry permits are required for overnight travel in the Alpine Lakes Wilderness. Information and permits can be obtained at a number of locations, including the North Bend Ranger Station; see number above.

Maps: Green Trails: Stevens Pass, Kachess Lake, and Snoqualmie Pass

Trail location: Drive Interstate 5 to Everett, take exit 194, and head east on U.S. Highway 2. Drive US 2 beyond milepost 64 to Stevens Pass, elevation 4,000+ feet. Immediately upon cresting the pass turn right and follow a short gravel road to the trailhead and parking area, elevation 4,100 feet. For the return home, travel I-90 to Snoqualmie Pass and take exit 52. Turn east, passing beneath the freeway, and take the first right on a short gravel road to the trailhead, elevation 3,100 feet.

The Pacific Crest Trail through the Alpine Lakes Wilderness offers a feast of outdoor bounty. Flirting with the Cascade Crest past Lakes Josephine, Mig, Hope, and Trap, the trail's steeper ascents and descents lead past Glacier, Deception, and Hyas Lakes. Mile after mile, every ridge climb is daunting, every mountain view rugged, and every nook filled with a splendid body of crystal liquid. Lakes are the defining glory of the Alpine Lakes Wilderness, and the PCT defines a glorious route through the wilderness befitting the stature of a National Scenic Trail.

DAY ONE 14 miles 4,100 feet gain

This first trekking day will immerse you deep within the rugged beauty of the Alpine Lakes. Leaving Stevens Pass, elevation 4,100 feet, ascend the PCT #2000 beneath the chairlifts and barren slopes of the ski area. Within an hour or so, climb through the ski area, cross beneath the powerlines, and walk across the service road, continuing toward the welcoming beauty of the pristine wilderness. Past Lake Susan Jane, climb to the true Cascade Crest and the junction with Icicle

1551

Josephine
Lake

Stevens Pass

T

2000

Hope
Lake

1

Icicle Creek

1060.1

2000

Glacier
Lake

1

Deception
Lakes

2

1059

Dece
Pa

2

2

Alpine Lakes

Wilderness

River

Skykomish

2

N
E
S
W

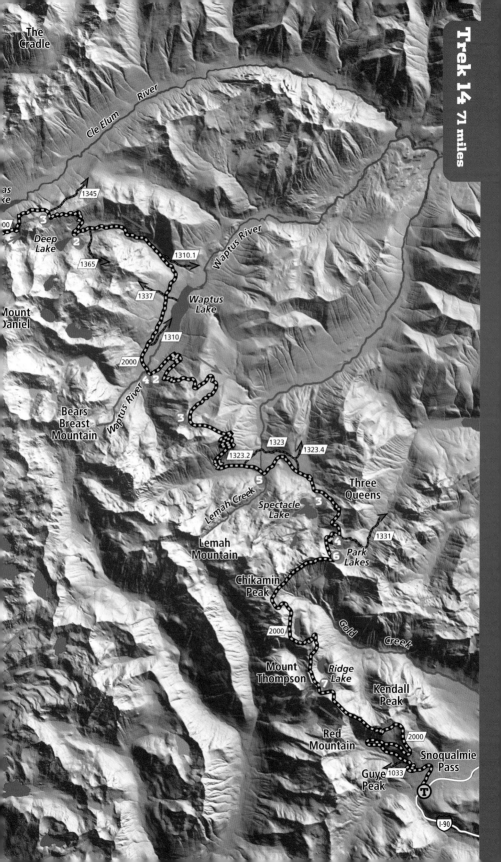

The Cradle

Cle Elum River

1345

3

2

Deep Lake

1365

Mount Daniel

1310.1

Waptus River

1337

Waptus Lake

1310

2000

4 2

Waptus River

Bears Breast Mountain

3

1323.2

1323

1323.4

5

Lemah Creek

Spectacle Lake

3

Three Queens

Lemah Mountain

1331

4

Park Lakes

6

Chikamin Peak

Gold Creek

2000

Mount Thompson

Ridge Lake

7

Kendall Peak

Red Mountain

2000

Snoqualmie Pass

Guye Peak

1033

T

I-90

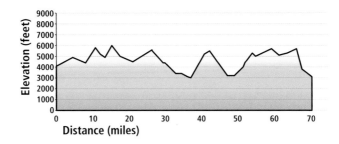

Creek Trail #1551, elevation 4,900 feet. Stay right and continue south on the PCT. Views of Lakes Josephine, Mig, and Hope will keep your camera shutter clicking.

Upon passing Tunnel Creek Trail #1061, elevation 4,400 feet, stay left on the PCT. The terrain is rugged, with a great deal of elevation gain and loss concealed from discovery by mere glances at the map. Traversing above Trap Lake and climbing to Trap Pass, enjoy views east to Icicle Ridge and west to Mount Index. Pass junctions with the Trap Pass Trail and Surprise Creek Trail, staying left on both occasions. Traverse above Surprise Lake before ascending a gentle incline to camp near Glacier Lake, elevation 4,900 feet.

Glacier Lake

DAY TWO 15+ miles 3,300 feet gain

Ascend alpine slopes above Glacier Lake toward Pieper Pass, with captivating views back down across the reflective waters of the lake and beyond to ridges of the crest. From Pieper Pass, descend then traverse to lovely Deception Lakes. Beyond the lakes, traverse subalpine greenery and then larger stands of old-growth forest, staying left at the Deception Creek Trail #1059.2 junction. After trekking about 7 miles from Glacier Lake, arrive at Deception Pass, elevation 4,500 feet. The pass presents an array of trail options leading to Deception Creek, Hyas Lake, and Marmot Lake. Choosing your path carefully; continue south on the PCT.

Having switched to the west side of the Cle Elum Valley from the east side of the Deception Creek Valley, the trail traverses beneath Mount Daniel in blazing sunshine on a nice day. Hyas Lake lies directly beneath the trail, brilliant blue in a wilderness of green. Cross roaring water flowing from the slopes of Mount Daniel, splashing through the foam. Angling steadily uphill, soon cross beneath immense Cathedral Rock, arriving in the meadows of Cathedral Pass.

Stay right at the junction with Cathedral Rock Trail #1345, then stay left at the intersection with Peggys Pond Trail #1375 and switchback down alp slopes toward lovely Deep Lake, which completely fills the basin below. Upon fording the shallow outlet and dancing across logs to avoid boggy terrain, find camp either along the lake or a few minutes farther along the PCT near Vicente Creek.

DAY THREE 12 miles 2,800 feet gain

From Deep Lake, continue along the PCT and in quick succession pass a trail leading left and one leading right, but keep your course steady on Trail #2000. The terrain moderates and for miles traverses through forest on gentle trail. Staying right at the junction with Spinola Creek Trail #1310.1, elevation 3,400 feet, curve into the Waptus River Valley and traverse above large and beautiful Waptus Lake. Passing straight through the junction with Spade Lake Trail #1337, continue past the Waptus River Trail junction and soon arrive beside the cool deep water of the river itself, Bears Breast Mountain looming directly above.

Beyond the Dutch Miller Gap Trail, the PCT climbs nearly 3,000 feet for the honor of traversing a mile or two atop Escondido Ridge before descending to Lemah Creek. Move up the ridge gradually on broad switchbacks. Putting the PCT over the top of Escondido Ridge was the result of a misplaced effort several years ago to put the PCT on the crest of something. This marginally useful trail has such a nonfunctional design that at times it is difficult to tell whether a switchback leads you up or down.

Focusing once again on the scenery instead of the path, fill your water containers at the second crossing of the stream descending from the ridge above, at about 5,000 feet elevation. Filling up here gives you the option of camping where you would like and negates the need for a water search atop the ridge. Stay right at

Waptus River and Bears Breast Mountain

junctions with the Waptus Burn Trail #1329.3 and find camp along the ridge. The views of Chimney Rock and Lemah Mountain are particularly impressive, just out of reach to the northwest. See remnants of the fire of 1994 that ravaged the slopes of Escondido Ridge. The views are broader now that all the trees are burned, but it will be a human lifetime before the terrain is largely restored.

DAY FOUR 15 miles 3,200 feet gain

The trek across the length of Escondido Ridge will likely take you an hour or so. Once again face the gentle switchbacks, this time headed downward. Eventually reach the wild and visually impressive valley of Lemah Creek. Standing near the roaring stream, adjust your gaze and marvel as above the valley rise the very rugged summits of Chikamin Peak, Lemah, Chimney Rock, and Summit Chief, the slopes steep and the relief impressive.

Descending as low as 3,200 feet, stay right at numerous trail junctions just uphill from Pete Lake, and about 4 miles after crossing Lemah Creek reach the second trail leading to the right a short distance to the shores of Spectacle Lake. Wildly rugged, with rock escarpments surrounding the octopus-like arms of clear blue water that radiate into the surrounding forests, the lake is indeed a spectacle to behold. Drop your pack and take the 10-minute walk to the lakeshore, both to see and touch the splendor.

Continuing to gain another 1,000 feet of elevation, crest a pass near Park Lakes Basin and earn an all-encompassing view of Spectacle Lake and the surrounding terrain. Dropping gently through the soft meadows of Park Lakes Basin, stay right on the PCT at the junction with Mineral Creek Trail #1331, and descend to one of the lakes for a relaxing and pleasant camp, elevation 5,000 feet.

DAY FIVE 15 miles 2,600 feet gain

The last trekking day is a grand finale, a day spent largely on ridge tops possessing some of the finest mountain views in the Alpine Lakes Wilderness. Surrounded by parkland with near views of Alta Mountain, Three Queens, and rugged Box Ridge, you will have to tear yourself away from Park Lakes Basin to begin the climb to Chikamin Pass, 700 feet above. Trekking uphill through open terrain to the pass, prepare yourself for the mind-blowing views of Mount Rainier, standing majestically over the Gold Creek Valley. Just as impressive is the near view of country soon to be visited: Huckleberry Mountain, Mount Thompson, and Kendall Peak along the true crest of the Cascades. Holding to near 6,000 feet elevation, the trail traverses very steep rocky slopes, sometimes blasted from the cliffs of Chikamin Peak. The scree rock of the trail bed is uneven and the sharp edges of rock will be quite hard on your trip-weary feet.

For more than an hour traverse the rocky hillside before reaching the crest near Huckleberry Mountain and regaining glorious meadows of heather, daisies, asters, and lilies. Once again enthralled, descend through a splendid alpine vale, refreshing yourself at a stream splashing down the mountainside. With views down to Joe Lake, back to Chikamin Ridge, and out to Mount Rainier, cross through a wooded saddle and climb sharply to near the meadow summit of Alaska Mountain. Traversing high above Alaska Lake, arrive at the small divide between Ridge and Gravel Lakes. Perhaps enjoy lunch here, one last splendid hour near the lovely alpine lakes. The lakes will be less busy and more enjoyable if you are finishing the trek on a weekday, but they are beautiful regardless.

Traverse the last remaining alpine slopes, crossing the exposed granite of the Kendall Catwalk, passing through the divide into Commonwealth Creek Valley, and descending the slopes of Kendall Peak. The views of the near peaks—Red, Snoqualmie, and Lundin—are impressive for their ruggedness. Staying left at the junction with Red Mountain Trail #1033, descend the gentle tread in tall timber to Snoqualmie Pass.

Trail Summary and Mileage Estimates

0.0	PCT #2000 South, Stevens Pass, elevation 4,100 feet
4.5	Icicle Creek Trail #1551, elevation 4,900 feet, stay right on PCT
8.0	Tunnel Creek Trail #1061, elevation 4,400 feet, stay left on PCT
12.0	Trap Pass Trail #1060.1, elevation 5,200 feet, stay left on PCT
13.3	Surprise Creek Trail #1060, elevation 4,900 feet, stay left on PCT
17.5	Deception Creek Trail #1059.2, elevation 5,000 feet, stay left on PCT
21.0	Multiple junctions at Deception Pass, elevation 4,500 feet, south on PCT
26.3	Cathedral Rock Trail #1345, elevation 5,600 feet, stay right on PCT
26.4	Peggys Pond Trail #1375, elevation 5,500 feet, stay left on PCT
29.4	Deep Lake Trail #1358, elevation 4,400 feet, stay left on PCT
29.9	Vicente Lake Trail #1365, elevation 4,400 feet, stay left on PCT
32.9	Spinola Creek Trail #1310.1, elevation 3,400 feet, stay right on PCT
34.5	Spade Lake Trail #1337, elevation 3,400 feet, straight ahead on PCT
36.2	Waptus River Trail #1310, elevation 3,100 feet, stay right on PCT
37.1	Dutch Miller Gap Trail #1362, elevation 3,000 feet, stay left on PCT
40.8	Waptus Burn Trail #1329.3, elevation 5,200 feet, stay right on PCT
47.2	Lemah Meadow Trail #1323.2, elevation 3,200 feet, stay right on PCT
49.1	Pete Lake Trail #1323, elevation 3,200 feet, stay right on PCT
51.5	Spectacle Lake Trail #1306, elevation 4,000 feet, stay left on PCT
52.0	Spectacle Lake Trail #1306, elevation 4,400 feet, stay left on PCT
54.9	Mineral Creek Trail #1331, elevation 5,000 feet, stay right on PCT
67.6	Red Mountain Trail #1033, elevation 3,800 feet, stay left on PCT
70.3	Snoqualmie Pass, elevation 3,100 feet

Josephine Lake near the Stevens Pass Trailhead

Suggested Camps Based on Different Trekking Itineraries

Night	15–20 mpd	10–15 mpd	10 mpd
One:	16+ miles - Deception Lakes	14 miles - Glacier Lake	8 miles - Hope Lake
Two:	36+ miles - Waptus River	29+ miles - Deep Lake	16+ miles - Deception Lakes
Three:	52+ miles - Spectacle Lake	42 miles - Escondido Ridge	27 miles - by Cathedral Rock
Four:		55 miles - Park Lakes Basin	36+ miles - Waptus River
Five:			46+ miles - near Lemah Creek
Six:			56 miles - near Chikamin Pass
Seven:			63+ miles - near Ridge Lake

TREK 15

The Stuart Range Traverse

Mount Stuart from Ingalls Creek

Difficulty:	Easier
Distance:	39 miles
Elevation gain:	8,800 feet
Best season:	Early July through mid-October
Recommended itinerary:	2 days (15–20+ miles per day)
Water availability:	Good throughout the trek
Logistics:	The trailheads are about 25 road miles apart, so either use two vehicles or arrange for a drop-off and pickup. For the hardcore, an option might be to stash a bike at trek's end and pedal back to your vehicle. If so, consider doing the trek in reverse for a largely downhill bike ride, as the Eightmile Lake Trailhead is 1,300 feet higher than Ingalls Creek Trailhead.

Jurisdictions:	Alpine Lakes Wilderness, 509-548-6977. Backcountry permits are required for overnight travel in the Alpine Lakes Wilderness. For permits and information, contact the Leavenworth Ranger Station at the above number.
Maps:	Green Trails: Chiwaukum Mountains, Mt. Stuart, and Liberty
Trail location:	Drive Interstate 5 to Everett, turning east on U.S. Highway 2 at exit 194. Follow US 2 to milepost 99, on the outskirts of Leavenworth. Turn right on Icicle Road and drive 8.4 miles to Bridge Creek Campground and Forest Service Road 7601. Turn left on Road 7601 and drive 3 miles to the Eightmile Lake Trailhead, elevation 3,300 feet. For the return trip, drive US 2 through Leavenworth and beyond milepost 104 to US 97. Turn right (west) on Highway 97 and reach Ingalls Creek Road near milepost 178. Turn right on Ingalls Creek Road and drive 1+ miles to the road end and trailhead, elevation 2,000 feet.

Scribe a great arc through the Stuart Range, savoring the spires of granite, narrow alpine passes, valleys of pine, and crystal flowing water of this prominent Cascade sub-range. These spectacular peaks, many approaching 9,000 feet elevation and crowned by the magnificent granite spires of Mount Stuart, elevation 9,415 feet, are circumnavigated in striking fashion by trekking the high ridges, mountain passes, and deep interconnecting pine-forested valleys of this Sierra-like terrain.

DAY ONE   17 miles   5,800 feet gain

Beginning on the Eightmile Lake Trail #1552 at 3,300 feet elevation, climb gently through forest for about 3 miles until adjacent to Little Eightmile Lake. Just beyond, reach the Lake Caroline/Windy Pass Trail #1554 junction. Turn right and begin the long climb toward Windy Pass, nearly 3,000 feet above. Move steadily uphill through wilderness pine forests charred by the fires of 1994. The golden heads of mountain grasses and lavender fireweed line the switchbacking path.

Transition to alpine terrain and expansive views as you climb to 6,400 feet elevation and the pass overlooking Lake Caroline. Before dropping to the lake, admire the view back into the Stuart Range of Aasgard Pass as well as Dragontail, Argonaut, and Colchuck Peaks. Upon reaching the shores of Lake Caroline, begin the meadow meander to Windy Pass. The roundabout nature of the path would be annoying except for the surrounding beauty. The brilliant flower fields dominate the near view, while Mount Stuart and its companion peaks fill the distance.

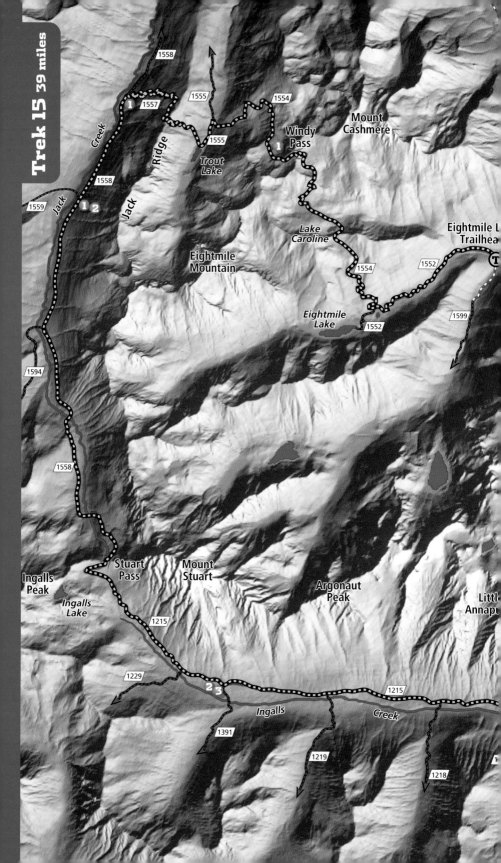

1558

1557 **1**

Creek

1555

1554

Jack Ridge

1 Windy Pass

Mount Cashmere

Trout Lake

1555

1559

1558

1 2

Jack

Lake Caroline

Eightmile Mountain

1554

Eightmile L Trailhea

1552

1599

Eightmile Lake

1552

1594

1558

Stuart Pass

Mount Stuart

Argonaut Peak

Littl Annap

Ingalls Peak

Ingalls Lake

1215

1229

2 3

Ingalls

Creek

1215

1391

1219

1218

Leavenworth

2

/601

Icicle Road

Alpine Lakes

Wilderness

N
W + E
S

Enchantment Lakes

97

Ingalls Creek
Trailhead
T

1215

1215

1215

Ingalls Creek

1216

vaho
eak

The gentle path in time attains the ridge of Windy Pass, 7,200 feet elevation, about 8 miles from the trailhead. Enjoy the climactic views not only of the Stuart Range but also of the Cascade Crest westward and to Icicle Creek and Icicle Ridge northward.

Moving along, the trail immediately descends through rocks and flowers. The steeper angle and narrow tread contrast noticeably with the path to Windy Pass. Curving through a seldom-visited alpine basin, continue descending toward Trout Creek. After 3 miles and 2,600 feet of elevation loss, cross Trout Creek and turn left on the Trout Creek Trail #1555. In 0.5 mile reach forested, marshy, and pretty Trout Lake, 4,800 feet elevation and 11+ miles from the trailhead. Ample camping room is available if your itinerary enables such a choice.

Leaving Trout Lake on the Jack Ridge Trail #1557, crest Jack Ridge at 5,800 feet elevation and revel in ever more expansive views. It is easy to get confused atop Jack Ridge. The real trail turns sharply right the moment the ridge crest is gained. Don't be fooled by the tread going left along the ridge. Soon the real trail crosses over the ridge and descends through open forest to the junction with Jack Creek Trail #1558, elevation 3,700 feet, 14.8 miles from the trailhead. Turn left.

Backlit grasses and fireweed along Windy Pass Trail

Trout Lake

The valley of Jack Creek is open forest. The trail gently ascends the valley floor, often in sight and always within sound of the stream. The mostly shaded valley will be welcome on a hot day. Good camps exist at the Jack Creek Trail junctions with the Jack Ridge, Meadow Creek, and Van Epps Trails, among others. Find your camp near Meadow Creek or, if you have the will, 3+ miles beyond at Van Epps Creek, or in between. Relax and relive your high-country experiences while enjoying the cool luxury of a forested camp near a lovely stream.

DAY TWO   22+ miles   3,000+ feet gain

While the itinerary calls for a day over 20 miles in trekking distance, the elevation gain is about one-half that experienced on the first day of trekking. Regain your stride alongside gently rolling Jack Creek. About 0.75 mile beyond the Van Epps Trail junction, Jack Creek is finally crossed. In 1+ miles, cross back over Jack Creek, this time in subalpine meadows with impressive views of Mount Stuart. The trail continues switchbacking, crossing numerous streams that are the very source of Jack Creek. Meadows of lupine, daisies, Indian paintbrush, and valerian occupy the mind instead of the ascending path. Soon the narrow profile of Stuart Pass is reached, 6,400 feet elevation and astride the very ridge connecting Mount Stuart with Ingalls Peak.

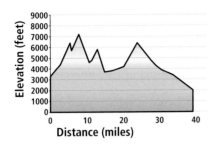

Enjoy the close-up views of the clean, sharp Mount Stuart granite contrasting with the graceful lines of nearby Jack Creek Valley and Icicle Creek Valley in the distance. Mount Stuart is among the largest granite peaks in the United States. A massive substrate of granite carved by multiple ice ages into the elegant ridges and massive walls is within reach of your outstretched arms as you recoup at Stuart Pass.

The descent into the headwater basin of Ingalls Creek parallels the flower-lined streambed. Water bubbles beside the path, following nature's course to join the Wenatchee River and then on to the Columbia. The very gentle path moves close beneath Mount Stuart. Meadows merge with rock ridges, gullies, and the steep faces of the massive and complex peak. Inevitably leave the meadows and enter the forested portion of the Ingalls Creek Valley. The valley of Ingalls Creek traversed by trail is the longest unblemished valley in the Alpine Lakes Wilderness; its relative remoteness, narrow profile, and precipitous walls offered protection from the logger's saw and road builder's dynamite until the area received the coveted Wilderness designation. Now follow the small river, passing numerous trail junctions ascending into the highland beauty near Navaho Peak. While passing straight through these junctions on the Ingalls Creek Trail, each one validates the distance traveled and offers the opportunity for further explorations. Good camps also reside near each trail junction.

The last 4 miles of the path track closely near the now full-blown river beneath you. Ups and downs are a bit more pronounced as the path winds around nature's obstacles of stone and steep slopes near the valley floor. The trail moves closer to the swift water of Ingalls Creek reaching the Ingalls Creek Trailhead in open forest adjacent to the creek.

Trail Summary and Mileage Estimates

0.0	Eightmile Lake Trailhead #1552, elevation 3,300 feet
2.8	Lake Caroline/Windy Pass Trail #1554, elevation 4,400 feet, turn right on Trail #1554
10.6	Trout Creek Trail #1555, elevation 4,600 feet, turn left on Trail #1555
11.3	Jack Ridge Trail #1557, elevation 4,800 feet, turn right on Trail #1557
14.8	Jack Creek Trail #1558, elevation 3,700 feet, turn left on Trail #1558
16.9	Meadow Creek Trail #1559, elevation 3,800 feet, stay left on Trail #1558
20.1	Van Epps Creek Trail #1594, elevation 4,200 feet, stay left on Trail #1558
23.8	Stuart Pass, elevation 6,400 feet, continue on Ingalls Creek Trail #1215
27.6	Turnpike Creek Trail #1391, elevation 4,800 feet, stay left on Trail #1215
29.0	Fourth Creek Trail #1218, elevation 4,300 feet, stay left on Trail #1215
30.5	Hardscrabble Creek Trail #1219, elevation 3,900 feet, stay left on Trail #1215
31.8	Cascade Creek Trail #1217, elevation 3,700 feet, stay left on Trail #1215
33.7	Falls Creek Trail #1216, elevation 3,400 feet, stay left on Trail #1215
39.2	Ingalls Creek Trailhead, elevation 2,000 feet

Suggested Camps Based on Different Trekking Itineraries

Night	15–20 mpd	10–15 mpd	10 mpd
One:	17 miles - Meadow Creek Trail	15 miles - Jack Creek Trail	9 miles - basin near Windy Pass
Two:		27+ miles - Turnpike Creek Trail	17 miles - Meadow Creek Trail
Three:			27+ miles - Turnpike Creek Trail

Ingalls Peak from Ingalls Creek

The Enchantment Traverse

Sunrise from Gnome Tarn

Difficulty:	Easier
Distance:	30 miles (with explorations)
Elevation gain:	9,900 feet (with explorations)
Best season:	Early July through mid-October
Recommended itinerary:	5 days (maximum enjoyment and exploration)
Water availability:	Good throughout the trek
Logistics:	The trailheads are 8 miles apart, so use two vehicles or stash a bike at trail's end. Or you may be able to catch a ride back up to Mountaineer Creek Trailhead given the heavy use of the entire Icicle Creek Valley by like-minded recreators. If you are uncomfortable with snow travel, do not traverse the Enchantments

before the last week of July. Aasgard Pass slopes will be largely snow-free by then. There are always brief, sometimes tricky, snow crossings in and around the lakes. Carry an ice ax and know how to use it. I use the lake names popularized by the Stark family over their years of exploration; Green Trails uses different names. To avoid confusion, I reference lake names in parentheses.

Jurisdictions: Alpine Lakes Wilderness, 509-548-6977. Access to the Enchantments is heavily regulated between June 15 and October 15. A longer than normal list of back-country rules exist, including an advance camping reservation system. Permits may be applied for beginning March 1 (mail) or March 31 (in person). For more information, contact the Leavenworth Ranger Station, 600 Sherbourne, Leavenworth, WA 98826, or at the above number.

Maps: Green Trails: The Enchantments

Trail location: Drive Interstate 5 to Everett and take exit 194. Travel east on U.S. Highway 2 just beyond milepost 99, entering Leavenworth and immediately turning right on Icicle Road. Drive 4+ miles to the Snow Lakes Trailhead and drop a vehicle here (optional). Continue up valley on Icicle Road another 4+ miles to Bridge Creek Campground and Forest Service Road 7601. Turn left on Road 7601 and drive the steep, narrow road about 4 miles to the parking lot at the Mountaineer Creek Trailhead, elevation 3,400 feet.

The Enchantments are the centerpiece of all the jewels displayed within the showcase Alpine Lakes Wilderness. Despite rugged and relatively technical approaches, the tender tread and fragile meadows were loved to death. Overuse was exacerbated when the Forest Service blasted, chipped, and glued together a better path up Trauma Rib and through the lower Enchantment Basin. The solution to this overuse was implementation in 1987 of the strictest reservation system in all of the Cascades. Sign up early, be flexible, and you can still enjoy the grandeur of the Enchantments.

DAY ONE   5+ miles   2,400 feet gain

Begin trekking up the Mountaineer Creek Trail, elevation 3,400 feet—your hiking goal for the day is the far end of Colchuck Lake, a slow 5+ miles away. The music

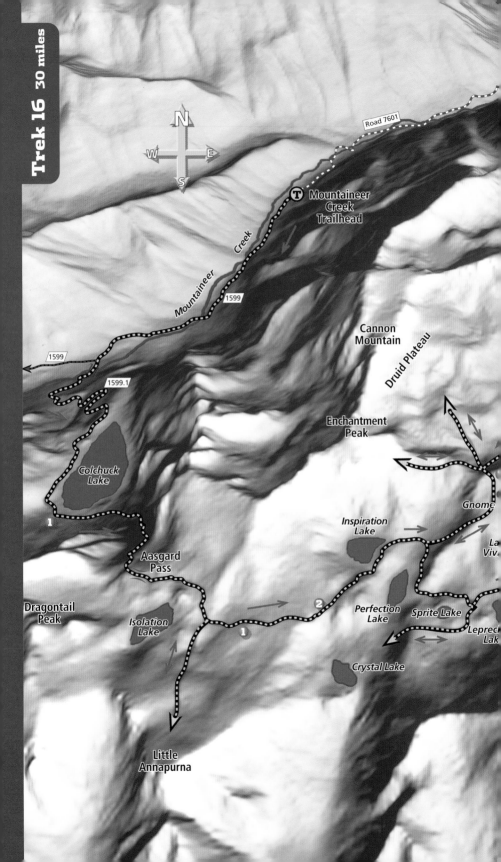

Road 7601

Ⓣ Mountaineer
Creek
Trailhead

1599

Mountaineer Creek

1599

1599.1

Cannon
Mountain

Druid Plateau

Enchantment
Peak

Colchuck
Lake

1

Gnome

Inspiration
Lake

La
Viv.

Aasgard
Pass

2

Dragontail
Peak

Isolation
Lake

1

Perfection
Lake

Sprite Lake

Leprec
Lak

Crystal Lake

Little
Annapurna

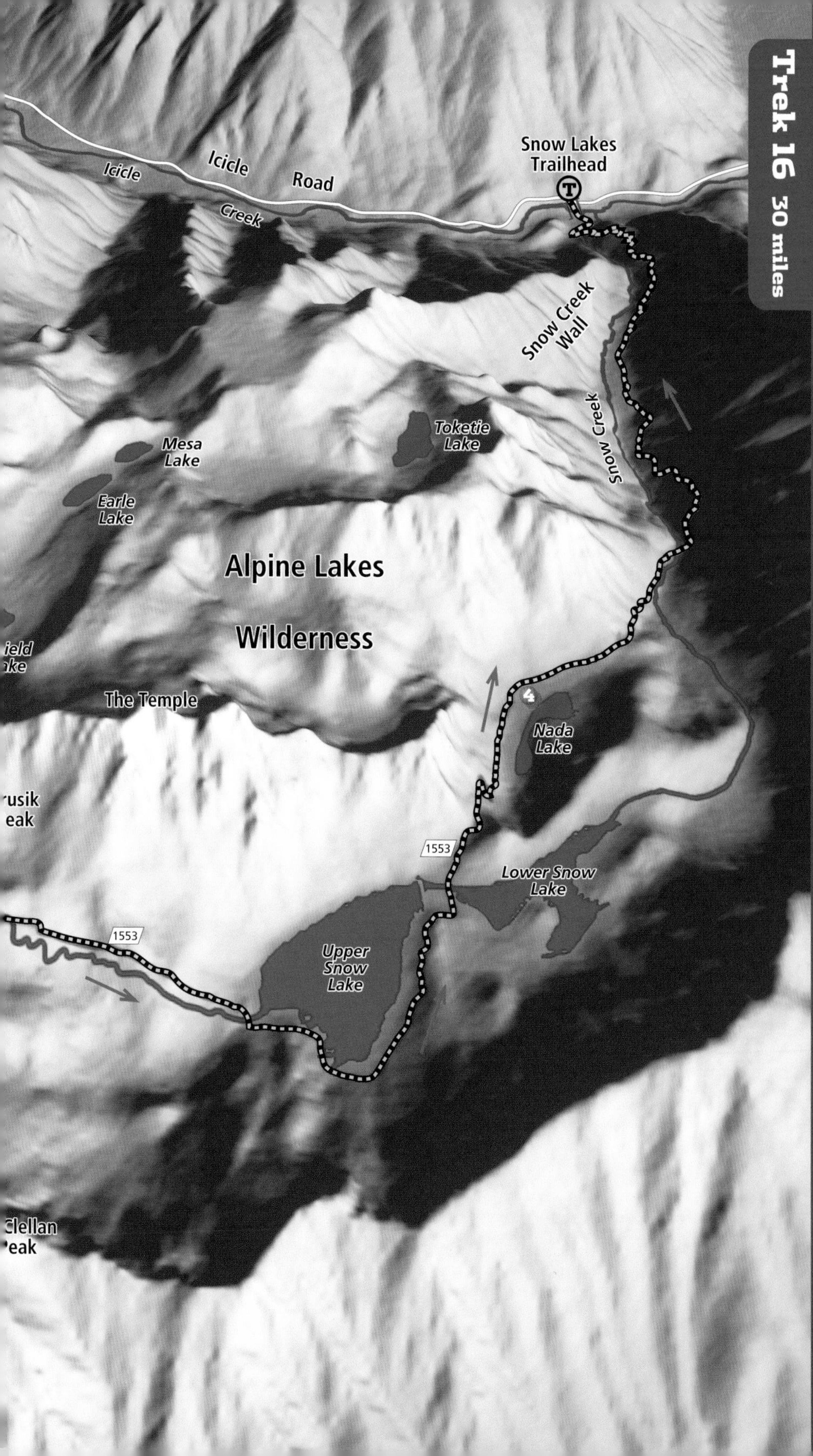

Snow Lakes
Trailhead

Icicle

Icicle   Road

Creek

Snow Creek Wall

Snow Creek

Mesa
Lake

Toketie
Lake

Earle
Lake

Alpine Lakes

Wilderness

ield
ke

The Temple

Nada
Lake

1553

rusik
eak

Lower Snow
Lake

1553

Upper
Snow
Lake

Clellan
eak

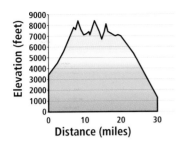

of Mountaineer Creek will provide a pleasant distraction from the pounding of your heart.

In a short hour cross over Mountaineer Creek on a sturdy bridge and enjoy a break near the stream. Moving again, switchback steadily uphill 500 feet before traversing gently to the Colchuck–Stuart Lake Trail junction, elevation 4,500 feet. Turn left toward Colchuck Lake and soon after cross the substantial stream on a sturdy bridge.

Toiling uphill through the woods, reach a scenic view on granite slabs overlooking the valley from Lake Stuart to Mount Cashmere. Climb the last 300 feet and abruptly exchange forest for spectacular alpine views on the shores of Colchuck Lake, elevation 5,600 feet. Walk the short distance left to the head of the lake and brilliant views to Dragontail and Colchuck Peaks, separated by the steep ice of Colchuck Glacier. Then regain the trail traversing the lakeshore. The ups and downs are very modest, and any time you choose the wrong trail, you will find it soon rejoins the "main" trail in a short distance. As you near the boulder field beneath Colchuck Peak, view the route to Aasgard Pass, rising directly from lakeshore to 7,800 feet.

DAY TWO   5 miles   3,200 feet gain

Day two takes you up and over Aasgard Pass into upper Enchantment Basin and on the excursion to the top of Little Annapurna. The slope to the pass remains shaded by the high peaks until midmorning. A sweltering climb in the afternoon sun, in the chill of morning the climb is cool and comfortable. The key to ascending Aasgard Pass is as follows: Travel on boot-built tread to the left of the stream flowing from the pass. Stay left of the broad rock band one-third of the way up the slope. Progress is easy to recognize as measured against ever-retreating Colchuck Lake. Continue ascending the steep switchbacks, moving right to more gentle terrain three-quarters of the way up the slope when steep rock blocks a direct route. At this juncture, traverse right on sandy slopes and ledges, crossing one stream but not the second; then climb sharply upward on rock slabs and edges. Stay off steep snow unless you have the skill to arrest a slip. The angle soon eases and by following large rock cairns the doors to the Enchantments open to you.

Amble across gentle ridges and along lakeshores of blue. Large patches of snow, some permanent, linger in the upper valley. As you descend by numerous small tarns, remaining snow gives way to meadows. Now face one final challenge: the ascent of Little Annapurna.

Obligatory side trip 1. From beyond Brynhild Lake (Isolation Lake), elevation 7,600 feet, choose the path of least resistance in order to gain the ridge that forms the southern boundary of the Enchantment Basin, from Dragontail on the west past Witches Tower to Little Annapurna on the east. Once on the ridge crest, travel east with modest ups and downs to the very top of Little Annapurna, elevation 8,400 feet. Figure on a round trip of 2 to 3 hours. The views from Little Annapurna are spectacular: Mounts Adams, Rainier, Stuart, and Baker highlight the state-long panorama. Below is the beautiful vertical south face of Prusik Peak, golden in the afternoon glow.

DAY THREE   6–8 miles   2,000–3,000+ feet gain

Pack up camp, for the spectacular views and camping near Gnome Tarn are a must to experience. To reach Gnome Tarn, descend past Talisman (Inspiration) Lake. A steep snow slope with a runout directly into Talisman Lake may cause you to pause. Pick your way around it if necessary and continue past the lake to the gently sloping meadow on the shores of Rune (Perfection) Lake, elevation 7,100 feet. Instead of ascending on boot-built tread to the obvious pass in the ridge to the north, Prusik Pass, ascend 90 degrees right of the pass to the ridge crest near Gnome Tarn and enjoy climax views of nearby Prusik Peak and the Enchantment Basin

Mount Cashmere reflected in Colchuck Lake

from Dragontail to McClellan Peaks. Fill your day with one or more of the following explorations.

Obligatory side trip 2. From near Gnome Tarn, scramble on or near the crest to Prusik Pass, elevation 7,400 feet. Descend gravely slopes to 7,100 feet elevation, then ascend gentle slopes northwest toward the high plateau near the very top of Cannon Mountain. Climb past lovely private lakelets, ideal for swimming, camping, and relaxing. Move through meadows of larch and scramble talus slopes to the Druid Plateau, elevation 8,400 feet. Marvel at the unusual rock meadow—acres of rounded stones interspersed with tufts of vegetation amongst pools of snowmelt—with unique and dramatic views of the Stuart Range. The plateau is rarely visited and will offer you a day of solitude, beauty, and satisfying off-trail exploration. Figure on a round trip of 4 to 5 hours from Prusik Pass.

Obligatory side trip 3. Also rarely visited, for the fisherman or lake lover, enjoy a day or afternoon at Shield and Earle Lakes. Follow the aforementioned route to Prusik Pass and then simply descend directly to the lakes in the broad meadow basin beneath you, elevation 6,700 feet. Figure on a round trip of up to 3 hours to all day, depending on how much time you spend at the lakes.

Obligatory side trip 4. From Prusik Pass, ascend the ridge crest west onto the small plateau at 8,100 feet beneath the summit of Enchantment Peak. Gain fabulous views of the basins on either side, as well as a profile view of all the grand rock spires on Temple Ridge, from Prusik to Comet. The peak itself, elevation 8,500+ feet, is a tricky scramble, so don't exceed your comfort zone in your quest for the tip-top. Figure on a round trip of 2 to 3 hours from Prusik Pass.

Regardless of your day's adventures, relaxing near Gnome Tarn as the evening light settles over the Enchantments will find you reveling in the experience.

DAY FOUR   7 miles   1,000 feet gain

Descending from Gnome Tarn, regain the trail near Rune (Perfection) Lake. Walk along the lakeshore trail, with the vertical profile of Little Annapurna rising above the water blue. One final essential exploration remains.

Obligatory side trip 5. Cross the torrent flowing from Rune Lake and contour around the ridge toe descending from McClellan Peak into the lovely basin of Crystal Lake. This delightful basin is very private, especially given that its location is only 30 minutes from the beaten path. Nestled beneath the rugged cliffs of Little Annapurna and draining steeply into the Ingalls Creek Valley, Crystal Lake offers a unique view and feel of the Enchantments. Figure on a round trip of 90 minutes.

If possible, Leprechaun Lake is even more stunning than Talisman and Rune, nestled in larch-filled meadows tucked beneath the spires of McClellan Peak. Viviane, though, is the climax. Crystal and deep, surrounded by white granite

Druid Plateau

cliffs dropping visibly beneath the liquid surface, the south face of Prusik Peak looms directly above it.

Once across the Lake Viviane outlet on spindly logs and boulder hops, stop to enjoy your last look up at the Enchantments and your first look across Trauma Rib and down to Snow Lakes. The path traverses a few hundred feet before descending toward the lake far below. Follow rock cairns and bits of dirt tread, dance across granite slabs, and carefully descend steps blasted or carved in steeper rock. At times the path traverses, even climbs. At times it drops directly beneath your feet. Such is the challenge of Trauma Rib. The route is easy to lose, but usually readily found. It is very easy to stumble and skin yourself up, even hurt yourself.

Reaching upper Snow Lake, follow the narrow trail through marshes and small trees near the water. Remove your shoes and tiptoe through ankle-deep water across the dam/intake structure regulating the Snow Lake outlet. Late in the season the foot-wide concrete dam stands several feet above the water's surface. Beyond Snow Lake, crest a small rise and enter a talus field with broad views over lovely Nada

Lake, shimmering water in a basin of tall timber and glistening granite. If Viviane is the most spectacular lake, Nada is the most elegant. Switchbacking through the boulders to the lakeshore, find a lovely camp near the lake.

DAY FIVE 5+ miles 300 feet gain

Pack up your gear and begin the descent toward Icicle Road on a trail that's a steady downward pound. The lower Snow Lake Valley is beautiful, it's just not the Enchantments. Views down the valley and across to Icicle Ridge are diversions from the knee-buckling grind. About halfway to the trailhead, the steep fang of Snow Creek Wall comes into view, one of the finest rock-climbing crags in Washington and a marvel to look at. Climbers can often be spotted high up on the 500-foot wall of nearly vertical granite, colorful clothing or the glint of sun reflecting off metallic carabiners often the only recognizable features of the spiderlike dots far up the cliff. Beyond Snow Creek Wall, the trail finally juts out of the valley and descends a broad ridge with views up valley into the headwaters of Icicle Creek and down valley to Leavenworth. In sweeping switchbacks descend the open slope to its abrupt end near Icicle Creek. A short distance downstream cross the sturdy wooden footbridge and ascend the narrow trail left (not the adjacent road) a few feet to the Snow Lakes Trailhead.

Trail Summary and Mileage Estimates

0.0	Mountaineer Creek Trail #1599, elevation 3,400 feet
2.5	Colchuck Lake Trail #1599.1, elevation 4,500 feet, turn left on Trail 1599.1
4.2	Aasgard Pass Route, at shores of Colchuck Lake, elevation 5,600 feet, turn right on the route to Aasgard Pass (visit the lake first)
5.2	Reach the far end of Colchuck Lake
7.0	Aasgard Pass, elevation 7,800 feet (becomes Snow Lakes Trail)
7.5	Brynhild Lake, elevation 7,600 feet, to Little Annapurna
9.0	Ascent of Little Annapurna and return to the basin
10.5	Gnome Tarn, elevation 7,200 feet
17.5	Cross-country to Druid Plateau, Shield Lake, and Enchantment Peak, and return to Gnome Tarn
18.5	Rune Lake outlet stream, elevation 7,000 feet, to Crystal Lake
20.0	Cross-country to Crystal Lake and return to basin
23.5	Snow Lake outlet stream, elevation 5,400 feet
30.0	Snow Lakes Trailhead #1553, elevation 1,300 feet

Note: The obligatory side trips are included in the mileage and elevation estimates.

Mountain goats and Prusik Peak

Suggested Camps Based on Different Trekking Itineraries

Night	Faster	Medium	Slower
One:	17.5 miles - Gnome Tarn	9.0 miles - Enchantment Basin	5+ miles - Colchuck Lake
Two:		17.5 miles - Gnome Tarn	9.0 miles - Enchantment Basin
Three:			17.5 miles - Gnome Tarn
Four:			24.5 miles - Nada Lake

Mount Rainier—
The Wonderland Trail

Indian Henrys Hunting Ground

Difficulty:	Most strenuous
Distance:	90 miles
Elevation gain:	25,500 feet
Best season:	August through mid-September
Recommended itinerary:	6 days (15–20 miles per day). Allows 1 day for bad weather, rest, or exploration.
Water availability:	Good throughout the trek, but in late season Klapatche Park and Devils Dream Camps may be dry. Glacial streams are silted and make a poor water source.
Logistics:	The trail network around Sunrise and Reflection Lakes can be very confusing. Follow the narrative descriptions or your own good judgment. The snow

crossing at Panhandle Gap requires care: carry an
ice ax and know how to use it.

Jurisdictions: Mount Rainier National Park, 360-569-2211. Permits
are required for overnight camping in the national
park backcountry. Contact the above number or the
Longmire Wilderness Information Center, 360-569-
HIKE.

Maps: Green Trails: Mt. Rainier West and Mt. Rainier East

Trail location: Drive Interstate 5 to exit 127. Turn east on State Route
512 and in about 2 miles exit onto SR 7. Follow SR 7
about 40 miles to the community of Elbe. Continue
east of Elbe on SR 706, driving about 13 miles to the
park entrance and then 6 miles farther to Longmire,
elevation approximately 2,800 feet.

Rising unmistakably as an icy cone from the lowlands that surround it, Mount
Rainier boldly dominates the eastern skyline from the central Puget Sound Basin.
Hiking the Wonderland Trail up, down, and around Mount Rainier is equally as
challenging and fulfilling as it is to stand atop this icy crown of the great Cascades.

DAY ONE   19+ miles   6,400 feet gain

The first major routefinding difficulty is figuring out where to start hiking. The
trick to the Wonderland Trail is that you start and finish on the same short trail
segment that begins near Longmire. Begin hiking on this signed trail and in a few
minutes reach the trail junction where the Wonderland Trail goes either left or
right around the mountain. Choose left to explore the west side of the mountain
first. In a few more minutes, cross the road leading to Paradise and ascend toward
Rampart Ridge. Trail conditions on the Wonderland Trail are generally perfect and
the steady climb to Rampart Ridge is easily completed. After gently descending to
Kautz Creek, 3,600 feet elevation, climb steadily back to 4,400 feet. The trail then
climbs and meanders to the enthralling meadows of Indian Henrys Hunting Ground,
and at 7 miles into the trek, enjoy the first of many climatic alpine vistas. Walk

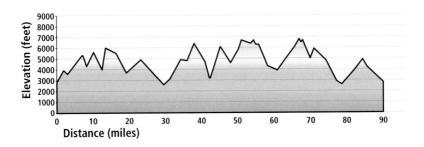

Wonderland
Trail

Carbon River

Alternate

2

Mowich Lake Road

Mowich
Lake

Wonderland
Trail

2

Mowich

River

North Mowich River

Spray

3

Park

Trail

Seattle Park

Carbon Glacier

M
L

2

South Mowich River

Golden
Lakes

2

Wonderland
Trail

Mount Rainier

National Park

North Puyallup River

Tahoma Glacier

1

Aurora
Peak

1

St.
Andrews
Lake

Mou
Raini

Aurora
Lake

Wonderland
Trail

South Ayallup River

1

Tahoma Creek

Wonderland
Trail

Henrys
Ground

Indian
Hunting

Wonderland
Trail

Nisqually-Parad

N

W   **E**

S

River

Nisqually

Wonderla
Trail

T
Longmire

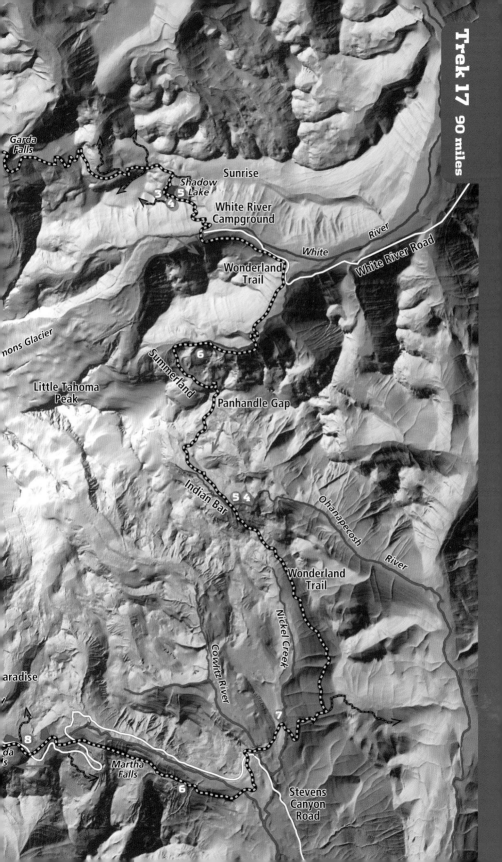

Garda
Falls

Sunrise

Shadow
Lake

3

5

4

White River
Campground

White River Road

White

River

Wonderland
Trail

nons Glacier

Summerland

6

Little Tahoma
Peak

Panhandle Gap

Indian Bar

S 4

Ohanapecosh

River

Wonderland
Trail

Nickel Creek

Cowlitz River

7

aradise

8

da
s

Martha
Falls

6

Stevens
Canyon
Road

Suspension bridge over Tahoma Creek

another mile through nearly flat fields of multicolored flowers in contrast with the stark mountain of tumbling icefalls and shattered rock towers.

Descend to the spectacular suspension bridge spanning Tahoma Creek, a muddy glacial torrent spilling through the deep, narrow chasm. The length is accentuated because the bridge is narrow, only one-person wide. After crossing the bridge, begin climbing again, this time through forest, then rock moraine, and finally to a meadow ridge at 5,600 feet elevation. The Tahoma Glacier dominates the view both above and below the trail. Above lies a crevassed and glistening mass of yawning, stretching, and moving ice. Below is the glacier terminus, a place of stale ice strewn with boulders and mineral deposits. The trek goes up and down over every single ridge around the mountain. The trail can't stay high because the massive glaciers cut too deeply into the valleys, barring consistent highland trail possibilities. From the ridge above the Tahoma Glacier, the trail once again drops to forest, bottoming out at the crossing of the South Puyallup River, elevation 4,000 feet. No longer a surprise, immediately trek back up to the meadows of St. Andrews Park, undulating between 5,600 and 5,800 feet elevation. From St. Andrews Lake, the trail continues through meadows, dropping gently across a ridge shoulder to Aurora Lake, about 16 miles from Longmire.

Once again, leave the sweeping beauty of the alpine terrain as the tread descends into magnificent stands of old-growth fir, cedar, and hemlock. The sight and thunder of the streams falling from the Puyallup Glacier above is awesome. It takes more effort to keep your eyes on the trail than to descend to the substantial bridge crossing at the North Puyallup River Camp.

DAY TWO 20+ miles 6,300 feet gain

Day two starts gently, the trail teasing at 3,600 feet elevation for nearly 2 miles before climbing to the high country. Ascending through fire-scarred terrain and abundant blueberries, the trail winds around and through Sunset Park. Pass by alluring Golden Lakes and the Golden Lakes Partol Cabin. Once again descend into deep woods, this time all the way down to 2,600 feet at the broad boulder-strewn floor of the Mowich River Valley. In 0.5 mile, begin reclaiming the elevation just lost as the trail rises steadily to a junction with the Mowich Lake Trail, elevation 4,900 feet.

At the Spray Park Trail junction you have a choice. The sign designating the current Wonderland Trail points to the left, toward Mowich Lake. Instead, the historic route of Wonderland Trail also goes to the right through Spray Park. Either choice represents about 8 miles of trekking before the routes reconnect along the Carbon River. To follow the Wonderland Trail proper, choose the lower route that proceeds along the road by Mowich Lake and down Ipsut Creek to the Carbon River. For some time out of the trees, follow the classic and higher line through Spray Park. Turning right, the trail undulates between 4,700 and 5,000 feet as it traverses toward Spray Creek, a clear tumbling waterfall of a stream. Upon reaching the stream, the tread turns sharply uphill, gaining 600 feet before breaking into the meadows of Spray Park. Climb 800 more feet as the path meanders through broad meadows, small tarns, and expansive views. Directly above rises the unobstructed dominance of Mount Rainier.

Upon reaching the culmination of Spray Park, elevation 6,400 feet, begin descending into Seattle Park. In this vicinity, the trail traverses several gentle snow patches. Rock cairns mark the way. Routefinding can be difficult on cloudy or foggy days. Descend through lovely Seattle Park and then along Cataract Creek to Cataract Valley Camp, elevation 4,600 feet. If you trekked via Mowich Lake, camp at the Carbon River Camp.

DAY THREE   16 miles   5,300 feet gain

Continue the descent of yesterday, rejoining the true Wonderland Trail near the Carbon River at elevation 3,200 feet. Cross the Carbon River on a suspension bridge—a milder version of the the Tahoma Creek crossing. The trail immediately climbs alongside the Carbon Glacier, its immense gravel-covered snout very near and impressive. Watch the gray glacial water pour forth in torrents from gaping holes in the ice—the very birthplace of a river! For more than 3 miles the trail climbs and traverses above the Carbon Glacier. Streams from the slopes of Moraine Park high above provide splendid waterfalls and an abundance of cool clear water. As roaring and cold as the Carbon River and the other glacial streams are, they are too silt-laden to be considered potable water sources. The ascent culminates by reaching a pretty valley, then a pass at 6,100 feet. Just ahead lies Mystic Lake, the small, attractive lake rests above timberline in a grassy meadow at 5,700 feet elevation.

Once again leave alpine terrain for a jaunt through forests. Mudflow activities periodically alter the path between Mystic Lake and the Winthrop Glacier, but other than a bit of grime and muck they cause no meaningful confusion as the trail is redesignated and easily followed. This time the trail does not drop quite as low.

Skirt the terminus of the Winthrop Glacier in boulders and trees at the near alpine elevation of 4,800 feet. Crossing beneath stunning Garda Falls, continue very close to the Winthrop Glacier. Then follow along beautiful Granite Creek for nearly 1 mile before crossing the stream and continuing upward through flower meadows and then gravelly slopes to the pass, elevation 6,700 feet, that marks the beginning of gorgeous Berkeley Park.

Berkeley Park is a broad, fabulous splash of green meadows and purple lupine. Traverse 2 miles across the park, descending to 6,300 feet before climbing back to 6,700 feet at aptly named Frozen Lake. Navigating through a confusing array of trails, soon transition to an old gravel roadbed, turn right, and walk down the road following signs to Sunrise Camp.

DAY FOUR   16 miles   3,500 feet gain

From Sunrise Camp, the Wonderland Trail may be labeled the "Sunrise Rim Trail." In either case, traverse the slope beneath Shadow Lake a short mile and upon reaching a clearly marked junction turn right on the Wonderland Trail as it switchbacks 2,000 feet down the slope in a short 3 miles to the valley floor and a major campground along the White River, elevation 4,300 feet. From the upstream end of the campground, gain a recently constructed segment of the Wonderland Trail. Crossing over the White River, continue downstream, descending to 3,900 feet until the trail begins to ascend the gentle valley of Fryingpan Creek. Stop to enjoy the waterfalls that tumble into the stream channel. Soon reach the splendid meadows and streams of Summerland, about 5,900 feet in elevation, nearly 7 miles from the campground.

Enjoy the ascent of Fryingpan Creek up through the meadows, streams, and expansive views of Summerland. Beyond the meadows, the route continues up through scree slopes and snow patches to snowy Panhandle Gap, elevation 6,800 feet, the highest point on the Wonderland Trail. Some caution needs to be exercised in determining where to walk on the snow. There are actually two passes to choose from. The correct pass is to the right, where most tracks will lead. Once through the gap, the trail stays high, traversing meadows, snow, and abundant creeklets. Whenever on snow, the route is marked by rock cairns (use your map, altimeter, and compass). After crossing a ridge at 6,500 feet elevation, the trail climbs back in rock and snow to 6,700 feet. Finally, the trail begins to descend toward Indian Bar.

The beauty that unfolds before you is astounding. Below the snow zone, flower fields of lupine, monkey flowers, daisies, Indian paintbrush, anemone, and asters envelop you. The closer you get to the valley floor, the richer the colors appear. The meandering stream that graces the gentle upper valley ends abruptly in a spectacular waterfall. Stand on the footbridge to look up valley at the water, as clear as crystal. The flower meadows touch the damp boulders and small rocks at the water's

Stream and flowers at Summerland

edge. Farther up, the flower meadows disappear onto steep slopes and into the clouds above. Looking down, the world seems to end as the water falls out of sight beyond the cliffs below. Make your camp here!

DAY FIVE   18 miles   4,000 feet gain

On your final day of trekking, the trail takes you closer to civilization than on the previous days. From Indian Bar, ascend through inspiring meadows to Cowlitz Divide, then travel along the divide for a few miles as it gently ascends in ups and downs to nearly 6,000 feet before dipping toward forests below 5,000 feet. It is nice to follow a ridge crest after having gone up and over so many. At the junction with the Cowlitz Divide Trail, elevation 4,800 feet, turn right, toward Nickel Creek. The descent through old-growth forests to Nickel Creek and beyond to the Box Canyon is captivating.

Walking on the hard-surfaced trail toward the Box Canyon overlook, mingle with those visitors strolling a short distance from their cars to witness the same view. The canyon is a narrow, vertical-sided cleft with the entire Cowlitz River pouring through it. Again civilization causes trail confusion. After crossing the bridge over the canyon, in a short distance the sign for the Wonderland Trail points to the right up a less substantial trail, meaning you should leave the asphalt path. The trick is that the Wonderland Trail goes over the top of the tunnel spanning Stevens Canyon Road, a little bizarre, but it beats crossing the highway.

Descend gently in forest to 2,600 feet elevation. Once again the beauty of a stream will capture your eye, this time of carved rock and clear pools, surely the work of a sculptor and not the force of water within Stevens Creek. Although the road above is periodically visible, the stream mutes most vehicle noise you might otherwise hear. Continuing up the valley, pass Martha Falls and almost touch the road just below Louise Lake. Walking along or near the road by Reflection Lakes, cross the road beyond the lakes and once again walk on the tread of the Wonderland Trail in forest. The final grand view is Narada Falls, where you will share a stunning view with people who walked a few steps instead of nearly 100 miles. The trek is completed amongst old-growth giants alongside the rolling gray Nisqually River, arriving at Longmire on the very stretch of trail on which you began.

Trail Summary with Mileage Estimates

0.0	Longmire, elevation 2,800 feet
0.1	Reach the Wonderland Trail, elevation 2,900 feet, turn left
0.3	Cross the highway leading to Paradise, regain trail on opposite side
1.8	Van Trump Park Trail, elevation 3,900 feet, stay left on Wonderland Trail
2.0	Rampart Ridge Trail, elevation 3,900 feet, stay right on Wonderland Trail
7.0	Kautz Creek Trail, elevation 5,300 feet, stay right on Wonderland Trail
7.3	Mirror Lakes Trail, elevation 5,300 feet, stay left on Wonderland Trail

12.5	South Puyallup Trail, elevation 4,000 feet, stay right on Wonderland Trail
16.4	Klapatche Ridge Trail, elevation 5,500 feet, stay right on Wonderland Trail
19.2	North Puyallup Trail, elevation 3,700 feet, stay right on Wonderland Trail
31.2	Paul Peak Trail, elevation 3,100 feet, stay right on Wonderland Trail
34.2	Spray Park Trail, elevation 4,900 feet, turn right on Spray Park Trail (the real Wonderland Trail)
42.2	Rejoin Wonderland Trail, elevation 3,200 feet at Carbon River Camp, turn right
42.4	Northern Loop Trail, elevation 3,200 feet, stay right on Wonderland Trail
53.7	Northern Loop Trail, elevation 6,400 feet, stay right on Wonderland Trail
54.5	Mount Fremont Lookout/Burroughs Mountain Trails, elevation 6,700 feet, continue straight on Wonderland Trail
54.6	Sourdough Ridge Trail, elevation 6,600 feet, stay right on Wonderland Trail
55.1	Sunrise Camp/Sunrise Rim Trail, elevation 6,300 feet, hike the Sunrise Rim Trail
55.9	Wonderland Trail, elevation 6,300 feet, turn right and descend to White River Campground
58.3	White River Campground, elevation 4,300 feet, trail continues from upper campground
61.0	Fryingpan Creek Trail, elevation 3,900 feet, stay right on Wonderland Trail
74.3	Olallie Creek Trail, elevation 4,800 feet, stay right on Wonderland Trail
77.2	Stevens Canyon Road, elevation 2,900 feet, cross over road on trail atop the tunnel
78.6	Stevens Creek Trail, elevation 2,600 feet, stay left on Wonderland Trail
82.3	Stevens Canyon Road, elevation 4,000 feet, cross the road and regain trail on opposite side
83.8	Walk the road near Reflection Lakes
84.4	Regain the Wonderland Trail, elevation 4,900 feet
85.6	Visit Narada Falls
90.0	Complete the Wonderland Trail Loop
90.1	Longmire, elevation 2,800 feet

Suggested Camps Based on Different Trekking Itineraries

Night	15–20 mpd	10–15 mpd	10 mpd
One:	19+ miles - North Puyallup Camp	16+ miles - Klapatche Park Camp	12+ miles - South Puyallup Camp
Two:	40+ miles - Cataract Valley Camp	30+ miles - Mowich River Camp	24 miles - Golden Lakes Camp
Three:	55+ miles - Sunrise Camp	45+ miles - Mystic Lake Camp	34+ miles - Eagles Roost Camp
Four:	70+ miles - Indian Bar Camp	55+miles - Sunrise Camp	45+ miles - Mystic Lake Camp
Five:		70+ miles - Indian Bar Camp	55+ miles - Sunrise Camp
Six:		81+ miles - Maple Creek Camp	67 miles - Summerland Camp
Seven:			78 miles - Nickel Creek Camp
Eight:			85 miles - near Reflection Lakes

Mount St. Helens— The Loowit Trail

Plains of Abraham and Mount Rainier

Difficulty:	Easier
Distance:	32 miles
Elevation gain:	6,300 feet
Best season:	Late June through September
Recommended itinerary:	2 days (15–20 miles per day)
Water availability:	Generally adequate. Because of volcanic and glacial influence (foul water), carry at least 2 quarts when leaving a "good" stream. Water is scarce from the South Fork Toutle River for more than 5 miles, until beyond Butte Camp.
Logistics:	Navigation is not purely by following the tread of a trail; rock cairns and wooden posts are followed for

significant stretches. As easy as the trek is in many respects, do *not* underestimate possible navigation difficulties in poor weather. The trek is mostly on open mountain slopes, offering little or no protection from the elements.

Jurisdictions: Mount St. Helens National Monument, 360-274-2100. Permits are not required to use the Loowit Trail, but check with the staff at the above number to be sure. Encourage the staff to designate camping spots within the currently "restricted area" to enable further enjoyment of this area and more sensible trekking itineraries.

Maps: Green Trails: Mt. St. Helens NW

Trail location: Drive Interstate 5 to Woodland and take exit 21. Turn east on State Route 503, driving 28 miles to Cougar. From Cougar, travel on Forest Service Road 90, then on Roads 83 and 830, following the signs for the Climbers Bivouac parking area and trailhead, elevation 3,800 feet.

To walk the Loowit Trail around this violent peak is to remember May 18, 1980, when the symmetrical cone of Mount St. Helens convulsed and burst forth, destroying itself and all life around it. While crowds clamber to scale what remains of this once beautiful peak, few take the time to know the mountain better and see the beauty that remains: sometimes stark and immense, sometimes colorful and delicate; a single flower in a field of stone. On this trek, you'll get to know the mountain better.

DAY ONE   12+ miles   2,900 feet gain

From Climbers Bivouac, ascend 900 feet over 2.1 miles in open forest to reach the junction with Loowit Trail #216, turn right (east), and begin your counterclockwise traverse around the mountain. The slopes of Mount St. Helens have an alpine feeling usually associated with elevations above 6,000 feet, even though you are traversing near 4,000 feet elevation. Watch for the elusive elk herds that roam throughout the South Cascades. Traverse above the junctions with the Swift Creek Trail #244 and June Lake Trail #216B, keeping to the left—with rare exception the norm all day long. The path is interspersed with boulder fields navigated by sighting stone cairns and the unique, solitary wooden guideposts. Streams rush down from high above, sometimes clear and sometimes muddy. In this case, Mount St. Helens is no different from other mountains. Glacier-melt streams run dirty, while snow-fed streams run clear.

216

216G

South Fork Toutle River

238

2

240

238A

N
W E
S

Ro

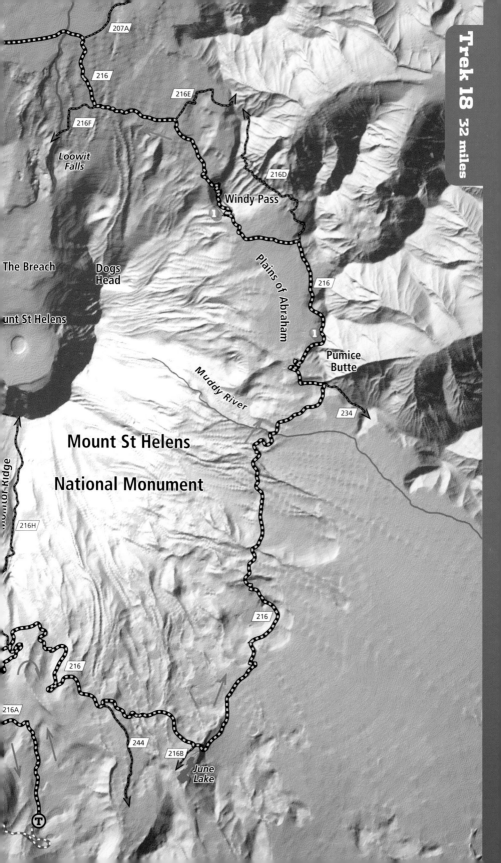

207A

216

216E

216F

Loowit Falls

216D

Windy Pass

1

The Breach

Dogs Head

Plains of Abraham

unt St Helens

216

1

Pumice Butte

Muddy River

234

Mount St Helens

National Monument

nitor Ridge

216H

216

216

216A

244

216B

June Lake

T

Guidepost and Mount Hood from Loowit Trail

From the June Lake Trail junction, the trail begins to ascend as it contours around the mountain. The majority of the traverse is on gravel or rock slopes, with direct views up to the crater rim and out to both Mount Adams and Mount Hood. Navigation continues to be supplemented by the wooden guideposts. A few of the stream crossings, including the Muddy River, are eroded owing to the action of water upon the unconsolidated gravel and dirt. While the crossings require some thought, the greatest danger is filling your shoes with dirt as you slide toward the streams or clamber up the opposite bank. Stay left at the junction with Ape Canyon Trail #234 and climb around Pumice Butte, approximately 10 miles into the trek.

Enjoy the 2-mile walk across the flat plain known as the Plains of Abraham. The view of white, ice-covered Mount Rainier, standing bright in the sunny blue sky, contrasts starkly with the barren tan-colored rock of the plain. Halfway across the plain, reach the junction with the Abraham Trail #216D. Turn left and trek toward Windy Pass, the obvious small saddle in the ridge rising from the plains to the crater rim above. The trail climbs very gently, then switchbacks quickly to the pass, elevation 4,900 feet. Before the pass is a stream that is your water source for the dry camp at the pass. Upon reaching Windy Pass, enjoy the dramatic views across the north-side devastation, toward Spirit Lake and Mount Rainier. Though largely in tones of brown and gray, the scene is stunningly immense, the powerful forces of nature never more apparent.

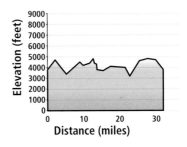

DAY TWO 19+ miles 3,400 feet gain

Descending from the pass, soon reach the junction with the Windy Trail #216E. Once again turn left on this contour 'round the mountain. Despite the modest altitude, the Loowit Trail retains its distinctly alpine feeling. The hike comes pretty easy so far, with no steady climbs of more than several hundred feet. Alpine ambiance and modest elevation changes are rare in combination and add to the allure of this mountain trek.

Rounding a corner, come upon lush vegetation and roaring water. A gushing spring of icy cold, clear water spews forth through nearby rocks. Refill your water bottles with the delicious spring water. You will see innumerable places that look ideal for camping, but they are off-limits because Windy Pass marks the edge of the "restricted area," where even so much as walking off the trail is forbidden. Continuing along, Loowit Falls comes into view, a spectacular series of waterfalls spilling brown liquid directly from the Breach, the gaping north-side expanse that bore the brunt of the May 18 explosion.

Recommended side trip 1: To further enjoy the falls, access the view from a short side trail, gaining 300 feet in 0.7 mile and placing you beneath the muddy water spilling over cliffs from the Breach. Figure on a round trip of 1 hour.

Leaving Loowit Falls, descend steadily near the stream. Traverse and climb the northwest shoulder of the mountain to high benches covered with the remnants of an entire forest, thousands of silver logs knocked down by the volcanic blast. In a few short seconds on that day in May, hundreds of years of nature were reversed. While meadows are forming amongst the destroyed forest, no forests will be seen here during our lifetimes. Farther along, in beautiful alpine meadows, encounter the silvery snags of trees killed but left standing by the blast.

From glacier remnants high above, see the source of the Toutle River as water spilling over boulders. Walk on a gentle ridge directly above the chasm. Turn left at the junction with Fairview Trail #216G and descend sharply into the void, boulder-hopping across the South Fork Toutle River. At 3,200 feet elevation, this is the lowest point reached by the Loowit Trail. Upon leaving the river, face the only steady climb of the entire circuit, the tread immediately ascending to 4,400 feet. Upon reaching timberline, the trail contours a few miles between 4,500 and 4,900

Dead sentinels along Loowit Trail

feet elevation. Staying left at trail junctions with the Sheep Canyon Trail #240 and Butte Camp Trail #238A, traverse the beautiful meadows and rock slopes. By early August, there will likely be no water available from the Toutle River until beyond the Butte Camp Trail. More than once, water visible above the trail disappears into the ground only to reappear a few hundred feet below the trail.

Time and distance pass quickly as you enjoy views up the mountain to the crater and across patchwork forests to Mount Hood. Soon cross beneath the Monitor Ridge climbing route, finding ample water cascading from the snow slopes above. Rounding beneath the ridge on boulders, join the Ptarmigan Trail #216A, your initial access to the Loowit Trail. Turn right on the Ptarmigan Trail to arrive back at Climbers Bivouac, your starting point.

Trail Summary and Mileage Estimates

0.0	Ptarmigan Trail #216A, elevation 3,800 feet
2.1	Loowit Trail #216, elevation 4,700 feet, turn right on Loowit Trail #216
4.2	Swift Creek Trail #244, elevation 3,800 feet, stay left on Trail #216
5.2	June Lake Trail #216B, elevation 3,400 feet, stay left on Trail #216
9.9	Ape Canyon Trail #234, elevation 4,200 feet, stay left on Trail #216
11.7	Abraham Trail #216D, elevation 4,400 feet, stay left on Trail #216
13.6	Windy Trail #216E, elevation 4,300 feet, stay left on Trail #216
13.0	Loowit Falls Trail #216F, elevation 4,400 feet, stay right on Trail #216
21.5	Fairview Trail #216G, elevation 4,000 feet, stay left on Trail #216
22.7	Toutle Trail #238, elevation 3,200 feet, stay left on Trail #216
25.4	Sheep Canyon Trail #240, elevation 4,600 feet, stay left on Trail #216
27.6	Butte Camp Trail #238A, elevation 4,800 feet, stay left on Trail #216
29.8	Ptarmigan Trail #216A, elevation 4,700 feet, turn right on Trail #216A
31.9	Trailhead at Climbers Bivouac, elevation 3,800 feet

Suggested Camps Based on Different Trekking Itineraries

Night	15–20 mpd	10–15 mpd	10 mpd—not feasible
One:	12+ miles - near Windy Pass	10+ miles - beyond Pumice Butte	
Two:		23 miles - near South Fork Toutle River	
		(0.25 down Trail #238 at spring)	

Note: The ideal camping spot would be in the vicinity of the spring at the base of the Dogs Head about 14+ miles into the journey. This isn't allowed because of the prohibition on camping in the "restricted area."

At 32 miles distance, there is no real differentiation between 10- to 15-miles-per-day and a 10-miles-per-day itinerary. Camping restrictions necessitate traveling between Windy Pass and the South Fork Toutle River in a single day. Thus, one of the first two days is a 12+ mile day. The camp beyond Pumice Butte has the advantage of a nearby stream as a good water source.

TREK 19

Mount Adams—
Round the Mountain (Truly)

Mount Adams and Klickitat Glacier

Difficulty:	Very strenuous
Distance:	35 miles
Elevation gain:	8,000 feet
Best Season:	Late July through September
Recommended itinerary:	3 days (10–15 miles per day)
Water availability:	Good throughout the trek
Logistics:	The itinerary presumes you arrived at the trailhead campground the prior evening or at a minimum begin trekking before midmorning. Follow the directions for the off-trail segments very carefully. Expect considerable snow crossings prior to August; carry an ice ax prior to mid-August. Crossing Big Muddy Creek

is a challenge at high runoff volumes. Avoid the crossing in late afternoons on hot days. If the crossing is too scary, cross above on snow, but be careful. The high trail on either side of Devils Garden is not well defined due to its rocky nature. Use the rock cairns for navigation, although in poor visibility this trail segment will be challenging to follow.

Jurisdictions: Mount Adams Wilderness, 509-395-3400 or 360-497-1100. Permits are required for overnight travel in the Mount Adams Wilderness. Generally permits are self-issued at the trailhead. Contact either the Trout Lake or Randle Ranger Stations for more information at the numbers above.

Maps: Green Trails: Mt. Adams

Trail Location: Drive Interstate 5 to exit 68. Turn east and follow U.S. Highway 12 to milepost 115. Turn right on Forest Service Road 23. After about 55 miles, reach a junction and stop sign. Turn left and in 1 mile turn left again on Road 80. Follow Road 80 until the junction with Road 8040. Follow Road 8040 (may also be labeled Road 500) and signs for the South Climb Trail to the road end at Cold Springs Campground and Trailhead, elevation 5,600 feet. Total distance on Roads 80 and 8040 is approximately 12 miles. If coming from the Columbia Gorge, travel State Route 14 to SR 141 and follow SR 141 to the junction with Road 23 in Trout Lake. Follow Road 23 to Road 80 and continue on Road 80 until the intersection with Road 8040.

Mount Adams has a hiking identity crisis. The Round the Mountain Trail doesn't go around the mountain. The Highline Trail starts, but stops. The Pacific Crest Trail cuts through, but it doesn't go around either. Maps show either no route whatsoever or a climber's traverse route winding up the mountain to nearly 9,000 feet elevation. But the directions for this trek enable you to circumnavigate Washington's second highest peak.

DAY ONE   11 miles   3,800 feet gain

After negotiating the challenging approach road, begin hiking up the South Climb Trail, from Cold Springs Campground, elevation 5,600 feet. Traveling briefly in forest and then in meadows, ascend to reach the Round the Mountain Trail #9,

Mount Adams

Wilderness

113

10

Adams C

112

2000

64

Sheep
Lake

2

2000

2000

9

9A

9

Aval

16

N
W   E
S

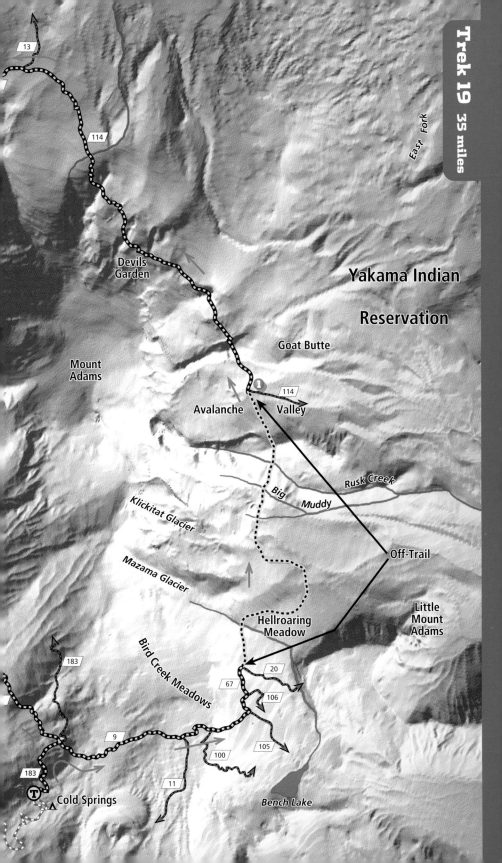

13

114

East Fork

Devils
Garden

Yakama Indian

Reservation

Goat Butte

Mount
Adams

114

Avalanche   Valley

Rusk Creek

Big   Muddy

Klickitat Glacier

Off-Trail

Mazama Glacier

Little
Mount
Adams

Hellroaring
Meadow

183

Bird Creek Meadows

20

67

106

9

100   105

183

11

Cold Springs

Bench Lake

elevation 6,300 feet. Turn right to begin your hike around the mountain. Note that much of the route to Devils Garden crosses tract D of the Yakama Indian Reservation, open to the public only during the summer.

The terrain is gentle and the meadows are lovely, with views down to forested Bird and Bench Lakes. In a short 3 miles reach the Bird Lake Trail #100 junction, elevation 6,200 feet. Stay left, entering lovely Bird Creek Meadows. In less than 1 mile, turn left on Flower Trail #106 and a short distance later again turn left on the Viewpoint Trail #67, climbing to the trail's end at a viewpoint panorama beneath the Mazama Glacier overlooking the Hellroaring Meadow, elevation 6,500 feet, 5.7 miles from the trailhead. The off-trail exploration begins.

Off-trail directions: From the viewpoint, move up the ridge 40 yards before descending on easy gravel slopes through alpine trees to the small flat at 6,100 feet. Traversing left (toward the mountain), cross a small ridge and then angle down and left through moderately steep bushes on a game trail. Pushing through dense alpine trees, break onto gentle grassy slopes of upper Hellroaring Meadow. Traverse the lovely basin at approximately 5,900 feet elevation, crossing numerous chilly watercourses. Once across the last tributary, descend easily along the edge of the valley floor. At 5,500 feet elevation, when brush begins to block progress along the edge of the valley floor, turn upward. Making certain to have skirted beneath the prominent cliffs in the slope above, turn uphill and ascend meadow slopes and light brush between rock outcroppings to the left of Little Mount Adams, heading toward the ridge above. Avoid the periodic patches of impenetrable brush by going around them. As the angle eases at 6,400 feet elevation, follow the terrain leftward toward the mountain, ascending to a glorious vantage of the Klickitat and Mazama Glaciers from 6,800 feet elevation on the Ridge of Wonders.

From 6,800 feet, descend on scree and loose gravel down an open slope leading to the basin below. Once there,

Kristy Woodmansee atop
Ridge of Wonders

traverse the entire moraine-filled basin between 5,900 to 6,000 feet elevation. Upon reaching the final torrent, which is the Big Muddy, pause to assess the crossing. The Big Muddy is neither very big nor very muddy. It is indeed a screeching glacial torrent though, draining the bulk of the Klickitat Glacier. You might have to ascend to about 6,200 feet

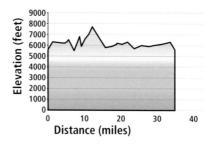

before finding a place to leap across. Or you might have to hike to about 6,500 feet elevation and cross the stream on snow at the base of the glacier. Remember, whenever choosing a snow crossing over a stream, make sure the snow is thick enough to support your weight by both visual observation and by probing with an ice ax, stick, or tent pole.

Climb over the cobbled, Indian-paintbrush-strewn moraine separating the Big Muddy and Avalanche Valleys. Avalanche Valley is easily traversed, but there are more little ridges and gullies than you might imagine. Avoid steep ravines below by traversing at 6,300 feet elevation and cross the first of four forks of Rusk Creek. Ascending to 6,450 feet, again to avoid gullies, easily cross the second and third forks of Rusk Creek. Climbing slightly higher still, cross the final splashing fork of Rusk Creek and make your way toward the obvious trail and camp visible across the meadow. Regain the Highline Trail at the camp below the obvious springs, elevation 6,600 feet.

DAY TWO 13 miles 2,400 feet gain

Day two is in theory on "real" trail, but don't be fooled. For 4 miles or more the trail traverses up to and then down from Devils Garden, a stark volcanic wasteland with scarcely a boot scuff. Mountain goats abound, so keep your eyes open.

Move along a short mile and ascend to the pass, elevation 7,000 feet, near aptly named Goat Butte on the divide between the Rusk and Wilson Glaciers. Descend slightly, traverse, and then ascend across ancient lava flows and rubble, with cairns often marking the way where the trail isn't obvious. Continuing on sketchy trail, ascend to wild, rocky, and lovely Devils Garden, elevation 7,700 feet, and the highest point on the trek. Descend through Devils Garden on rubble and through rock formations toward the meadows below following a rushing stream draining the Lyman Glacier. Continuous unobstructed views of the mountain along with views out to Mount Rainier and the Goat Rocks make for a spectacular scene. Upon reaching the Muddy Meadows Trail #13 junction, elevation 5,800 feet, stay left on the Highline Trail. Meandering through lovely meadows, reach the trail junction with the PCT #2000, elevation 5,900 feet. Stay left as the Highline Trail melds with the PCT.

Big Muddy Valley with Avalanche Valley and Goat Butte beyond

Passing the simultaneous junctions with Killen Creek Trail #113 on the right and High Camp Trail #10 on the left, continue through on the PCT. From this point until the last turn down the South Climb Trail toward your vehicle, stay left at every trail junction.

Crossing beneath the spectacular Adams Glacier is enthralling! Log-hop and ford the broad, shallow torrents streaming from the snow and ice above. In continuous high-country beauty, pass Divide Camp Trail #112, round ridges, gullies, and meadows, and climb up to 6,300 feet before descending to the Riley Camp Trail #64, elevation 5,700 feet. Find camp just beyond the junction, near Sheep Lake.

DAY THREE   11 miles   1,800 feet gain

The final day's trek includes the dramatic yet fast trail around the southwest side of Mount Adams. The trail undulates continuously but upon leaving Sheep Lake and climbing above 6,000 feet it does not drop below 5,900 feet until very near the trailhead. Therefore the elevation gain is modest and the alpine scenery continuous.

From Sheep Lake, climb uphill several hundred feet, continuously meandering through meadows and past lakelets and streams. Upon reaching Horseshoe Meadow, elevation 5,900 feet, stay left on the Round the Mountain Trail #9 as the PCT turns right and heads toward the Columbia River, still 90 miles away. Come around to the south side of Mount Adams. Staying left at the junction with Looking Glass Lake Trail #9A, soon reach the Shorthorn Trail #16, elevation 6,100 feet. The junction is slightly confusing, as the Round the Mountain Trail ascends a hundred feet through boulders before continuing the traverse. Do not be fooled by the Shorthorn Trail, which traverses into the junction just below the Round the Mountain Trail. Stay left, climb uphill, and then resume the traverse.

Descend slightly and then climb to 6,400 feet elevation to enjoy your last hour of exploration on the slopes of Mount Adams. Once again stand at the South Climb Trail junction, elevation 6,300 feet. Having circumnavigated Mount Adams, turn right and in 20 minutes or so reach the trailhead and parking lot at Cold Springs Campground.

Trail Summary and Mileage Estimates

0.0	South Climb Trail #183 at Cold Springs, elevation 5,600 feet
1.3	Round the Mountain Trail #9, elevation 6,300 feet, turn right on Trail #9
4.0	Bird Lake Trail #100, elevation 6,200 feet, stay left on Trail #9
4.7	Flower Trail #106, elevation 6,200 feet, turn left on Trail #106
5.2	Viewpoint Trail #67, elevation 6,300 feet, turn left on Trail #67
5.7	Begin off-trail travel at the viewpoint, elevation 6,500 feet
10.2	Regain Highline Trail #114 at camp below obvious springs, turn left
15.8	Muddy Meadows Trail #13, elevation 5,800 feet, stay left on Trail #114
17.5	PCT #2000, elevation 5,900 feet, stay left on PCT
18.8	Killen Creek Trail #113, elevation 6,100 feet, stay left on PCT
18.9	High Camp Trail #10, elevation 6,200 feet, stay right on PCT
20.3	Divide Camp Trail #112, elevation 6,100 feet, stay left on PCT
23.6	Riley Camp Trail #64, elevation 5,700 feet, stay left on PCT
27.8	Round the Mountain Trail #9, elevation 5,900 feet, stay left on Trail #9
28.9	Looking Glass Trail #9A, elevation 6,000 feet, stay left on Trail #9
31.0	Shorthorn Trail #16, elevation 6,100 feet, stay left on Trail #9
33.5	South Climb Trail #183, elevation 6,300 feet, turn right on Trail #183
34.8	Cold Springs Trailhead, elevation 5,600 feet

Suggested Camps Based on Different Trekking Itineraries

Night	15–20 mpd	10–15 mpd	10 mpd—not feasible
One:	18+ miles - near Killen Creek	10+ miles - near Avalanche Valley	
Two:		24 miles - near Sheep Lake	

Note: If 10 miles per day is your limit, you will probably not have the wherewithal to complete the off-trail segment of this trek.

TREK 20

The Wild Goat Rocks Divide

Mount Rainier from above Elk Pass

Difficulty:	Strenuous
Distance:	30 miles
Elevation gain:	8,500 feet
Best season:	Late July through September
Recommended itinerary:	2 days (15–20 miles per day)
Water availability:	Water is plentiful, *except* for the first 5 or so miles to Sheep Lake and the last 12 miles of the trek. Carry 2 quarts of liquid to start your journey and 2 to 3 quarts when leaving McCall Basin, refilling if possible beyond Tieton Pass or anticipate the possibility of a side trip to Shoe Lake for water.
Logistics:	The trailheads are about 50 road miles apart, so either leave a car at the trek's end near White Pass or arrange

for a drop-off and pickup. In threatening weather, think very carefully before committing to the exposed crossing between Snowgrass Flats and Elk Pass. If you commit, bundle up before starting the traverse, stick together, and if the weather deteriorates, set up your tent and sit it out. Camping beyond the Packwood Glacier and the spiny rock ridge assure you an afternoon (best time of day) snow crossing of the glacier and put the most challenging aspects of the trek behind you. If you are not adept at snow crossings, learn how to use an ice ax or do this trek after mid-August and anticipate using a snow-free crossing high on Old Snowy.

Jurisdictions: Goat Rocks Wilderness, 360-497-1100. Permits are required for wilderness use. Generally permits are available on a self-issued basis at trailheads. Contact the Cowlitz Valley Ranger District for more information at the above number.

Maps: Green Trails: Walupt Lake and White Pass

Trail location: To reach Walupt Lake and the trek's beginning, travel on Interstate 5 to exit 68 (or if coming from eastern Washington, exit 31A on I-82), and drive U.S. Highway 12 to between mileposts 128 and 129. Turn south on Forest Service Road 21 and follow it approximately 20 miles to Road 2160. Turn left on Road 2160 and drive approximately 5 miles to Walupt Lake and the trailhead, elevation 3,900 feet. To drop a car off or be picked up, drive US 12 to between mileposts 151 and 152, 1 mile east of the White Pass summit, to the trailhead for the PCT, heading south from White Pass.

The Goat Rocks straddle the very crest of the Cascades, forming the spine of the mountain range from White Pass south to Mount Adams. This stretch of crest splendor competes with the fabled scenic beauty and ruggedness of the North Cascades. Miles of meadows line ridges and cover basins. Streams and waterfalls pour forth from mountaintop snowfields. The most rigorous snow crossings you will encounter on a "trail" in the state of Washington are found in the Goat Rocks.

DAY ONE   16 miles   5,900 feet gain

Walk away from the Walupt Lake Campground and parking area, elevation 3,900 feet, with the tempting smell of pancakes and bacon heavy in the air. Selecting the

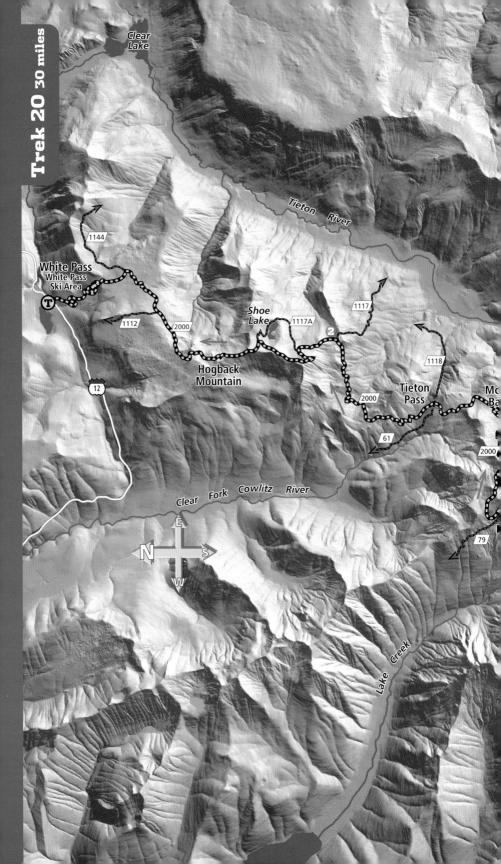

Clear
Lake

Tieton River

1144

White Pass
White Pass
Ski Area

T

1112   2000   Shoe
Lake   1117A

1117

2

Hogback
Mountain

2000   Tieton
Pass

1118

Mc
Ba

61   2000

Clear Fork Cowlitz River   79

N
E
S
W

Lake Creek

12

Klickitat River

Gilbert Peak

Goat Rocks

Wilderness

Cispus Pass

2000

2000

Sheep Lake

101

Nannie Peak

Old Snowy Mountain

Snowgrass Flats

2000

Cispus

1

96

97

86

98

River

Walupt Lake

Road 2160

Sheep Lake

Nannie Ridge Trail #98, climb steadily toward the blue sky and sunlight above. Soon reach timberline and savor breathtaking views of Mount Adams to the south and the Goat Rocks to the east. Dropping 300 feet to round cliffs, regain the gentle alpine ridge and for 2 miles stride along the bumpy crest, until arriving at the shores of picturesque Sheep Lake. Immediately thereafter, reach the junction with the Pacific Crest Trail #2000, elevation 5,800 feet, about 5 miles from the trailhead. Turn left and head north on the PCT, your choice of travel for the remaining trek distance.

All-encompassing alpine splendor stretches around. For 4 miles climb, traverse and descend through basins and across ridges. The waterfalls of Cispus Basin are enthralling: the splashing streams tumble over cliffs shrouded in alpine foliage. Upon reaching junctions with first the Lily Basin Trail #97 and then the Snowgrass Flats Trail #96, stay right and enter magnificent Snowgrass Flats on the PCT, aptly named, as the unique puffballs of white are everywhere. Gently climb through meadows, then cross scree and snow patches toward the shoulder of Old Snowy. The views grow climactically as Mount Rainier looms to the north, Mounts Adams and St. Helens appear to the south, and the Goat Rocks are on display all around.

Upon reaching the shoulder of Old Snowy, before you stretches a 0.25-mile Packwood Glacier snow crossing, angling at about 25 to 30 degrees. Beyond is the rock-pinnacled ridge of the Cascade Crest, which functions as a barrier to storms.

Weather systems that started in the Pacific Ocean and dropped precipitation in the western portion of the state are forced up and over this divide before they can spill into eastern Washington and dissipate in force and effect. The crest is a poor place to be in a storm because of the velocity of winds and the moisture-laden clouds that create blurry whiteout conditions. The 4 trail miles between Snowgrass Flats and Elk Pass are the most dangerous of Washington's PCT. They represent the highest elevation reached by the PCT in Washington and the trail can be difficult to find in poor visibility. The challenge is compounded by the lengthy snow crossing of the Packwood Glacier and adjacent slopes. It is possible in August to find a way above or between glacial remnants and avoid snow by ascending higher than the 7,100-foot trail, going nearly or over the top of Old Snowy in the process. The trouble is, in poor visibility with a storm pounding you, this option is likely slower and even more dangerous.

If you are adept at snow travel and know how to use an ice ax, the crossing is no big deal. Beyond the snow, pick your way over scree slopes to the blasted trail segment spanning the pinnacled ridge. The ridge is narrow and exposed, very impressive for hiking terrain. Although the trail is always visible when you scan the ridge ahead, beneath your feet it is not so obvious because the blasted rock melds with the scree slopes. Behind you rises the significant bulk of Old Snowy—the setting looks more like a climbing scene than a hiking scene.

Trail through Cispus Basin headwaters

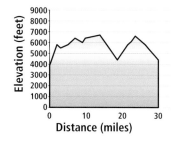

Once off the rock rib, drop to Elk Pass and continue beyond into gorgeous upper McCall Basin. Camp here amidst the splendor of small streams and wildflowers while soaking up the grandeur of Mount Rainier across the valley.

DAY TWO   14 miles   2,600 feet gain

Day two begins as day one ended, strolling down through McCall Basin, alive with waterfalls and flowers. The brief climb from the basin onto the forested ridge northward is a warm-up for the stern climb ahead. The gently weaving trail leads to the forested saddle of Tieton Pass and junctions with the Clear Fork Trail #61 and the North Fork Tieton Trail #1118. Continue ahead on the PCT.

Traversing nearly level for 1 mile, the trail then crosses over the divide into eastern Washington and begins an ambling ascent through rugged terrain. The

Shoe Lake

rock outcroppings and stunted trees stand in testimony to the harsh reality of life on the crest. Climbing back to 6,600 feet elevation, once again hike the backbone of Washington. Look back toward the splendor and challenge of Old Snowy and the cluster of Goat Rock summits, the distance lending some perspective to the terrain so recently traveled.

Staying left at intersections with Hidden Springs Trail #1117 and Shoe Lake Trail #1117A, finish the long climb from Tieton Pass and traverse first above Shoe Lake and then just beneath the summit of Hogback Mountain. Completing the traverse beneath Hogback Mountain, descend through the pass above Miriam Creek and angle toward White Pass and the PCT junction with US 12. Walk gently down through forest on a very roundabout path. Arrive at the trailhead on US 12 just east of White Pass, elevation 4,400 feet, about 30 miles from Walupt Lake.

Trail Summary and Mileage Estimates

0.0	Walupt Lake Trail #101, elevation 3,900 feet
0.1	Nannie Ridge Trail #98, turn left on Nannie Ridge Trail
5.0	PCT #2000, elevation 5,800 feet, turn left on PCT
9.0	Lily Basin Trail #97, elevation 6,000 feet, stay right on PCT
9.8	Snowgrass Flats Trail #96, elevation 6,400 feet, stay right on PCT
13.8	Coyote Trail #79, elevation 6,700 feet, stay right on PCT
18.6	Tieton Pass junction with Trails #61 and #1118, elevation 4,400 feet, continue ahead on PCT
21.5	Hidden Springs Trail #1117, elevation 5,800 feet, stay left on PCT
22.5	Shoe Lake Trail #1117A, elevation 6,100 feet, stay left on PCT
26.4	White Pass Chairlift Trail #1112, elevation 5,800 feet, stay right on PCT
27.4	Round Mountain Trail #1144, elevation 5,400 feet, stay left on PCT
30.0	Pacific Crest Trailhead near White Pass, elevation 4,400 feet

Note: This trek's distance can vary by up to 3 miles, depending on the map or information source you use. The mileage estimates above are based on the Green Trails map series, with slight adjustments from personal experience. Thirty miles is one of the shorter estimates.

Suggested Camps Based on Different Trekking Itineraries

Night	15–20 mpd	10–15 mpd	10 mpd—not practical
One:	16 miles - upper McCall Basin	11 miles - past Snowgrass Flats	
Two:		22 miles - near Hidden Spring	

Note: To reach Hidden Spring and camps, follow Trail #1117 a couple hundred yards off the PCT and then you will need to snoop around farther east to find the spring atop a meadowed area.

The Enchanted Loop

Quinault River

Difficulty:	Strenuous
Distance:	60 miles
Elevation gain:	10,100 feet
Best season:	Mid-July through mid-October
Recommended itinerary:	4 days (15–20 miles per day)
Water availability:	Good *except* for the nearly 7-mile trek segment from the Duckabush to Dosewallips Rivers via La Crosse Pass. Carry 2 to 3 quarts of liquid when leaving the Duckabush Valley.
Logistics:	If coming from the Seattle area, the drive to the trailhead takes 4 hours, so consider leaving the night before. There is a campground at the trailhead as well as camping and lodging near Lake Quinault, including the famed Lake Quinault Lodge. One goal of this trek is to spend a night in the midst of the

	Enchanted Valley, 13 miles from the trailhead.
Jurisdictions:	Olympic National Park, 360-288-2444. Permits are required for overnight backcountry travel. A daily fee is applied as well. Permits can be obtained from the Quinault Ranger Station or by self-issue at the trail-head. Contact the Quinault Ranger Station at the above number for information.
Maps:	Green Trails: Mt. Christie and Mt. Steel
Trail location:	Travel Interstate 5 to Olympia and take exit 104. Travel west on State Routes 8 and 12 to Aberdeen/Hoquiam. Drive U.S. Highway 101 North from Aberdeen/Hoquiam to beyond milepost 125. Turn right on Lake Quinault South Shore Road and travel about 13 miles to Graves Creek Road. Turn right on Graves Creek Road and drive approximately 6 miles to the road end and trailhead, elevation 600 feet.

Trekking old-growth forests abundant with wildlife along the Quinault River to the Enchanted Valley and beyond to the La Crosse Lakes Basin, then looping back via La Crosse and Anderson Passes, is a defining experience in the Olympic National Park. The astounding size of the conifers, the entrancing aura of the Enchanted Valley, and the sparkling basin of Marmot, Hart, and La Crosse Lakes offer unsurpassed visual splendor. The wildlife bounty of deer, elk, and black bears remain among my most memorable trekking sights.

DAY ONE   13 miles   1,500 feet gain

In less than 5 minutes, cross Graves Creek on a high sturdy bridge and pass the Graves Creek Trail, staying left on the broad path leading up the Quinault Valley. The old road gives way to trail at spectacular Pony Bridge. The bridge spans a narrow chasm through which the Quinault River pours. Always beautiful, the site is wildly spectacular at high water. Beyond, the trail climbs gently through the deep green beauty of the rain forest. When I trekked this stretch of trail, the sharp snap of a limb announced the presence of a magnificent herd of elk moving silently down the valley.

Passing O'Neil Creek and then Pyrites Creek Camps, the trail is immersed in groves of ancient maple trees, the twisting trunks and limbs ensconced with clinging moss. Throughout the valley, the voracious appetite of the resident elk herd contains the growth of ground-cover vegetation, creating a maintained parklike setting beneath the giant trees. After crossing the Quinault River on a footbridge, you are rewarded with glimpses of Mount Anderson rising far above the adjoining ridges.

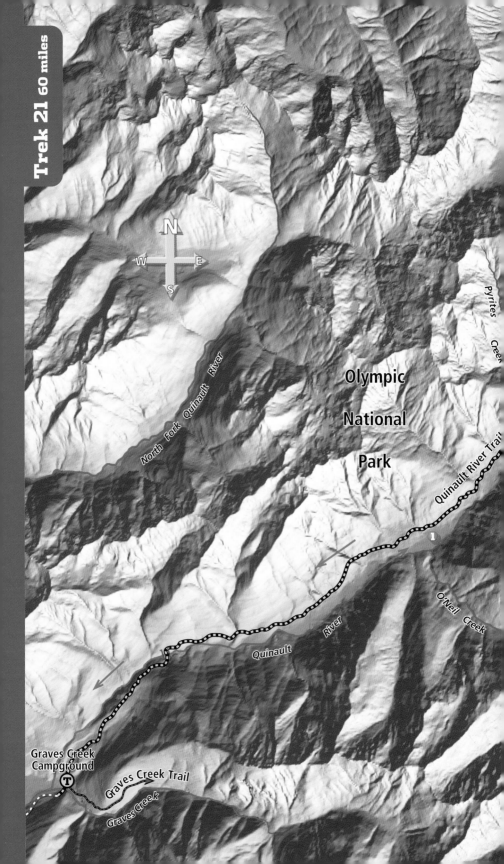

Olympic

National

Park

Pyrites Creek

North Fork Quinault River

Quinault River Trail

O'Neil Creek

Quinault River

Graves Creek Campground

Graves Creek Trail

Graves Creek

Mount
Anderson

West Fork
Dosewallips Trail

Chimney
Peak

**5 3
3**

Anderson Pass

La Crosse Pass Trail

Enchanted Valley

Mount
La Crosse

Enchanted
Valley
Camp

Lake
La Crosse

**1
2**

O'Neil Pass Trail

Quinault

Duckabush   River   Trail

Duckabush River

ault River Trail

**2
2**

4

Marmot
Lake

3

Upper Duckabush River Trail

O'Neil
Pass

Mount
Duckabush

O'Neil
Peak

O'Neil Creek

Warming hut and ranger station in Enchanted Valley

The gentle trail allows for fast walking, so before you realize it you will arrive at what can only be described as the Enchanted Valley. The open meadow is laced with alders, an unusual sight given the dominance of conifers in the old-growth scheme of nature. In the middle of the meadow stands a wooden chalet, two stories tall, built around 1930 as a "resort" prior to establishment of the national park in 1938. Beyond, a twisting river of blue-gray water spills in rapids down the valley. Above this scene rise the cliff-strewn valley walls, topped by Anderson Glacier and peak.

Explore the meadow, the valley, and the combination ranger station and gathering place. Ample camping is available in the open trees near the river.

DAY TWO 15 miles 4,600 feet gain

The trail on this second day gains 1,300 feet of elevation as it climbs out of the valley floor and provides a clear view toward Anderson Pass, enmeshed in trees at the valley's head. Upon reaching a trail junction 3 miles from the Enchanted Valley, turn right on the O'Neil Pass Trail. The trail climbs steadily in forest, crossing a pleasant stream, and then contours around a timbered rib at 4,000 feet elevation before continuing on a roundabout course toward O'Neil Pass. Climbing higher, Mount Anderson is now in plain view, from valley floor to summit cairn. Down valley, see all the way to Lake Quinault, more than 25 miles distant. Higher, contour for miles in open meadows as the tread gradually creeps up the slope, winding toward the far end of the ridge that extends from Mount La Crosse to Mount Duckabush.

Finally, attain the broad expanse of O'Neil Pass, elevation 5,400 feet, 10+ miles from the Enchanted Valley. The pass is a gorgeous expanse of boulder-strewn alpine meadows, with views to nearby peaks and down the Duckabush Valley. Move ahead the long mile downhill to Marmot Lake where you can easily spend an afternoon or day sunning, swimming, bear watching, or fishing—the options are many. Set up camp in the vicinity of Marmot Lake and enjoy the side trip to Hart and La Crosse Lakes without a heavy pack, or carry your gear to more private camps deeper in the splendid basin near the other lakes.

Obligatory side trip 1: Take the way trail toward Hart and La Crosse Lakes to enjoy the dramatic lake views. Climb 400 feet on the way trail leading north from Marmot Lake, traversing above larger Hart Lake before traversing to Lake La Crosse in 1.5 miles. The basin is open and explorations are delightful. Figure on a round trip of 2 hours or more.

Mount Anderson from near O'Neil Pass

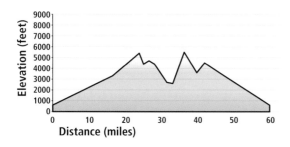

DAY THREE
12+ miles
3,300 feet gain

Leaving the splendor of La Crosse Basin, descend steadily to the Duckabush Trail and continue down valley a short 2 miles to the La Crosse Pass Trail, elevation 2,600 feet. After filling your water bottles, turn left and come to grips with the 3,000-foot climb to La Crosse Pass. The trail climb to the pass is consistent and efficient. As the forest gives way to meadows, the tight switchbacks begin to alternate with lovely meadow traverses. The pass becomes visible as you climb higher, providing motivation to reach the top. Finally, reach the rocky and airy pass, elevation 5,500 feet. The path of descent arcs beneath you in a sweeping contour of the hillside. To the south Mount Hopper and Mount Steel rise above First Ridge. To the north, the black silhouette of Mount Anderson dominates.

Continuing on, walk through grass meadows and alpine nooks. Watch for elk herds as the trail descends to reach the West Fork Dosewallips River Trail in just over 3 miles. Turning left, climb 400 feet in 1 mile to Anderson Camp, elevation 4,000 feet, situated closely beneath Anderson Pass.

DAY FOUR   20 miles   700 feet gain

Scarcely warmed up, crest Anderson Pass, elevation 4,500 feet, and cruise downhill, soon in familiar terrain. Stay right at the known junction with the O'Neil Pass Trail and arrive once again in the Enchanted Valley, 6 miles into the day's trek. Again, spend a bit of time here, perhaps enjoying a late breakfast or, if you are really slacking, an early lunch. Resuming the down-valley march, enjoy views of the river as sunlight gradually peers through the needles of the old-growth monarchs above. Keep your eye out for bear, deer, and elk as you retrace your route of a few days before, crossing the Pony Bridge and returning to the starting trailhead.

Marmot Lake

Trail Summary and Mileage Estimates

0.0	Quinault River Trailhead, elevation 600 feet
16.3	O'Neil Pass Trail, elevation 3,300 feet, turn right on O'Neil Pass Trail
23.7	O'Neil Pass, elevation 5,400 feet, continue on Upper Duckabush Trail (no junction)
24.9	La Crosse Basin Trail, elevation 4,400 feet, turn left for 1.5-miles out-and-back side trip
27.9	Upper Duckabush Trail, elevation 4,400 feet, return to Marmot Lake from side trip
31.3	Duckabush River Trail, elevation 2,700 feet, stay left on Duckabush River Trail
33.0	La Crosse Pass Trail, elevation 2,600 feet, turn left on La Crosse Pass Trail
39.7	West Fork Dosewallips Trail, elevation 3,600 feet, turn left on West Fork Dosewallips Trail
41.8	Anderson Pass, elevation 4,500 feet, continue on Quinault River Trail (no junction)
59.8	Quinault River Trailhead, elevation 600 feet

Note: The obligatory side trip is included in the mileage and elevation estimates.

Suggested Camps Based on Different Trekking Itineraries

Night	15–20 mpd	10–15 mpd	10 mpd
One:	13 miles - Enchanted Valley	13 miles - Enchanted Valley	6+ miles - O'Neil Creek Camp
Two:	28 miles - La Crosse Basin area	28 miles - La Crosse Basin area	13 miles - Enchanted Valley
Three:	40 miles - Anderson Camp	40 miles - Anderson Camp	25 miles - Marmot Lake
Four:		50 miles - Pyrites Creek Camp	31+ miles - Duckabush Camp
Five:			40 miles - Anderson Camp
Six:			50 miles - Pyrites Creek Camp

TREK 22

The Hoh Valley-Bogachiel Traverse

Elk in lower Hoh Valley

Difficulty:	Easier
Distance:	74 miles
Elevation gain:	16,000 feet
Best season:	Mid-July through mid-October
Recommended itinerary:	4 days (15–20 miles per day)
Water availability:	Good except for the climb to Hoh Lake and on High Divide, and again at trek's finale. Carry 2 quarts when ascending to Hoh Lake and 2 quarts when leaving Hoh Lake. Also carry 2 to 3 quarts when leaving the Bogachiel Valley for the traverse back to the Hoh Valley.
Logistics:	The trailheads are about 6 road miles apart, so stash a bicycle as an option for retrieving your vehicle at

trek's end. Stay off the Blue Glacier unless you are trained and equipped for glacier travel. Before embarking upon this trek prior to mid-July, contact the ranger station regarding whether the Bogachiel River is fordable.

Jurisdictions: Olympic National Park, 360-374-6925. Permits are required for overnight backcountry travel. A daily fee is applied as well. Permits can be obtained from the Hoh Visitor Center or by self-issue at the trailhead. Contact the Hoh Ranger Station/Visitor Center at the above number for information.

Maps: Green Trails: Mt. Tom, Mt. Olympus, and Spruce Mountain

Trail location: Travel Interstate 5 to Olympia and take exit 104. Travel west on State Routes 8 and 12 to Aberdeen/Hoquiam. Drive U.S. Highway 101 North from Aberdeen/ Hoquiam to beyond milepost 178. Turn right on Upper Hoh Road about 13 miles before reaching the official park entrance. Just before the entrance gate is the Snider-Jackson (Hoh Ridge) Trailhead. Beyond the entrance, drive approximately 6 miles to the Hoh Campground, parking lot, and trailhead, elevation 500 feet. The trailhead can also be reached via Port Angeles and Forks, the Upper Hoh Road being about 12 miles south of Forks.

The trek along the Hoh to the white ice of Olympus is to see firsthand the power and effect of rain and water, from lush vegetation and roaring falls to deep glacial ice. Elk, deer, bear, and other wildlife abound in this fertile jungle, where human presence is limited to the beaten path.

DAY ONE   19 miles   5,000 feet gain

The trekking goal of day one is to reach Glacier Meadows Camp and view Mount Olympus and the Blue Glacier on your first afternoon. The rain forest is enchanting despite the steady stream of day hikers, backpackers, and climbers. Hike through the unbelievable beauty of cedars, giant firs, hemlocks, and vine maple, with moss draped from limb upon limb. The trail is a corridor through a sea of green moss and flourishing ground cover.

Pass by the Olympus Guard Station and the trail to Hoh Lake, contouring up the valley past a lovely campsite along the river about 12.5 miles from the trailhead. Climbing a couple hundred feet higher, stop in amazement of the chasm beneath

N
W · E
S

Twenty
Mile
Cam
5

Bogachiel River

North Fork

Hyak
Camp
3 4

Bogachiel River Trail

Bogachiel
River
Trail

Flapjack
Camp
6

Ford

Bogachiel   River

Hoh Rain
Forest
Visitor
Center
T

Snider

Jackson

Trail

Upper Hoh Road

Hoh River

T

Upper Hoh Road

Hoh
River

South Fork Hoh River

Mink Lake Trail

Mink Lake

kwood ke

Little Divide Trail

Sol Duc River

Deer Lake Trail

Deer Lake

High Divide Trail

Lunch Lake

Sol Duc River Trail

Heart Lake

gachiel

River

2 3
4

Bogachiel Peak

High Divide Trail

Cat Peak

Hoh Lake

Olympus Guard Station

Hoh River Trail

High Hoh Bridge

Hoh River Trail

3

Hoh River

2

Hoh

River Trail

er

Olympic

National

Park

Elk Lake

Glacier Meadows

1
2

Glacier Meadows Camp

Blue Glacier

Mount Olympus

South Fork Hoh River

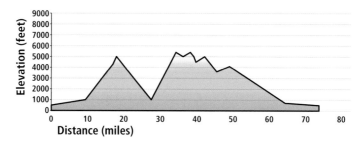

your feet. Although spanned by a sturdy bridge, the view down through the narrow rock walls to the frothy Hoh River will make you shudder. After crossing the Hoh, climb steadily up the hillside, reaching the forested shores of Elk Lake, elevation 2,700 feet, 15 miles from the trailhead and a gathering place for hikers and climbers alike.

Continue toward Glacier Meadows, with views all around except for Mount Olympus, which remains tucked behind a ridge out of view. Reaching Glacier Meadows, elevation 4,300 feet, set up camp and prepare to view the mountain. Quickly passing a ranger's encampment and breaking through timberline, trek either or both the glacier overlook trail and the moraine trail. Ultimately reach the crest of the moraine and the shockingly beautiful view of Mount Olympus and the Blue Glacier. The entire trek is worth every step just for this view alone and you don't get any of the Mount Olympus view until you take the final steps. Beneath your feet lies the broad Blue Glacier, filling the valley below. Up toward the multiple peaks of Mount Olympus are cirques of tumbling ice walls, ice cliffs, crevasses, and fluted ridges of ice streaming from the rock peaks to the valley glacier. Unless you are bent on climbing Mount Olympus, there is no reason to go beyond the crest of the moraine. The view from the moraine is the best in the land and descending the moraine is unpleasant if not dangerous.

DAY TWO   20+ miles   5,800 feet gain

For a trek with a valley orientation, the first two trekking days are very challenging, the significant elevation gain indicative of striving to gain ridge tops from the valley floor. The day's trekking distance also includes trekking 2 miles out along High Divide toward Heart Lake as well as descending to Lunch Lake, so let your energy and ambition be your guide. Arise, pack your gear, and turn down the valley past Elk Lake, where hikers are stirring, and continue down through the forest.

After descending 7.5 miles, reach the Hoh Lake Trail junction once again. Turning right, begin the climb, but fill up with water the first time the trail nears Hoh Creek for the climb is stern and warm. Ascend through forest and then an old burn before crossing beneath Hoh Creek, entering meadows, and tackling the final rise to the lake itself, which is set in a lovely alp basin just beneath High Divide.

From the lake, complete a contour through meadow slopes with expanding

Lunch Lake

views to the very top of High Divide, a few feet below the summit of Bogachiel Peak. Scramble the peak for the best views along the beautiful divide. Below to the left lies Heart Lake; indeed, the shape of a valentine heart surrounded by delicate meadows. To the right lies the sweeping curve of the Hoh Valley, the incredible snout of the Blue Glacier protruding beneath the shining ice of Mount Olympus. Drop your pack and walk a mile or more along the divide toward Cat Peak before turning back toward Bogachiel Peak. The lakes of Seven Lakes Basin beckoning, pass by the Hoh Lake Trail junction and soon reach the junction with Seven Lakes Basin Trail (Lunch Lake). Giving up the divide for the moment, turn right and in a few minutes find a camp near Lunch Lake.

DAY THREE   16 miles   2,400 feet gain

Ascend from Lunch Lake back to High Divide within a few minutes and resume the trek toward the Bogachiel Valley. Hiking early, you may discover nature's creatures still foraging. Climbing several hundred feet above Deer Lake, the trail then holds directly on top of the forested ridge, with views to Mount Olympus and Mount Tom. Staying left at the Mink Lake Trail junction, continue descending

Bogachiel Valley

down the forested ridge. The trail clings to the ridge top, undulating over every bump in the terrain before abandoning the ridge altogether and reaching the banks of the Bogachiel River at Twentyone Mile Camp. The trail bed is grown over with moss and grass, and it weaves a narrow path through the immense trees and dense vegetation of the rain forest. The light filtering through the trees to the shadowy valley floor is captivating. Find camp in the deserted valley near Hyak Shelter.

DAY FOUR 17+ miles 2,800 feet gain

From Hyak Camp, continue down the moderately steep valley of the North Fork Bogachiel River. Passing Fifteenmile Camp, reach the flat valley floor and continue to Flapjack Camp, elevation 700 feet. The trail weaves and bobs around the massive trees and deep brush of the valley.

At Flapjack Camp, make your way to the river and find a ford or, hopefully, a log crossing. After successfully crossing the river, find a trail leading in 0.5 mile to the Snider-Jackson Trail (formerly Hoh Ridge Trail). Turn left and ascend a forested rib over the top of Hoh Ridge and continue down a similar rib to trek's end at the Upper Hoh Road, adjacent to the national park entrance.

Trail Summary and Mileage Estimates

0.0	Hoh River Trailhead, elevation 500 feet
9.5	Hoh Lake Trail, elevation 1,000 feet, stay right on Hoh Trail
17.0	Glacier Meadows Camp, elevation 4,300 feet
18.0	Top of Blue Glacier moraine, elevation 5,000 feet
27.5	Hoh Lake Trail, elevation 1,000 feet, turn right on Hoh Lake Trail
34.2	High Divide Trail, elevation 5,400 feet, turn right and go out and back on High Divide
38.2	Hoh Lake Trail, elevation 5,400 feet, continue toward Seven Lakes Basin
39.1	Lunch Lake Trail, elevation 5,000 feet, turn right and descend to Lunch Lake
42.1	High Divide Trail, elevation 5,000 feet, turn right on High Divide Trail
45.4	Deer Lake Trail, elevation 3,600 feet, turn left on Little Divide Trail
49.0	Mink Lake Trail, elevation 4,100 feet, stay left on Bogachiel River Trail
64.5	Flapjack Camp, elevation 700 feet, ford the Bogachiel River
65.1	Snider-Jackson Trail, elevation 700 feet, turn left on Snider-Jackson Trail
73.8	Upper Hoh Road, elevation 500 feet

Suggested Camps Based on Different Trekking Itineraries

Night	15–20 mpd	10–15 mpd	10 mpd
One:	19 miles - Glacier Meadows Camp	13+ miles - near Hoh Bridge	9 miles - Olympus Guard Station
Two:	40 miles - Lunch Lake	25+ miles - near Hoh Bridge	19 miles - Glacier Meadows Camp
Three:	56 miles - Hyak Camp	40 miles - Lunch Lake	28+ miles - Olympus Guard Station
Four:		56 miles - Hyak Camp	40 miles - Lunch Lake
Five:			52 miles - Twentyone Mile Camp
Six:			64.5 miles - Flapjack Camp

The Grand Loop

Trail sign at Grand Pass

Difficulty:	Strenuous
Distance:	46 miles
Elevation gain:	12,600 feet
Best season:	Late July through September
Recommended itinerary:	3 days (10–15 miles per day)
Water availability:	Good except that the water pump at Deer Park Campground is the only certain water source over the last 14 miles. Leave Three Forks Camp with at least 2 quarts of liquid and walk off the trail a short distance to get water at the aforementioned pump.
Logistics:	Before mid-August anticipate ascending steep snow leading up to Cameron Pass. Carry an ice ax and know how to use it.
Jurisdictions:	Olympic National Park, 360-565-3100. Permits are required for overnight backcountry travel. A daily

fee is applied as well. Permits can be obtained from the Wilderness Information Center or by self-issue at the trailhead. Contact the center at the above number for information.

Maps: Green Trails: Mt. Angeles and Tyler Peak

Trail location: Drive U.S. Highway 101 to Port Angeles. Beyond milepost 249, turn left on Race Street, which becomes Heart O' the Hills Road. Formally enter the Olympic National Park and drive 12 miles beyond the entrance to Obstruction Point Road. Turn left on Obstruction Point Road and drive approximately 7 miles to the road end and trailhead, elevation 6,100 feet.

In this national park of valley trails and near sea-level trailheads, the Grand Loop breaks the mold. The succession of high passes will challenge your body, while miles of meadow travel and dramatic views will have your spirits soaring. Call this trek Grand.

DAY ONE   16 miles   4,500 feet gain

The first trekking day is bold and aggressive, climbing up and over three passes before finally nestling into camp in subalpine meadows. Shoulder your pack and stumble along the Grand Pass Trail, elevation 6,100 feet, the stumbling directly related to the stunning alpine views all around. After contouring the ups and downs of the ridge crest with spectacular 360-degree views, cross over a shoulder and dip into the Grand Valley, passing the Badger Valley Trail a swan dive above Grand Lake.

Ascending the Grand Valley is captivating. Moose Lake is just as pretty as and even closer to the trail than Grand Lake. Crystal flowing water is always near, with flower-strewn alpine benches all around. Higher, the gentle valley gives way to a winding ascent up scree slopes, across easy snow patches, and among rock outcroppings to spectacular Grand Pass, elevation 6,400 feet, the first pass of the day. Only 6 miles into the trek, the expansive mountainous views create an aura of deep wilderness.

Leaving the pass, switchback steeply into the rocky, snowy basin below, picking up thin but good tread where meadow meets the gravel and snow. The short descent into the Cameron Valley is delightful, the trail always near and sometimes in the stream that splashes down from the basin

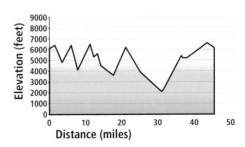

Deer Ridge Trail

Lower Gray Wolf Trail

Gray Wolf River

Three Forks Trail

2

Gray Wolf River Trail

4

Deer Park
Campground

Gray   Wolf   River

Deer
Park
Road

Cameron Creek Trail

Cameron

Elk Mountain Trail

Grand

Creek

Creek

Maiden
Peak

Grand
Lake

Moose
Lake

Badger
Valley
Cutoff
Trail

Trail

Elk

Mountain

Badger

Valley

Trail

Olympic

Grand

Pass

National

T Obstruction
Peak

Park

Obstruction Point Road

Gray Wolf
Pass

Gray Wolf River Trail 1

Gray

Wolf

3

River

Cedar Lake
Trail

Cedar
Lake

Dosewallips River Trail

Dosewallips

River

Thousand
Acre
Meadow

1
2

Mount
Cameron

Sentinel
Peak

Cameron

on

Creek

and
ss

Creek

Trail

Cameron
Pass

1

Cameron Pass Trail

Lost
Pass

Mount
Fromme

E

N   S

W

Grand Lake

above. At 4,100 feet elevation, turn right on the Cameron Creek Trail and head up the valley toward as yet unseen Cameron Pass. Surrounded by high ridges culminating in Cameron Peak, the Cameron Creek Valley is even more beautiful than the Grand. Broad valley meadows with Cameron Creek bubbling nearby finally give way to the starker upper basin. Spying the pass and tread switchbacking up possibly snow-covered scree slopes, climb to pass number two. If the upper slope is snow covered, this means ascending 30- to 35-degree snow slopes, terrain suitable only for the experienced and surefooted. The consequences of a slip are a fast ride down slope to a scraping stop in the rock scree below. As you walk over tundralike turf into the glorious saddle of Cameron Pass, the chilly northern slopes give way to among the best flower fields in the Olympics, including vast fields of lupine with Indian paintbrush, daisies, and other species.

Leaving the pass amidst the flowery beauty and inspiring mountain views, pass by a nice camp as you complete the diagonal descent and brief climb through Lost Pass, the third and final pass of the day. Savor the views back to Cameron Pass and out to serene Thousand Acre Meadow, an incongruent and immense flat space amidst the mountainous terrain. Turn left on the Dosewallips River Trail, elevation 4,500 feet, and in less than 2 miles reach Bear Camp, elevation 3,900 feet.

DAY TWO   15 miles   2,900 feet gain

After a brief stroll down valley, face the day's only ascent as you turn left on the Gray Wolf Pass Trail and climb back to more than 6,200 feet elevation at Gray Wolf Pass. The immense rock facades of Warrior Peak and Mount Constance dominate the views down the Dosewallips Valley and up to the pass. Measure your uphill progress against these rock faces as you transition into alpine terrain and cross the rocky divide of Gray Wolf Pass. The north-side slopes again hold snow late into the season, but they are gentler than the Cameron Pass slopes. Plunge-step down the snow or try to follow the twisting switchbacks as they appear and disappear amidst the slippery white surface.

Upper Gray Wolf Basin is a delightful blend of meadows and outcroppings, running streams, and small tarns, ideal for a rest break or exploration. Beyond the basin, the trail switchbacks sharply to the floor of the upper valley, staying very near the Gray Wolf River all the way to its confluence with Cedar Creek. Upon reaching the Cedar Lake Trail, stay right on the Gray Wolf River Trail and in a few moments pass Falls Camp.

Beyond Falls Camp the tread continues to drop in an easy fashion all the way to Gray Wolf Camp near Three Forks, elevation 2,100 feet. Relax amidst the earthiness of the deep old-growth forest and the abundance of flowing water where three valleys merge into one.

DAY THREE   14+ miles   5,200 feet gain

After spending half of your previous day in the deep valley of Gray Wolf Creek, prepare yourself for the traverse along the highest ridge trail in the Olympic National Park.

Near Gray Wolf Camp is a junction. Turn left, taking the trail that leads up Cameron Creek a short distance to the Three Forks Trail. Head up valley and turn right in about 0.5 mile on Three Forks Trail, elevation 2,200 feet. Be sure to fill up with water before leaving the junction because the next sure water source is a pump at Deer Park Campground, more than 5 miles and 3,000 feet in elevation away. Ascending steadily, the trail climbs through a burn and into alpine meadows with broadening views before reaching the Deer Ridge Trail, elevation 5,400 feet. Turn left and in a short distance reach Deer Park Road and the campground. As you briefly intersect civilization, anticipate encountering a modest number of people and their vehicles as you gracefully clear the campground area and walk the road to the ranger station, where the Elk Mountain Trail is gained.

Because the traverse of Elk Ridge will likely be waterless, follow the signs directing you a short distance into Deer Creek Campground to a large, obvious manual water pump and spout. Proceed to the Elk Mountain Trail and descend a few hundred feet in forest before climbing steadily along the gentle ridge crest. To

Slopes leading to Cameron Pass and Peak

the northeast, Port Angeles, the Strait of Juan de Fuca, and Puget Sound loom far below, with Mount Baker dominating the Cascade view eastward. To the south and west extend ridge after ridge of Olympic peaks separated by old-growth valleys. Beneath your feet and on the surrounding slopes grow brilliant alpine flowers, melding with the forests far below.

Approaching 7,000 feet elevation, the marvelous scenery continues. Views below to Grand and Moose Lakes indicate the trek is nearly completed. Passing the Badger Valley Cutoff Trail, elevation 6,600 feet, stay right and enjoy the final traverse through splendid alpine basins. Nearing the trek's end, cross or go around a steep snow slope, a Park Service–installed rope hand-line reduces the crossing danger. In a few moments, pass the Badger Valley Trail and reach the trailhead at Obstruction Point.

Trail Summary and Mileage Estimates

0.0	Grand Pass Trailhead, elevation 6,100 feet
3.5	Badger Valley Trail, elevation 4,800 feet, stay right on Grand Pass Trail
7.8	Cameron Creek Trail, elevation 4,100 feet, turn right on Cameron Creek Trail
14.2	Dosewallips River Trail, elevation 4,500 feet, turn left on Dosewallips Trail
17.7	Gray Wolf Pass Trail, elevation 3,600 feet, turn left on Gray Wolf Pass Trail
25.2	Cedar Lake Trail, elevation 3,900 feet, turn right on Gray Wolf River Trail
31.0	Lower Gray Wolf Trail, elevation 2,100 feet, turn left on Cameron Creek Trail
31.4	Three Forks Trail, elevation 2,200 feet, turn right on Three Forks Trail
36.5	Deer Ridge Trail, elevation 5,400 feet, turn left toward Deer Park
36.9	Deer Park Campground, elevation 5,200 feet, walk the road to the ranger station
38.0	Elk Mountain Trail, elevation 5,200 feet, adjacent to the ranger station
43.5	Badger Valley Cutoff Trail, elevation 6,600 feet, stay right on Elk Mountain Trail
45.3	Badger Valley Trail, elevation 6,200 feet, stay right on Elk Mountain Trail
45.5	Grand Pass Trailhead, elevation 6,100 feet

Suggested Camps Based on Different Trekking Itineraries

Night	15–20 mpd	10–15 mpd	10 mpd
One:	22+ miles - upper Gray Wolf Basin	16 miles - Bear Camp	9+ miles - upper Cameron Basin
Two:		31 miles - Gray Wolf Camp	16 miles - Bear Camp
Three:			25+ miles - Falls Camp
Four:			37 miles - Deer Park

The Black Bear Traverse

Three Lakes Basin

Difficulty:	Most strenuous
Distance:	107 miles
Elevation gain:	25,000 feet
Best season:	Late July through September
Recommended itinerary:	6 days (15–20 miles per day)
Water availability:	The ridge tops and climbs to passes tend to be dry. When leaving Three Lakes, the West Fork Dosewallips River, and the North Fork Skokomish River, carry at least 2 quarts of liquid and don't pass up opportunities to fill up.
Logistics:	The trailheads are about 10 miles apart, so consider leaving a bicycle near Graves Creek Campground for the 40-minute pedal back to your vehicle.
Jurisdictions:	Olympic National Park, 360-288-2444. Permits are

required for overnight backcountry travel. A daily fee is applied as well. Permits can be obtained from the Quinault Ranger Station or by self-issue at the trailhead. Contact the Quinault Ranger Station at the above number for information.

Maps: Green Trails: Mt. Christie, Mt. Steel, Mt. Angeles, Tyler Peak, and The Brothers

Trail location: Travel Interstate 5 to Olympia and take exit 104. Travel west on State Routes 8 and 12 to Aberdeen/Hoquiam. Drive U.S. Highway 101 North from Aberdeen/Hoquiam to beyond milepost 125. Turn right on Lake Quinault South Shore Road and travel about 13 miles to Graves Creek Road. Turn right on Graves Creek Road and drive approximately 6 miles to the road end and exit trailhead, elevation 600 feet. Leaving a bike or vehicle here, return to the Graves Creek–Lake Quinault Road junction. Turn right, crossing the Quinault River, and immediately turn right again on North Fork Quinault River Road, traveling 3+ miles to the Three Lakes/Irely Lakes Trailhead (before the road end), elevation 500 feet.

The black bear symbolizes the mystique, strength, and diversity of Olympic National Park. The black bear owns the park, foraging and traveling at will through earthy old-growth stands and alpine meadows, swimming the lakes, and splashing across streams and rivers. Sustained on a diet that ranges from salmon to glacier lilies and blueberries, the black bear is master of its environment. Feared by most, with some justification, a face-to-face meeting with a bear is never forgotten. This trek honors the black bear, for it too roams freely through stands of old growth and alpine meadows, and splashes across streams and rivers. Those trekkers who can manage the distance, the elevation gain, and the significant navigational challenges of the Black Bear Traverse master the paths of Olympic National Park.

DAY ONE   14 miles   4,700 feet gain

The goal of day one is to establish yourself high on the Skyline Trail close beneath the ridge's high point, Kimta Peak. Passing Irely Lake and ascending the narrow valley of Big Creek, switchback to Three Lakes and the start of the Skyline Trail, elevation 3,200 feet and 6.5 miles from the trailhead. Prior to reaching Three Lakes, walk the marked side trail a short distance to view the world's largest yellow cedar.

Gently ascending and contouring through the subalpine beauty of Tshletshy

Mount
Olympus

N
W   E
S

Elwha
Basin
Trail

Lake
Beauty
Trail

Mount
Seattle

Low
Divide
Trail

Elwha Ri

Elwha Tr

*Lake
Beauty*

2

Low
Divide

2

Martins
Park
Trail

Kimta
Peak

Trail

11

Quinault

River

Olympic

Quinault

National

Trail

Quinault

Park

Skyline

Elip Creek Trail

Fork

Fork

North

River

Three

Fork

Three
Lakes

Lakes

North

Quinault

Graves   Creek

Trail

T

Graves

T

Graves

Creek

North Fork Road

River

Graves Creek Road

Quinault

Wynoochee
Pass Trail

Sund
Pa
Tra

Hayden

Pass

Trail

Hayes

River

Iwha
Trail

Cameron
Pass
Trail

Mount
Fromme

Dosewallips

Gray Wolf
Pass Trail

Dosewallips

River

4

3

Thousand
Acre
Meadow

Constance
Pass Trail

Hayden
Pass

River

Trail

Mount
Anderson

West Fork Dosewallips Trail

5

Dosewallips River

West   Fork   Dosewallips   River

Honeymoon
Meadows
Camp

4

La Crosse Pass Trail

Mount
La Crosse

River   Trail

Duckabush   River

Duckabush

Duckabush

Home Sweet
Home

Mount
Steel

6

Mount
Hopper

Quinault

River

Skokomish   Trail

Mount
Hopper Trail

North

Fork

Skokomish

River

Seven   Stream

Six   Ridge

5

Ridge   Trail

North

Fork

Ix

Six   Stream

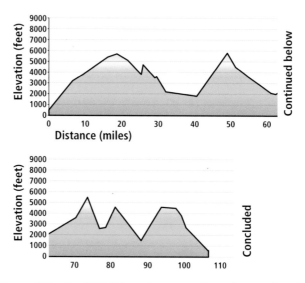

Continued below

Concluded

Ridge, pass by the Elip Creek Trail junction 9.5 miles and 3,800 feet elevation gain from the day's beginning. Starting at 500 feet elevation makes for long climbs to the mountaintops. Past the junction, the terrain transitions to alpine flora as the tread climbs toward timberline. Depending on the season, enjoy lovely flower gardens, blueberries, or blazing fall colors. Whenever you look up, admire views across the Queets Valley to Mount Olympus, up the Quinault to Low Divide, and above the divide to Seattle Peak.

Traverse on or near the spectacular ridge crest to a small alpine basin just short of Kimta Peak. This is likely to be the only place on Skyline Divide with water, so make camp here at elevation 4,500 feet. Scout for small water courses draining the slopes of the basin or descend a few hundred feet toward the valley until the primary stream channel is reached.

DAY TWO   15+ miles   4,000 feet gain

Within an hour of camp, scramble a few feet above the trail to the summit of Kimta Peak, elevation 5,400 feet. In addition to impressive views to Mount Olympus and ridge after ridge of Olympic summits, look west and spy the Pacific Ocean, sparkling with sun in the distance! From Kimta Peak, the tread descends a recently burned slope and then regains all of the just-lost elevation, reaching a glacial shelf above Promise Creek. Typical of a recovering burn, innumerable blow downs make the going slow. After reaching the unusual shelf of glacier-scoured rock and numerous lakelets, the trail becomes very sketchy. Follow bits of tread, rock cairns, and your map to navigate the rock fissures and ribs of the plateau.

The reward for navigating the plateau is attaining the ridge overlooking Lake Beauty and a trail junction leading to the lake. The scene looking over Lake Beauty, across the Queets Valley and out to Mount Olympus, is among the best in the park.

Brilliant foliage along Skyline Trail

Recommended side trip 1. If time allows, descend the 300+ feet to the lake to enjoy even more Olympic splendor. Anticipate a round trip of 1 hour, plus time for roaming or merely soaking up the scenery.

From above Lake Beauty, contour and descend to the rugged Seattle Creek Basin; then continue on to the gentle lower slopes of Mount Seattle. After crossing Seattle Creek, gain back 1,000 feet of the elevation just lost and wind through high meadows with views straight ahead to Mount Christie. Finally reaching Low Divide, turn left at the junction with the North Fork Quinault River Trail and stroll into camp.

DAY THREE   22 miles   4,500 feet gain

After the challenging two-day ridge-top traverse, day three sets the pattern for the upcoming days: a descent through a pristine old-growth valley followed by a steady climb through an alpine pass and a descent into a valley once again.

Just past Low Divide immediately descend to Lakes Margaret and Mary. Traveling in the early morning as you are, stop to admire the reflections of the surrounding scenery on the calm waters. Descending into the Elwah River Valley, enjoy impressive Martins Falls as it plummets in a roar from the slopes of Mount Christie. Upon reaching Chicago Camp and the Elwah River Trail junction, stay right and continue down valley through the beautiful old-growth forest. Recrossing

Elwah River

the Elwah on a sturdy log, wind ever farther down valley. Continuing on in splendid forest with fabulous river views past Camp Wilder and beyond, cross the Hayes River on a sturdy bridge. Immediately reaching the junction with the Hayden Pass Trail, turn right and begin the 10+-mile trek up and over Hayden Pass.

Gaining 4,200 feet elevation on this upward route, the trail contours alpine slopes high above the Hayes River Valley, with views back to now distant Mount Olympus and near views of impressive Mount Anderson. The last 4 ascending miles traverse lovely meadows across the slopes of Mount Claywood and Mount Fromme as Hayden Pass remains always out of reach below Sentinel Peak. Finally reaching the pass, transition into the enchanting walk down through Thousand Acre Meadow and continue on to Dose Meadows Camp.

DAY FOUR   18+ miles   2,200 feet gain

Day four is the only trekking day that does not involve at least one climb to a high mountain pass; instead, you will spend the entire day walking the length of two river valleys. Rest up, because day five has two climbs.

The straightforward trek down the Dosewallips River Valley is gentle and scenic. Upon passing the Gray Wolf Pass Trail junction, the views are dominated by the sheer rock walls of Mount Constance and Warrior Peak, each rising a vertical mile from the valley floor. Staying right at the Constance Pass Trail junction, soon reach the West Fork Dosewallips Trail junction. Turn right and begin ascending the gentle valley.

The West Fork Dosewallips Trail is a bridge builder's dream for the trail crosses the river no less than five times. After crossing and recrossing the river in short order, contour for miles a few hundred feet above the river. Beyond Diamond Meadows Camp, once again cross the river, now following the riverbank closely. Just below Honeymoon Meadows, a bridge once again spans the river as the lovely meadows and camp reveal themselves from the shadows of Mount Anderson and Anderson Pass.

DAY FIVE   19 miles   4,500 feet gain

Day five has the potential to be exciting, for I have seen a magnificent elk herd on both my treks over La Crosse Pass.

Upon reaching the La Crosse Pass Trail, elevation 3,600 feet, turn left. Fill up with water at your fifth and final crossing of the West Fork Dosewallips, now a small stream, as water isn't available until reaching the Duckabush Valley. Climb very directly to 4,800 feet elevation before breaking into meadows as you begin contouring the hillside up to the pass.

Keep an eye out for any sign of the elk herd that frequents the valley. Winding through the alp slopes and crossing through the rock outcroppings of the pass, immediately descend into the Duckabush Valley. Views directly across the valley to

First Ridge offer a clear look at the day's second climb. From La Crosse Pass at 5,500 feet elevation, descend to 2,600 feet in the Duckabush Valley only to climb back 2,000 feet higher to the crest of First Ridge. In between, walk along the lovely Duckabush River Trail before crossing the river on a log and turning left at the junction with the North Fork Skokomish Trail, headed for First Ridge. Climbing steeply through deep forest, reach the lovely meadows and shelter of Home Sweet Home and then switchback beyond to the top of First Ridge, the divide between the Duckabush and Skokomish Rivers.

Descend directly into the Skokomish Valley beneath Mounts Duckabush and Steel, reaching the flat lower valley at 2,000 feet elevation near Nine Stream Camp. Nine, eight, seven, six, five . . . count them, the streams are named numerically. Six Ridge then is between Seven Stream and Six Stream. Continue trekking near the North Fork Skokomish River deeper into the valley beneath Mount Cruiser and others, reaching the Six Ridge Trail junction about 3.7 miles from Nine Stream Camp. Camp in this vicinity, as the final day's trek is up Six Ridge all the way to Sundown Lake and then beyond to Graves Creek. If necessary, camp at Big Log Camp a short distance farther down the valley trail, realizing you'll have to backtrack a bit in the morning.

DAY SIX   18 miles   5,100 feet gain

Hoist your by now light backpack and greet Six Ridge Trail, which is like few others in the Olympic National Park. Cross Seven Stream on a burly old-growth log and begin the ascent. In serious need of some maintenance, the trail gains 2,000 feet elevation directly to the subalpine ridge crest. With brush periodically hanging thick over the trail, continue the gentle ascent along the ridge crest, with ever-growing views out to Lake Cushman and back across First Ridge. After traversing the ridge to alpine terrain, the thin trail leaves the crest, descending slightly and contouring the slope high above Six Stream. Upon dropping to 3,900 feet elevation along the traverse, the tread becomes thin enough that choosing the proper path becomes difficult. Ignoring game trails and paths created by confused hikers, pay attention to your map and altimeter. The proper route does not drop below 3,800 feet elevation on the traverse, and it is marked by flagging, cairns, and periodically even a trail. Follow this sketchy path and markings for 1 to 2 hours through bogs, across spongy slopes, and around the bushes crowding the route. Do not head down into Six Stream.

Upon reaching the tiny but pleasant basin of McGravey Lakes, the trail improves as the route ascends through an alpine basin toward Six Ridge Pass, now visible ahead. Traverse through the pass, elevation 4,600 feet, and continue down to Sundown Lake. Still on rough and tumble terrain with thin tread, stay right at both the Sundown Pass and Wynoochee Pass Trails and descend along Graves Creek. After fording Graves Creek near Success Camp, traverse Graves Creek Canyon on good trail at last. Drifting away from the stream as the trail nears the Quinault Valley, reach the Quinault River Trail junction, elevation 600 feet. Turn left and walk the remaining few steps to the trek's completion at the Quinault River Trailhead.

One final challenge likely remains: the 10-mile bike ride to your vehicle. Reach the South Shore Road junction. Turn right and cross the Quinault River Bridge, then immediately turn right again and pedal up the North Fork Road.

Trail Summary and Mileage Estimates

0.0	Three Lakes Trail, elevation 500 feet
6.6	Three Lakes, elevation 3,200 feet, becomes Skyline Trail
9.5	Elip Creek Trail, elevation 3,800 feet, stay left on Skyline Trail
21.6	Lake Beauty Trail, elevation 5,100 feet, stay right on Skyline Trail
29.0	North Fork Quinault Trail, elevation 3,600 feet, turn left on North Fork Trail
29.5	Low Divide, elevation 3,600 feet
32.0	Elwah Basin Trail, elevation 2,200 feet, stay right on Elwah River Trail
40.6	Hayden Pass Trail, elevation 1,800 feet, turn right on Hayden Pass Trail
51.3	Cameron Pass Trail, elevation 4,500 feet, stay right on Dosewallips River Trail
54.8	Gray Wolf Pass Trail, elevation 3,600 feet, stay right on Dosewallips River Trail
61.2	Constance Pass Trail, elevation 2,100 feet, stay right on Dosewallips River Trail
62.4	West Fork Dosewallips Trail, elevation 2,000 feet, turn right on West Fork Dosewallips Trail
70.5	La Crosse Pass Trail, elevation 3,600 feet, turn left on La Crosse Pass Trail
76.9	Duckabush River Trail, elevation 2,600 feet, turn right on Duckabush River Trail
78.6	North Fork Skokomish River Trail, elevation 2,700 feet, turn left on North Fork Skokomish Trail
88.2	Six Ridge Trail, elevation 1,500 feet, turn right on Six Ridge Trail
99.3	Sundown Pass Trail, elevation 3,800 feet, stay right on Graves Creek Trail
100.6	Wynoochee Pass Trail, elevation 2,700 feet, stay right on Graves Creek Trail
106.6	Quinault River Trail, elevation, 600 feet, turn left on Quinault River Trail
106.8	Quinault River Trailhead, elevation 600 feet

Suggested Camps Based on Different Trekking Itineraries

Night	15–20 mpd	10–15 mpd	10 mpd—not feasible
One:	14 miles - basin before Kimta Peak	14 miles - basin before Kimta Peak	
Two:	29+ miles - Low Divide Camp	27 miles - Seattle Creek Basin	
Three:	51+ miles - Dose Meadows Camp	40+ miles - Hayes River Camp	
Four:	70 miles - Honeymoon Meadows	53 miles - Bear Camp	
Five:	89 miles - Big Log Camp	67+ miles - Diamond Meadows Camp	
Six:		81 miles - Home Sweet Home	
Seven:		96 miles - McGravey Lakes	

TREK 25

The Cougar Traverse

Horseshoe Basin

Difficulty:	Toughest
Distance:	242 miles
Elevation gain:	46,500 feet
Best season:	Mid-July to mid-October
Recommended itinerary:	10 days (20–25+ miles per day)
Water availability:	Good except as specifically noted in the description
Logistics:	None
Jurisdictions:	Pasayten Wilderness, 509-996-4000. Permits are required for overnight travel in the Pasayten Wilderness. They are generally available by self-issue at trailheads.
Maps:	Green Trails: Mt. Logan, Diablo Dam, Ross Lake, Jack Mountain, Pasayten Peak, Billy Goat Mountain, Coleman Peak, and Horseshoe Basin

Trail location: Drive Interstate 5 to Burlington and take exit 230. Turn east and follow State Route 20 until past milepost 141. Turn left into the Canyon Creek parking area and trailhead, elevation 1,900 feet.

The Cougar Traverse is as elegant and challenging as it is simple. Strike deep into the heart of Washington's wilderness core, stretching to the very east edge of the Pasayten Wilderness, and then slingshot back across the wilderness to the heart of the North Cascades. To my knowledge, the Cougar Traverse offers the longest uninterrupted wilderness trek in the Lower 48. For nearly 250 miles you will not once touch a road, brush civilization, or walk the same trail segment twice. This trek is presented last because it is like no other. The cougar owns the Pasayten Wilderness, capable of roaming 30 miles per day with little food or water. The big cat has no natural predators (barring humans), because no animal is as quick, powerful, and adept at navigating mountainous terrain. Like the cougar, trekkers traversing this area will be extremely fit, have wilderness savvy, and be able to match any of nature's challenges.

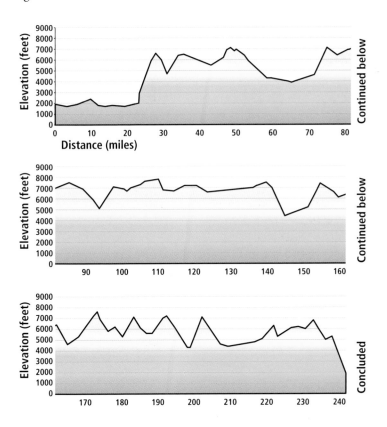

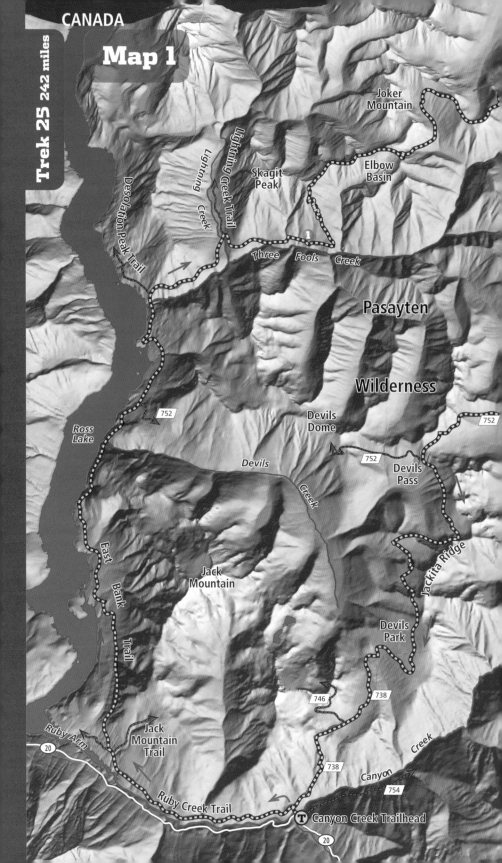

CANADA

Map 1

Joker Mountain

Elbow Basin

Skagit Peak

Lightning Creek Trail

Lightning Creek

Desolation Peak Trail

Three Fools Creek

Pasayten

Wilderness

752

Devils Dome

Ross Lake

Devils Creek

752

752

Devils Pass

East Bank Trail

Jack Mountain

Jackita Ridge

Devils Park

746   738

Jack Mountain Trail

Ruby Arm

20

738   Canyon Creek

754

Ruby Creek Trail

T Canyon Creek Trailhead

20

Bunker
Hill

533

533

533

456

461

454

533

477

477

533

533

3

Hopkins
Pass

2

533

478

485

478

498

472

473

Rock   Creek

Woody
Pass

East
Fork
Pasayten
River

Tatoosh
Buttes

8

477

River

Pasayten

West   Fork   Pasayten   River

Buckskin Ridge

Middle Fork Pasayten River

2000

Holman
Pass

472A

9

2000

Sky Pilot
Pass

472

754

N

W   E

S

Trek 25 overview

Map 1

Map 2

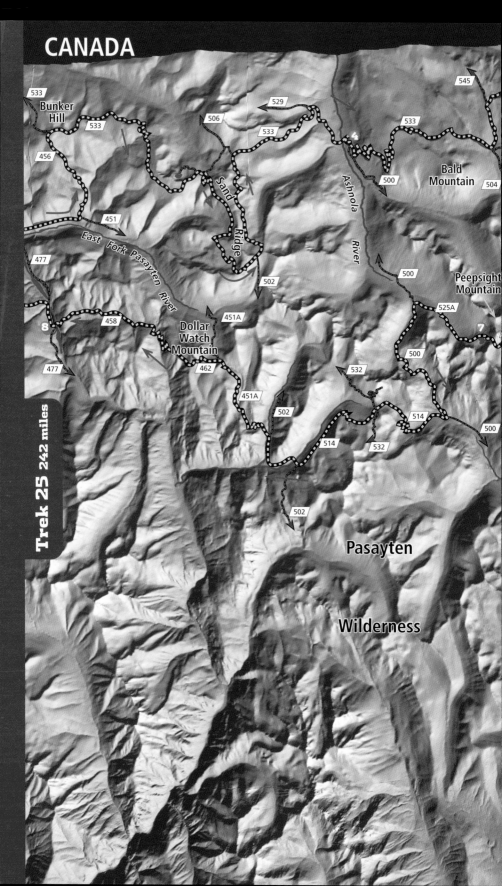

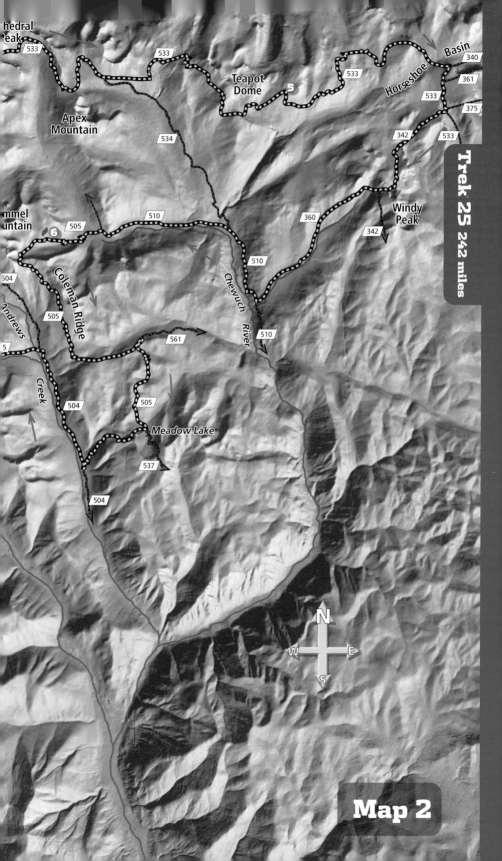

hedral
eak
533

533

Apex
Mountain

534

Teapot
Dome

5

533

Horseshoe

Basin

340

361

533

375

342

533

mmel
untain

6
505

510

505

360

342

Windy
Peak

342

Coleman Ridge

504

Andrews

505

510

510

Chewuch River

5

Creek

504

561

505

504

Meadow Lake

537

504

N

W   E

S

Map 2

DAY ONE 27 miles 2,700 feet gain

The goal of day one is to immerse yourself in the wild lands of the Pasayten. No one knows with certainty where the name *Pasayten* originated. Native American lore suggests a meaning of "water flowing from gentle mountains." At the close of day, find yourself camped along a stream flowing from the gentle mountains.

Begin at Canyon Creek, crossing Granite Creek on a footbridge and Canyon Creek via a foot log, both within 0.25 mile of the trailhead. Immediately upon crossing Canyon Creek, turn left and descend along the roiling waters of the combined stream flows, now called Ruby Creek. Follow Ruby Creek for about 6 miles as it transitions from rampaging white water to fjordlike Ruby Arm, compliments of Ross Dam and the resulting unnatural but beautiful Ross Lake. At the junction with the Ruby Pasture and Jack Mountain Trails, the East Bank Trail turns right and begins the gentle 600-foot climb through Hidden Hand Pass before gently descending and reaching the shores of Ross Lake after 12 miles.

On or near the lakeshore, enjoy the splendid views across the lake in all directions as you trek toward the Lightning Creek Trail far up the lake. After more than 19 miles of gentle travel with little more than ups and downs to surmount, reach Lightning Creek and the trail junction just beyond. Turn right on the Lightning Creek Trail and face the first of countless stern climbs. Climb sharply above the lake 800 feet, achieving commanding regional views before contouring with ups and downs the steep cliffs above Lightning Creek. After 4 miles, cross Lightning Creek on a sturdy bridge and turn right on the Three Fools Trail #749. Climb and descend in a twisting contour of the terrain above Three Fools Creek, entering the Pasayten Wilderness and then finding a lovely camp along the creek itself before the trail leaves the stream and climbs to the sky above.

DAY TWO 19+ miles 7,600 feet gain

Don't let the distance fool you, the shortest trekking day also enjoys 50 percent more elevation gain than any other day. You will climb and descend, again and again. Once you leave Three Fools Creek, there is no on-trail water for approximately 7 miles and more than 4,000 feet elevation gain. Carry 2 to 3 quarts of fluid to start and figure on getting thirsty. Start early, if you can.

The part of the word *Pasayten* that suggests "gentle mountains" does not apply to this day. Immediately ascend the lung-searing switchbacks up Skagit Peak, reaching 6,000 feet elevation before the switchbacks relent, replaced by an ascending contour of the very steep mountainous slopes. After humping your load to more than 6,600 feet, regain your perspective while traversing the flowery green brilliance of Elbow Basin. When not staring at the lupine and Indian paintbrush near your feet, the sharp Hozomeen Spires transfix your gaze to the north while the glacier-clad shoulders of Jack Mountain rise powerfully to the south. To traverse Elbow Basin is to begin to understand the magnificence of the Pasayten.

Trekking in Elbow Basin

After crossing the Elbow Basin–Big Face Creek Divide, descend alp slopes sharply toward the forest below. Find good tread in the forest before traversing the sketchy tread into the very waters of Big Face Creek, the crossing a foot-soaking dance. Test your legs by climbing nearly 2,000 feet across Big Face Basin, with dominating views to Jack Mountain and the very crest of the Cascades stretching toward Mexico. Only the inspiring views of Castle Peak, Mount Winthrop, and the meadows at your feet will enable you to survive the debilitating ups and downs on and around the flower-strewn ridge crest leading to Castle Pass.

At Castle Pass, turn right on the Pacific Crest Trail #2000 and walk the gentle but ascending trail 3+ miles to Hopkins Pass. Leave the main trail and find a delightful camp near alpine Hopkins Lake. Soak your feet or take a swim and rebuild your resolve, for every day will feel like this one.

DAY THREE   23+ miles   2,500 feet gain

This is a recovery day, the only remaining trekking day that you don't gain at least 4,000 or 5,000 feet elevation. Fill up on water, regaining the trail near Hopkins Pass, then surmount your only challenging ascent, the climb of Devils Stairway and on to Lakeview Ridge. For nearly 6 miles enjoy the high meadow traverse with expansive views west 50 miles to Mount Baker and to the east toward Cathedral

Peak. Cross through Woody Pass and a short distance beyond leave the PCT, turning left on the Rock Creek Trail #473. The hard work done, descend with ups and downs 6 miles to the Pasayten River Trail #478. Turn left and in a short distance pass a Forest Service patrol cabin and then walk along a bizarre Pasayten feature: the "airport." The grass landing strip was created in the 1930s by the Civilian Conservation Corps before this area was designated as a wilderness. Unused for years, the strip is slowly being reclaimed by nature as pine trees sprout amongst the blades of grass.

Past the airport, join the Boundary Trail #533 where it descends near Soda Creek. Continue along the Pasayten River nearly 6 miles before turning right on the Boundary Trail and immediately crossing both the main and east forks of the river. Upon reaching the Hidden Lakes Trail #477, turn right and walk closely along the East Fork Pasayten River nearly 4 miles before finding a delightful camp at the junction of the Hidden Lakes and East Fork Pasayten River Trails.

DAY FOUR   24+ miles   5,500 feet gain

Today's trekking starts low by Pasayten standards, at 4,400 feet elevation. Once timberline is gained, revel in alpine beauty and adventure for nearly 20 miles. Follow the East Fork Pasayten River Trail 2 miles until reaching the Dean Creek Trail #456. Turn left and climb to far above timberline near the summit of Bunker Hill at 7,200 feet elevation. Be sure to fill up with water at the stream crossing near 5,600 feet elevation, for there are few sure water sources along this high-country ramble. Near Bunker Hill, turn right on the Boundary Trail #533 and descend several hundred feet before gaining it all back along the scrambling contour of Quartz Mountain.

Passing the Quartz Lake Trail junction, turn right within a short distance on the Whistler Basin Trail. For 8 miles admire magnificent flower meadows and expansive views as the route circumnavigates Sand Ridge. With continual ups and downs, dipping only occasionally below 7,000 feet, the thin tread traverses Whistler Basin before climbing through Whistler Pass and crossing over to McCall Gulch. White-tailed deer and mountain goats abound in the lush, steep meadow terrain and on rocky ridge crests. Cougar, too, if you are lucky enough to see one. The 360-degree views are only of wilderness, valleys of pine forests, ridge after graceful ridge adorned with sharp spires, and in the distance massive glaciers. Joining the Larch Creek Trail #502 above McCall Gulch, continue north amidst the splendor, rejoining the Boundary Trail near Peeve Pass. Still near 7,000 feet elevation, continue the traverse with views into the Ashnola River Valley and across Bald Mountain to stunning Cathedral Peak, getting closer with every step. Nearing the end of an exhausting but unforgettable day, drop abruptly to the boiling rapids of the Ashnola, crossing the river on a foot log before reaching the comfortable camp and lean-to shelter along the boulder-strewn shore.

DAY FIVE   24+ miles   4,500 feet gain

For days you have glimpsed the magnificent rock spire of Cathedral Peak, without question the dominant peak in the eastern Pasayten Wilderness. Today you will touch the appealing granite and continue past, heading for the very eastern edge of Washington's wilderness. Pack your gear and climb the gentle tread that in 4 long miles finally gains the 2,000 feet elevation necessary to cross the divide below Bald Mountain. Indeed, the mountain is bald; expansive gentle meadows and open rocky slopes offer continual panoramas and hours of exploring for the less schedule-challenged wilderness hikers.

Cresting the ridge, traverse gently downward to the confluence of several trails at expansive Spanish Camp, which offers a trekkers' camp, horse camp, and even a Forest Service cabin. Just after the stream crossing, turn left and continue on the Boundary Trail #533, heading first to lower Cathedral Lake then on to stunning upper Cathedral Lake. Just beneath Cathedral Peak, the upper lake offers dramatic views of both Cathedral and Amphitheater Mountain from its larch-speckled, granitic perch. Leaving the lake, scramble solid granite to the 7,600-foot pass, higher than many Cascade peaks and literally on the ridge of Cathedral Peak. Walk astounded beneath the even more spectacular south face of Cathedral, these very towers and graceful columns of golden granite providing the inspiration for naming the peak. The 6-mile traverse across rock gardens to Apex Pass and across the slopes of Wolframite Peak and upper Tungsten Creek offer easy trekking and vast wilderness views across the international border, which at some points is less than 1 mile away.

Before leaving the Tungsten Creek area, with its mining relics and maintained outbuildings, fill up with water, because from this point east to Horseshoe Basin, water is at a premium as the trail traverses ridge tops and slopes far above the established water courses. After traversing through Scheelite Pass, ascend the open slopes across Bauerman Ridge, with impressive views east to Windy Peak, the easternmost prominent summit in the Pasayten Wilderness. Descend slightly and find camp in one of the lightly watered basins beneath Teapot Dome, ever watchful for the conspicuous white fur of a mountain goat on the granite monoliths above.

DAY SIX   25+ miles   4,200 feet gain

Continue the high-country ramble paralleling the international border, enjoying the broad meadows and gentle peaks of Horseshoe Basin before nearly touching the top of Windy Peak and turning west toward the main range of the Cascades. Once past tiny but picturesque Louden Lake, continue by the Long Draw and Smith Lake Trails before reaching Horseshoe Creek, the first significant water source since Tungsten Creek. Once again carry your fill of water, as the route remains dry for about 8 miles until reaching Basin Creek.

At Sunny Pass beneath Pick Peak, leave the Boundary Trail in favor of the path leading toward Windy Peak. Contour and descend along the very edge of Horseshoe

Basin before climbing 1,000 feet to a trail junction just below Windy Peak.

Recommended side trip 1: If time and energy allow, drop your pack and scramble up 900 feet in 0.5 mile to the 8,334-foot summit of Windy Peak to revel in views of all you have accomplished and survey the challenges yet to come. Figure on a round trip of 90 minutes.

To continue, turn right on Basin Creek Trail #360 and contour the rocky slopes of Topaz Mountain near 7,500 feet elevation before gaining the forested ridge top beyond and finally descending into Basin Creek. The Basin Creek Trail is only adequately maintained, but readily followable. When my wife, Kristy, and I descended this path in 2002, the trail was marked as "closed" due to hazardous conditions caused by the disastrous Thirtymile Creek Fire in 2001. However, the fire did not reach within 3 miles of Basin Creek, so we chose to walk the path as did other trekkers we encountered along the way.

Upon reaching the Chewuch River Trail #510, turn right and continue up valley on the broad path for more than 6 miles, passing the Tungsten Creek Trail, until you reach the Coleman Ridge Trail #505. Turn left on the Coleman Ridge Trail and ascend 1,500 feet before reaching the outlet stream and rudimentary trail junction of Four Point Lake. Turn right and within a few minutes find a camp near 6,800 feet elevation along the rocky open shoreline of Four Point Lake.

DAY SEVEN 20 miles 5,500 feet gain

Today you will witness much beauty and face many challenges, including some of the sparsest tread on the entire route. Regain the Coleman Ridge Trail upon leaving Four Point Lake and climb the rocky open slopes high on the shoulder of Remmel Mountain, crossing over a lovely waterfall en route to Coleman Ridge proper. Ascend and traverse on good trail across steep terrain until reaching a larch-dotted ridge, elevation 7,400 feet. Descend and then traverse the open basin ahead on sketchy tread, keeping a lookout for rock cairns or bits of path that mark the way. In all other respects, the going is very easy on the route. Ultimately, regain good tread and traverse along the slopes of Coleman Ridge near 7,200 feet elevation, with expansive views over Andrews Creek and out to the eastern Washington highlands beyond.

Transition into the headwaters of Fire Creek, reaching a trail junction near 6,100 feet elevation that leads to Meadow Lake. Turn right and trek through meadows and scrub forest to the marshy flat of Meadow Lake. With the profusion of trails in this area—the result of cattle grazing in past decades—it is easy to select paths to nowhere. Don't be tempted to turn toward Meadow Lake too soon, even if there is a marked junction of sorts near 6,600 feet. From Meadow Lake, continue on good trail to a switchbacking descent into Andrews Creek.

Upon reaching the gentle Andrews Creek Trail #504, turn right and trek up valley to the Peepsight Lake Trail junction, elevation 5,300 feet. Turn left, descending briefly to a log crossing of Andrews Creek before steadily gaining 2,000 feet elevation over 4 miles in the Peepsight Creek Valley. At 7,200 feet elevation reach the trail junction with Rock Lake. Stay left and pick your way on sparse tread through a meadow basin beneath Peepsight Mountain, intending to cross through Peepsight Pass, at 7,600 feet elevation the low point in the ridge extending south from Peepsight Mountain. If you lose the trail, it might be because you trended too far right, directly beneath the mountain. Eyeball the ridge above and likely climb up and left, heading toward the low point in the ridge. A route that follows the path of least resistance should lead you to good tread heading up and over the pass, then down to a pretty camp near Peepsight Lake.

DAY EIGHT   24+ miles   4,300 feet gain

Pay careful attention when leaving Peepsight Lake, for the aged unmaintained tread leading down the Ashnola River is easy to lose. A hundred feet below Peepsight Lake is a lovely flat meadow with a stream flowing through it. From the far right (north) edge of this meadow, pick your way down valley. Regardless of what your

Peepsight Lake

map indicates, the tread crosses the Ashnola River (a small stream here) at about 6,500 feet elevation. The sketchy trail then largely parallels the river down the boggy valley for 2 miles, never recrossing the river, and providing a manageable route downward.

After crossing through an old burn with countless blow downs, reach the Lake Creek Trail #500 junction adjacent to Spotted Creek. Turn left and on much better trail climb gently past quiet Fawn Lake, over Ashnola Pass, and down into the Lake Creek drainage. Turn right on the Diamond Jack Trail #514 and climb steadily into the open basin and then high pass at 7,100 feet elevation beneath Diamond Point. Descend Diamond Creek 3.5 miles to the junction with Larch Creek Trail. Turn right and follow the Larch Creek Trail #502 for 1.5 miles until veering left on the Tony Creek Trail. Finally, cross Larch Creek and then climb 1,500 feet along Tony Creek to the lovely meadow terrain of Dollar Watch Pass. Turn left on the Middle Mountain Trail #462 and in a short mile reach the junction with Dollar Watch Mountain Trail.

Recommended side trip 2: Take a deep breath, drop your pack, and scramble the 500 feet over 0.5 mile to the top of Dollar Watch Mountain, an outstanding viewpoint over the Pasayten Wilderness. Survey the terrain all around, much of which you've traversed over the past several days, or will yet travel. Figure on a round trip of 1 hour.

Back at your pack, descend near the ridge of Dollar Watch before traversing through Deception Pass and down along Stub Creek to the Forest Service outpost and lovely camp in deep forest near Middle Hidden Lake.

DAY NINE   22+ miles   4,900 feet gain

From Middle Hidden Lake, trek north a short mile to the Tatoosh Buttes Trail #485 junction, just before Big Hidden Lake. Turn left and climb 3,000 feet over 4 miles to the wondrous meadows and expansive views along Tatoosh Ridge. Scramble a short distance to the crest, looking down on the Pasayten River confluence and out again over the vast wilderness—for to stand here you must trek more than 20 miles by the shortest route. Descend the gentle ridge crest for 3 miles before dropping more sharply through forest to the flat and broad Pasayten River Valley.

Upon reaching the valley trail junction, turn right and within a short distance cross the Middle Fork Pasayten River on a sturdy bridge. After climbing sharply up and out of the river crossing, immediately cross a bridge over the West Fork Pasayten River, and reach the trail junction with the West Fork Pasayten River Trail #472. Turn left and begin the gentle ascent up the West Fork Pasayten River Valley. The trail does not stay close to the river for 4 miles, until after crossing Kid Creek. Beyond, the trail more closely follows the river until reaching the Holman Creek Trail junction. In total, 400 feet elevation, plus ups and downs, is all that is gained along the 7-mile route up the West Fork Pasayten River Valley. Turn right and continue

Tungsten mine ruins near Tungsten Creek

the meandering ascent to forested Holman Pass, elevation 5,100 feet, and a reunion with the PCT.

Instead of traveling the PCT, continue through Holman Pass on the Devils Ridge Trail #752, your ticket back to civilization. Beyond the crossing of Canyon Creek, ascend sharply 700 feet and find camp in the watered basin beneath Shull Mountain.

DAY TEN 21+ miles 4,800 feet gain

Congratulations! Today you will complete a trek that few are able to even imagine. The Pasayten will not let you go easily, for while the day is spent largely traversing beautiful alpine ridges, basins, and passes, the elevation gain nearly reaches a vertical mile. From beneath Shull Mountain, traverse easily the long mile to Sky Pilot Pass, a terrific spot in which to roam or camp except for the absence of water. Descend into the boggy forest near Deception Pass, your second Deception Pass of the trek, only to contour back above timberline on the delightful traverse of parklands with views back to the Cascade Crest and ahead to Devils Pass.

Upon reaching Devils Pass, elevation 6,100 feet, turn left on the Jackita Ridge Trail #738 and continue the beautiful traverse of alp slopes, the view now dominated by 9,000-foot-high Jack Mountain rising dramatically across the Devils Creek Valley. Descend into the forested headwaters of the North Fork of Devils Creek before climbing 900 feet to regain alpine terrain beneath Jackita Ridge. Traverse rugged terrain in and out of lovely basins for 2 miles before climbing several hundred feet up steep scree switchbacks to 6,800 feet elevation and the beginning of magnificent Devils Park.

The work nearly done, gently traverse and descend the flower-strewn meadows, with views deep into the heart of the North Cascades. Past Devils Park Shelter the tread dips into and out of Nickel Creek, climbing 300 feet through subalpine McMillan Park and its abundant blueberries in season. Stay left at the Crater Mountain Trail junction and begin the descent for home! In 4 miles, the abrupt descent ends back at vaguely familiar Canyon Creek where your trek began so long ago. Cross the same foot log and bridge as you did ten days prior, to complete the longest wilderness trek in the Lower 48!

Trail Summary and Mileage Estimates

0.0	Canyon Creek Trailhead #754, elevation 1,900 feet
0.2	Jackita Ridge Trail #738, elevation 1,900 feet, stay left on Trail #738
0.3	Ruby Creek Trail, elevation 1,900 feet, turn left on Ruby Creek Trail
3.3	East Bank Trail, elevation 1,700 feet, continue on East Bank Trail
6.1	Ruby Pasture/Jack Mountain Trails, elevation 1,900 feet, turn right on East Bank Trail
15.7	Devils Dome Trail, elevation 1,800 feet, continue on East Bank Trail
19.3	Lightning Creek Trail, elevation 1,700 feet, turn right on Lightning Creek Trail
23.1	Three Fools Trail #749, elevation 2,000 feet, turn right on Trail #749
43.0	PCT #2000, elevation 5,500 feet, turn right on PCT
43.2	Boundary Trail #533, elevation 5,500 feet, continue on PCT
52.3	Rock Creek Trail #473, elevation 6,400 feet, turn left on Trail #473
58.4	Pasayten River Trail #478, elevation 4,300 feet, turn left on Trail #478
59.6	Boundary Trail #533, elevation 4,300 feet, stay right on Trail #533
64.2	Harrison Creek Trail #454, elevation 4,000 feet, stay right on Trail #533
65.2	Border Trail #461, elevation 3,900 feet, stay right on Trail #533
65.9	Hidden Lakes Trail #477, elevation 4,000 feet, turn right on Trail #477
69.6	East Fork Pasayten River Trail #451, elevation 4,400 feet, turn left on Trail #451
71.4	Dean Creek Trail #456, elevation 4,600 feet, turn left on Trail #456
74.9	Boundary Trail #533, elevation 7,100 feet, turn right on Trail #533
80.7	Quartz Lake Trail, elevation 6,900 feet, stay right on Trail #533
81.0	Whistler Pass Trail, elevation 6,900 feet, turn right on Whistler Pass Trail
85.5	Larch Creek Trail #502, elevation 7,500 feet, turn left on Trail #502
89.2	Boundary Trail #533, elevation 6,900 feet, turn right on Trail #533
92.1	Sheep Mountain Trail #529, elevation 5,900 feet, stay right on Trail #533
93.8	Lake Creek Trail #500, elevation 5,100 feet, stay left on Trail #533
101.4	Andrews Creek Trail #504, elevation 6,700 feet, stay left on Trail #533
102.5	Beaver Creek Trail #545, elevation 7,000 feet, stay right on Trail #533
105.2	Lesamiz Trail #565, elevation 7,300 feet, stay left on Trail #533

111.4	Tungsten Creek Trail #534, elevation 6,800 feet, stay left on Trail #533
136.0	Long Draw Trail #340, elevation 7,000 feet, stay right on Trail #533
136.2	Smith Lake Trail #361, elevation 7,000 feet, stay right on Trail #533
137.2	Albert Camp Trail #375, elevation 7,200 feet, stay right on Trail #533
137.3	Windy Creek Trail #342, elevation 7,200 feet, turn right on Trail #342
139.8	Basin Creek Trail #360, elevation 7,500 feet, turn right on Trail #360
144.9	Chewuch River Trail #510, elevation 4,400 feet, turn right on Trail #510
147.2	Tungsten Creek Trail #534, elevation 4,700 feet, stay left on Trail #510
151.2	Coleman Ridge Trail #505, elevation 5,200 feet, turn left on Trail #505
159.7	Fire Creek Trail #561, elevation 6,100 feet, turn right on Trail #505
165.2	Andrews Creek Trail #504, elevation 4,600 feet, turn right on Trail #504
168.2	Peepsight Creek Trail #525, elevation 5,300 feet, turn left on Trail #525
172.3	Spotted Creek Trail #525A, elevation 7,200 feet, turn left on Trail #525A
176.3	Lake Creek Trail #500, elevation 5,800 feet, turn left on Trail #500
180.3	Diamond Jack Trail #514, elevation 5,300 feet, turn right on Trail #514
187.0	Larch Creek Trail #502, elevation 5,600 feet, turn right on Trail #502
188.5	Tony Creek Trail #451A, elevation 5,600 feet, turn left on Trail #451A
191.6	Middle Mountain Trail #462, elevation 7,000 feet, turn left on Trail #462
198.3	Hidden Lake Trail #477, elevation 4,300 feet, turn right on Trail #477
199.1	Tatoosh Buttes Trail #485, elevation 4,300 feet, turn left on Trail #485
209.3	Pasayten River Trail #478, elevation 4,400 feet, turn right on Trail #478
209.7	Buckskin Ridge Trail #498, elevation 4,400 feet, stay right on Trail #478
209.8	West Fork Pasayten River Trail #472, elevation 4,400 feet, turn left on Trail #472
216.8	Holman Creek Trail #472A, elevation 4,800 feet, turn right on Trail #472A
218.8	PCT/Devils Ridge Trails, elevation 5,100 feet, continue on Devils Ridge Trail #752
222.0	Chancellor Trail #754, elevation 6,300 feet, stay right on Trail #752
226.8	Jackita Ridge Trail #738, elevation 6,100 feet, turn left on Trail #738
238.1	Crater Mountain Trail #746, elevation 5,300 feet, stay left on Trail #738
242.0	Canyon Creek Trailhead, elevation 1,900 feet

Suggested Camps

Night

One:	near Three Fools Creek
Two:	Hopkins Lake
Three:	East Fork Pasayten River
Four:	Ashnola River
Five:	beneath Teapot Dome
Six:	Four Point Lake
Seven:	Peepsight Lake
Eight:	Middle Hidden Lake
Nine:	beneath Shull Mountain

Sunrise over Cascade River from Sahale Arm (Trek 6)

Appendix A:
Gear and Meal Planning

Sample Packing List

Here's what I consider to be a sensible minimum of gear and clothing necessary for treks lasting a few days. Items with an asterisk (*) are part of the Mountaineers Ten Essentials: A Systems Approach, a list of minimum safety gear.

Gear

Tent*: bivy bag (1 pound), solo tent (2 pounds), two-person tent (4 pounds), or three-person tent (7 pounds)

Stove (I prefer white or multigas stoves as compared to disposable cartridges)

Cooking pot

Bowl, mug (large plastic with lid), spoon, fork

Sleeping pad: full-length, closed-cell foam

Sleeping pad: half-length, ultralight inflatable pad

Sleeping bag: down, 30-degree bag (2+ pounds)

Small flashlight or miniheadlamp*

Miscellaneous gear: multifunction knife or tool, waterproof/windproof matches*, lighter*, and sunglasses*

Personal gear: toilet paper, comb, toothbrush/paste, sun cream, lip balm, and biodegradable soap

First aid*: Band-Aids, mole foam, gauze pads, alcohol swabs, blister kit, tape/ace bandage, and ibuprofen

Water containers: 2- or 3-quart bottles or a 3- to 4-quart bladder-type bag

Water bag (I carry an 8-quart plastic/nylon water bag for convenience at camp)

Water filter

Repair kit*: heavy needle/thread, duct tape, wire, cord, extra flashlight batteries/bulb, and safety pins

Map* (carry in a plastic bag)

Altimeter

Compass*

Camera/film

Hiking shoes/boots: low-top or above-ankle, lightweight, with a little
wiggle room

Clothing (including extra clothing for safety*)

Stocking cap

Sun cap/visor

Lightweight polypropylene gloves

Mid-weight gloves

Lightweight hiking socks (1 extra pair)

Lightweight hiking pants (nylon, short convertible)

Short-sleeved nylon active-wear shirt (1 extra)

Long-sleeved nylon active-wear shirt

Long-sleeved insulating shirt/sweater

Lightweight down or synthetic fiber jacket

Lightweight Gore-Tex or equivalent pants

Lightweight Gore-Tex or equivalent jacket

Undies (1 extra)

Shammy towel

Sample trekking menu

For general planning purposes, anticipate carrying and consuming 24 to 32 ounces of food per day, divided into three meals, plus morning and afternoon snacks. Your goal is to come up with a diet equal to about 2,500 to 3,000 calories per day. The Mountaineers also suggest carrying extra food and extra water as part of their Ten Essentials list. A day's worth of trekking meals would look something like the following:

Breakfast

One bowl oatmeal (two packets)

Gourmet raspberry hot chocolate (one-and-a-half packets)

One coffee single (completes the backcountry mocha)

Morning snacks (eaten at hourly breaks over course of morning)

One-quart sport drink (carry powdered form)

Energy/nutrition bars (one or two)

Dry roasted peanuts and/or trail mix

Dried fruit

Lyman Lake and Chiwawa Mountain (Trek 10)

Lunch

One-quart sport drink

Crackers

Cheese (3 ounces or so)

Dried fruit

Afternoon snacks (eaten at hourly breaks over course of afternoon)

One-quart sport drink

Energy/nutrition bars (one or two)

Dry roasted peanuts and/or trail mix

Dried fruit

Dinner

Macaroni and cheese or pasta with a tasty powdered sauce; supplement
    with fresh peppers on first day or two or with little cans of specialty
    goodies

Hot chocolate (one-and-a-half packets)

Any snacks left over from the day of trekking

Sunset above Park Creek Pass (Trek 6)

Appendix B: Agency Contacts

There are numerous ways to glean information and insights regarding the managed lands, trails, and experiences you are about to embark upon. The following is a list of a few places to start. Realize, however, that websites, phone numbers, addresses, regulations, roads, and sometime even trailheads can change. In my earliest days of trekking I always felt that getting the necessary permits and finding my way to the trailhead was the hardest part. That never changes. Good trekking to you.

National Parks
Mount Rainier National Park
www.nps.gov/mora

Mount Rainier National Park Headquarters
Tahoma Woods, Star Route
Ashford, WA 98304
360-569-2221

Longmire Ranger Station
Located at Longmire within the national park
360-569-2211, extension 3305

Longmire Hiker Information Center
Located at Longmire within the national park
360-569-HIKE

North Cascades National Park Complex
(including Lake Chelan and Ross Lake National Recreation Areas)
www.nps.gov/noca

North Cascades National Park Headquarters
810 State Route 20
Sedro-Woolley, WA 98284
360-856-5700

Wilderness Information Center
7280 Ranger Station Road
Marblemount, WA 98267
360-873-4500, extension 39

Glacier Ranger Station (Forest Service)
1094 Mount Baker Highway
Glacier, WA 98244
360-599-2714

Purple Point Information Center
Stehekin, WA 98852
360-856-5700, extension 340, then 14

Olympic National Park
www.nps.gov/olym

Olympic National Park Wilderness Information Center
600 East Park Avenue
Port Angeles, WA 98362
360-565-3100

Olympic National Park Visitor Center
600 East Park Avenue
Port Angeles, WA 98362
360-565-3130

Hoh Rain Forest Ranger Station/Visitor Center
18113 Upper Hoh Road
Forks, WA 98331
360-374-6925

Quinault Ranger Station
913 North Shore Road
Amanda Park, WA 98526
360-288-2444

There are several other Olympic National Park ranger stations, including summer-only or intermittent ranger stations at on-route locations, including Graves Creek, North Fork Quinault River, Deer Park, and Heart O' the Hills.

National Monuments
Mount St. Helens National Monument
www.fs.fed.us/gpnf/mshnvm

Mount St. Helens Visitor Center
3029 Spirit Lake Highway (State Route 504)
Castle Rock, WA 98611
360-274-2100

Wilderness Areas
Alpine Lakes Wilderness
www.fs.fed.us/r6/wenatchee
www.fs.fed.us/r6/mbs

Wenatchee National Forest
Leavenworth Ranger Station
600 Sherbourne Street
Leavenworth, WA 98826
509-548-6977

Mount Baker–Snoqualmie National Forest
North Bend Ranger Station
42404 SE North Bend Way
North Bend, WA 98045
425-888-1421

Mount Baker–Snoqualmie National Forest
Skykomish Ranger Station
74920 NE Stevens Pass Highway
Skykomish, WA 98288
360-677-2414

Glacier Peak Wilderness
www.fs.fed.us/r6/mbs

Mount Baker–Snoqualmie National Forest
Darrington Ranger Station
1405 Emmens Street
Darrington, WA 98241
360-436-1155

Goat Rocks Wilderness
www.fs.fed.us/r6/gpnf/wilderness

Gifford Pinchot National Forest
Cowlitz Valley Ranger District
10024 U.S. Highway 12
Randle, WA 98377
360-497-1100

Lake Chelan-Sawtooth Wilderness
www.fs.fed.us/r6/wenatchee/recreate/wilderns.html#sawtooth

Okanogan National Forest
Twisp Ranger Station
502 Glover Street
Twisp, WA 98856
509-997-2131

Okanogan National Forest
Winthrop Visitor Center
Building 49, State Route 20
24 East Chewuch Road
Winthrop, WA 98862
509-996-4000

Mount Adams Wilderness

www.fs.fed.us/r6/gpnf/wilderness

Gifford Pinchot National Forest
Mount Adams Ranger Station
2455 State Route 141
Trout Lake, WA 98650
509-395-3400

Gifford Pinchot National Forest
Cowlitz Valley Ranger District
10024 U.S. Highway 12
Randle, WA 98377
360-497-1100

Pasayten Wilderness

www.fs.fed.us/r6/oka

Okanogan National Forest
Winthrop Visitor Center
Building 49, State Route 20
24 East Chewuch Road
Winthrop, WA 98862
509-996-4000

Okanogan National Forest
Tonasket Ranger Station
1 West Winesap
Tonasket, WA 98855
509-486-2186

Appendix C:
Trek Summaries

Trek	Difficulty	Scenery	Solitude	Days	Miles	Elevation gain
#1	Most strenuous	5	4	8–10	141	27,000
#2	Strenuous	4	3	4–7	70	13,100
#3	Strenuous	4	5	3–6	48	12,600
#4	Easier	4	3	2–4	43	9,200
#5	Easier	5	3	3–5	52	12,000
#6	Strenuous	5	3	4–6	55	13,500
#7	Most strenuous	5	4	7–10	124	24,500
#8	Easier	4	2	3–5	43	9,900
#9	Very strenuous	5	3	6–10	86	20,400
#10	Easier	5	2	4–7	47	11,000
#11	Most strenuous	5	5	6–9	91	18,900
#12	Strenuous	5	3	3–5	46	12,600
#13	Very strenuous	5	4	3–5	45	13,500
#14	Strenuous	4	3	4–8	71	16,000
#15	Easier	4	3	2–4	39	8,800
#16	Easier	5	2	2–5	30	9,900
#17	Most strenuous	5	2	5–9	90	25,500
#18	Easier	4	3	2–3	32	6,300
#19	Very strenuous	4	3	2–3	35	8,000
#20	Strenuous	5	3	2–3	30	8,500
#21	Strenuous	5	3	4–7	60	10,100
#22	Easier	5	2	4–7	74	16,600
#23	Strenuous	5	3	2–5	46	12,600
#24	Most strenuous	5	5	6–8	107	25,000
#25	Toughest	5	5	10	242	46,500

Mount Olympus

Scenery. Scale of 1–5 with 5 being the most beautiful. All of the treks in *Trekking Washington* offer an overabundance of scenery. Therefore the differentiation is between the amazingly beautiful and the sublime.

Solitude. Scale of 1–5 with 5 offering the most solitude. All of the treks offer high-quality experiences that will not be negatively affected by crowds of any sort. No treks are rated as 1, meaning you will never be part of a stream of people trekking along a path. The 2 rating means you should expect to encounter people on either a sporadic basis over the trek or at key gathering points along the route. Ratings of 3–4 mean you will encounter progressively fewer people, likely a handful per day at most. The 5 rating means you can expect to travel a day or more at a time without encountering people. Outside the peak hiking weeks of mid-July through August, and on weekdays, there will be far fewer people utilizing trails and off-trail routes. Treks rated as 3 due to use during the peak hiking weeks would likely become a 5 in September.

Length in days. The trek length in days represents the shortest and longest recommended trek length for which camps and itineraries are provided as part of each trek description. Of course it is possible to do the treks in more or fewer days than described.

Climbers on Mount St. Helens (Trek 18)

Index

About the Author

Mike Woodmansee has hiked and climbed throughout Washington for 30 years. Born and reared in the Skagit Valley, home to the North Cascades National Park and Glacier Peak Wilderness, Mike was lured by the mountains when he was a teenager. Since then he has been a ceaseless traveler of country high and wild, not only in Washington State but in more than a dozen states and six countries. Mike

Photo by Kristy Woodmansee

hiked the 508-mile Washington Pacific Crest Trail in 19 days. He has also led successful expeditions to the summits of Denali, Aconcagua, Orizaba, Ixta, and Cotopaxi. Mike has summited over 300 different peaks and has logged more than 13,000 trail miles on his mountain travels.

In the spring of 2000, Mike and his wife, Kristy, attempted to stand atop the summit of Mount Everest (29,035 feet elevation). Twice they reached the south col, but were ultimately turned back below 27,000 feet because of oxygen-system failures.

Melding a passion for the outdoors with his passion for people and life, Mike has instructed mountaineering and taken countless youth on esteem-building hiking and climbing adventures.

Mike holds bachelor's and master's degrees from the University of Washington. Mike and Kristy, along with children, Aaron and Angie, reside in the Skagit Valley.

The mission of Backpacker magazine is to provide accurate, useful, in-depth, and engaging information about wilderness recreation in North America.

BACKPACKER
The Magazine Of Wilderness Travel

33 East Minor Street
Emmaus, PA 18098
(800) 666-3434
www.backpacker.com

THE MOUNTAINEERS, founded in 1906, is a nonprofit outdoor activity and conservation club with 15,000 members, whose mission is "to explore, study, preserve, and enjoy the natural beauty of the outdoors. . . ." The club sponsors many classes and year-round outdoor activities in the Pacific Northwest, and supports environmental causes through educational activities, sponsoring legislation, and presenting educational programs. The Mountaineers Books supports the club's mission by publishing travel and natural history guides, instructional texts, and works on conservation and history.

Send or call for our catalog of more than 500 outdoor titles:

The Mountaineers Books
1001 SW Klickitat Way, Suite 201
Seattle, WA 98134
800-553-4453
mbooks@mountaineersbooks.org
www.mountaineersbooks.org

Leave No Trace strives to educate visitors about the nature of their recreational impacts, as well as offer techniques to prevent and minimize such impacts. Leave No Trace is best understood as an educational and ethical program, not as a set of rules and regulations.

For more information, visit www.LNT.org, or call 800-332-4100.

Other titles you might enjoy from The Mountaineers Books

Available at fine bookstores and outdoor stores, by phone at (800) 553-4453, or on the Web at www.mountaineersbooks.org

Best Loop Hikes in Washington edited and compiled by Dan Nelson, photography by Alan Bauer. $16.95 paperbound. 0-89886-866-1.

100 Classic Hikes in™ Washington by Ira Spring and Harvey Manning. $19.95 paperbound. 0-89886-586-7.

Best of the Pacific Crest Trail: Washington: 55 Hikes by Dan Nelson. $16.95 paperbound. 0-89886-703-7.

Hiking the Triple Crown: How to Hike America's Longest Trails by Karen Berger. $18.95 paperbound. 0-89886-760-6.

More Everyday Wisdom: Trail-Tested Advice from the Experts by Karen Berger. $16.95 paperbound. 0-89886-899-8.

More Backcountry Cooking: Moveable Feasts from the Experts by Dorcas Miller. $16.95 paperbound. 0-89886-900-5.

Wilderness 911: A Step-By-Step Guide for Medical Emergencies and Improvised Care in the Backcountry by Eric A. Weiss, M.D. $16.95 paperbound. 0-89886-597-2.

Conditioning for Outdoor Fitness: A Comprehensive Training Guide by David Musnick, M.D. and Mark Pierce, A.T.C. $21.95 paperbound. 0-89886-450-X.

100 Best Cross-Country Ski Trails in Washington, 3rd Edition by Vicky Spring and Tom Kirkendall. $16.95 paperbound. 0-89886-806-8.

100 Classic Backcountry Ski and Snowboard Routes in Washington by Rainer Burgdorfer. $17.95 paperbound. 0-89886-661-8.

Snowshoe Routes: Washington by Dan Nelson. $16.95 paperbound. 0-89886-585-9.

50 Trail Runs in Washington by Cheri Pompeo Gillis. $16.95 paperbound. 0-89886-715-0.

75 Scrambles in Washington: Classic Routes to the Summits by Peggy Goldman. $18.95 paperbound. 0-89886-761-4.

Washington State Parks: A Complete Recreation Guide, 2nd Edition by Marge and Ted Mueller. $16.95 paperbound. 0-89886-642-1.

Exploring Washington's Wild Areas: A Guide for Hikers, Backpackers, Climbers, Cross-Country Skiers, and Paddlers, 2nd Edition by Marge and Ted Mueller. $18.95 paperbound. 0-89886-807-6.

Hiking Washington's Geology by Scott Babcock and Robert Carson. $16.95 paperbound. 0-89886-548-4.

Northwest Mountain Weather: Understanding and Forecasting for the Backcountry User by Jeff Renner. $10.95 paperbound. 0-89886-297-3.

Wilderness Navigation: Finding Your Way Using Map, Compass, Altimeter, and GPS by Mike Burns and Bob Burns. $9.95 paperbound. 0-89886-629-4.